GETTING OUT ALIVE

GETTING OUT
ALIVE

NEWS, SPORT & POLITICS AT THE BBC

ROGER MOSEY

Biteback Publishing

First published in Great Britain in 2015 by
Biteback Publishing Ltd
Westminster Tower
3 Albert Embankment
London SE1 7SP
Copyright © Roger Mosey 2015

ISBN 978-1-84954-831-1

10 9 8 7 6 5 4 3 2 1

A CIP catalogue record for this book is available from the British Library.

Set in Adobe Garamond Pro

Printed and bound in Great Britain by
CPI Group (UK) Ltd, Croydon CR0 4YY

MIX
Paper from
responsible sources
FSC® C020471
FSC
www.fsc.org

CONTENTS

PREFACE

PREFACE

I was jammed into a Tube train on my way home one night in 2009 when I saw my face in the paper being read by the man next to me. A little further along the District Line, the crowd thinned enough for me to open my own copy of the *Evening Standard* and read the story. It was accusing BBC executives of being overpaid, which was true, and aboard a gravy train, which was not an accurate description of my working day and my journey that evening. But the item was fair game: the BBC and its employees should be accountable. Those tend to be the introductions that most people, like my fellow Tube travellers, have to

BBC executives; and in recent years the stories have been supplemented by the periodic crises that the corporation has endured. We became used to the idea that we might become the target of the moment as we watched colleagues becoming embroiled in controversies and sometimes defenestrated. Yet many of the commuters alongside me would be going home to watch BBC programmes, which mostly they would enjoy. The BBC has thrived in the digital age in a way that its critics didn't expect, and it remains one of the world's most successful public service broadcasters.

I first thought about writing this book when I myself experienced so vividly this contrast between the glories of the BBC and its profound lows. In 2012, I led the BBC's coverage of the London Olympics, which was praised to the highest of heavens, and then I was one of the executive team during the Savile crisis as we saw our reputation plummet and the director-general obliged to resign. George Entwistle's departure was marked on the front page of *The Sun* by the initials BBC spelling out 'Bye Bye Chump'. With the passing of the years, which included my leaving the BBC and moving to become the head of a college in Cambridge, I wanted to give a sense of what it had been like in those times. Of course, BBC executives have written previously about what it's like inside the corporation, but that was some years ago. I liked the idea of updating the narrative – taking in more recent developments in news and sport, along with an account of the experience of working on the Olympic Games. I hope I can best do that by telling my own story, and offering snapshots of the people I met, not only in my thirty-three years as a servant of the corporation but also before and after the BBC.

This is not, therefore, a treatise on BBC Charter renewal or the future of the licence fee. Those are matters for the new Conservative majority government and the corporation's current leadership team. I trust that this book has some pointers about when the BBC is at its best, and I owe a lot myself to mentors who were evangelistic about journalistic rigour and a spirit of independence and intellectual challenge. I was inspired as an employee, and I continue to be captivated as a consumer, by programming with soaring ambition. I shy away from the mass-produced 'stuff' that merely fills a schedule; and I believe the BBC is most effective when it frees its staff to be creative, and resists the itch to control even more from the centre.

These are personal opinions, just as the book is my own narrative. There is consequently a health warning. You cannot get to the level I reached in the BBC without having detractors as well as supporters. Not everyone will agree with my view of events. But I was always cheered up when I was being criticised, internally or externally, by the realisation that it was my opponents who would sometimes portray me as unknowable or too much of a corporate politician. My friends, however, would always know precisely what I was up to, and they reprimanded me if I threw myself over-enthusiastically into the gamesmanship of BBC power. The news presenter Huw Edwards, for instance, had the uncanny ability to read my mood of the day without any contact with me. I would receive texts from him correctly analysing what I was thinking about a topic that he knew, by instinct, was on my mind. And this must surely be the right way round: imagine if you were transparent to your detractors but unreadable to your allies. So I am grateful every day for the profound friendships I have made in the BBC, and to the three godchildren I have acquired from colleagues, along with shared trips and holidays, food and drink. I couldn't have kept going during the bad times without the comradeship and humour of friends and colleagues, and they were the people with whom I shared the proud moments too.

Many of those individuals have helped me in the writing of this book. I'd like to thank Les Sheehan, Michael Forte, Chris Rybczynski, Conrad and Annabel Walker, my agent Alex Armitage, George Entwistle, Dominic Coles, my cousins Brenda Hunter and Lucy Pilkington, Anthony Lewis, Michael Tilby the Vice-Master of Selwyn College, Simon Heffer, Joanna Manning-Cooper, Jackie Brock-Doyle, James and Eleanor Naughtie, John Humphrys, Dave Gordon, Mark Thompson, Mark Byford, Amanda Farnsworth, Lorraine Heggessey, Paul Reynolds and many more who read sections of the book and helped sharpen my memory of events. Memoirs by Kevin Marsh, Greg Dyke and John Birt were useful accounts of BBC times that I lived through, as was *All Our Todays* by Paul Donovan. Finally, I'm grateful to Iain Dale, my editor Olivia Beattie, and the team at Biteback for encouraging me to write the book I wanted to write, for which freedom I am deeply appreciative.

CHAPTER I

2012

FOR SEVEN YEARS I had known that 2012 would be the biggest year in my professional life. For the three years that I spent as the BBC's director of London 2012, I was working towards just one goal: delivering a successful year of events for the BBC. What I could never have envisaged was that it would turn out to be such a combination of elation and dejection. In 2012 there were the proudest moments of my BBC career but also the ghastliest lows, during which I became certain that I needed to get out of the corporation.

When the New Year's Eve fireworks signalled the start of London 2012, forming Olympic rings above the crowds lining the Thames, I felt a sense of relief that it was finally here. The story that had begun with the IOC making its choice of London seven years earlier was entering its final and most exciting stage. There was trepidation, too, about what lay ahead. Many of the public believed the Games would be a national embarrassment, and the easiest way of getting a laugh in a comedy show at that time was to predict what a dud London 2012 would be. Those of us involved in the planning realised the scale of what was being attempted in the intermittent chaos of our capital city, and I doubted that we would get through the summer without terrorism or transport chaos or public derision. So it was one of life's most joyous surprises when London surpassed all expectations with the triumphs of its Olympic year, and the BBC shared the plaudits too. But only a few weeks later, BBC executives were clambering from the wreckage of one of the corporation's worst crises.

One of the pleasures of being the director of London 2012 in the run-up to the Games was that I had little to do with BBC politics. There was more than enough real politics with the government, the mayor, the IOC and the rest. But through the first half of 2012 there was the background of the search for a new director-general, after the BBC Trust chairman Lord Patten had – unhelpfully for the incumbent Mark Thompson – signalled the start of the process in January. He had used a *Times* interview to reveal that headhunters were being employed to develop 'a succession plan', and he told the paper that the successful candidate would need 'renaissance talents ... It's a big management job, it's an editorial job, it's a creative job and it's an important part of our national culture. When the time comes, some people will crawl over broken glass to get the chance of doing it.' Few of us on the management side had any doubt that this was Patten pushing the idea that it was time for Mark to go, and for himself as the new chairman to install his own man or woman. The curiosity was that we had always expected that Mark would leave after the Olympics anyway, and in March he confirmed that was his plan.

There was some amusing campaigning by the *papabili*. Caroline Thomson got herself profiled in *The Guardian*, cheerily telling colleagues at a management meeting that her mother *loved* the photo – while unprofiled colleagues seethed quietly. Caroline later made a rare visit to the BBC Olympics team to commune with the workers. 'Supporters' and 'friends' of Caroline and of Helen Boaden spoke to *The Times* about the case for a woman DG: one of the friends talked about men having 'a game plan' and 'being ambitious', which were apparently not characteristics of BBC women applying for the top job. George Entwistle did what BBC blokes do and announced an eye-catching restructuring of his division, while the sounds of whirring activity floated in as usual from Tim Davie. External candidates were beneath the radar, with only the Ofcom chief executive Ed Richards a fixture in the media speculation. It was predominantly long-standing staff members of the BBC who risked the broken glass.

After the first round of interviews, the only candidates we knew to be definitely still in the process were the internal duo of Thomson and Entwistle. In the early summer I shared a car back from an Olympic launch at Westminster with Mark Thompson, who was in relaxed and gossipy mode. He said he knew little about what was going on in the DG process but asked me who I favoured. 'George' was the unequivocal answer – because, I said, I thought he was clever and utterly decent and got the BBC, whereas Caroline had never struck me as being as commanding editorially. I had been George's boss when he was editor of *Newsnight*, and we had kept in touch over the years as he moved between news, science and arts into ever more senior roles.

'Any doubts about George?' asked Mark, as we sat in a traffic jam in Piccadilly.

'Only that he's never been through a real storm,' I said. This was not, in fact, entirely true: George had been caught up in the aftermath of the Hutton Inquiry in 2004 in a way I knew had been thoroughly unpleasant. But he had not been one of the main public characters to the extent that Greg Dyke or Richard Sambrook had, and the question was a real one: how would he, or anyone else, cope with the kind of mega-row that is pretty much inevitable in a BBC DG's career? Mark Thompson was known for having the thickest of skins, and John Birt similarly. But George was kinder and more emotionally intelligent than the average broadcasting executive, and this was always my niggling doubt about his candidature for the top job.

It was reinforced while the DG race was still unresolved by the furore around the Diamond Jubilee pageant. In a weekend of generally very good coverage of the Jubilee – church service, concert and beacons – the Sunday river pageant broadcast was very bad indeed. It was not really anyone's fault. The weather was terrible, causing technical problems for the outside broadcast. The mood of the programme, which might have worked on a sunny day, felt wrong from the start. The casting of the talent was not right. There were unforced errors in the presentation and commentary.

This happens, and it was a collective failure for which I, as one of the members of the Jubilee steering group, will accept my share of blame. But since George was director of television, he was more obviously in the firing line and, from whatever inside sources, there was a repeated and ludicrous effort to get his name into the papers as the 'Guilty Man' who had ruined the Queen's big day. This did need careful handling, but in the scale of BBC crises it was no more than 'medium'. George, however, was unsettled by it – and from our conversations at the time I got the sense that he even considered pulling out of the DG race because of his sense of responsibility as the overall man in charge. This was noble but also way out of proportion for the offence, and he did not go through with it. But it confirmed my unease about George's decency and the danger of the inevitable storms, even before the hurricane that hit us in the autumn.

The summer, though, was golden, and not just in Olympic Park. In early July, George got the job. To most of us inside he was so obviously the best candidate that there was rejoicing in the sane choice that Patten had made. I had not been making any calculations about my personal advantage because I had not been expecting to stay in the BBC after the Olympics. I didn't have a job once 2012 was over, and anyone at my level of seniority is at the mercy of a new DG, who could have been from anywhere in the broadcasting spectrum. But I was delighted to be asked by George to act in his place as director of television – the biggest job apart from DG – until a permanent appointment was made, and it felt like the BBC was going to be run by 'people like us', which was a comforting thought as we took up residence in east London for the Olympics.

I could not have been happier in Games time about our brace of DGs. Mark had a whiff of freedom in his nostrils, and was the perfect supportive editor-in-chief, with the bounce and humour that represented him at his best. George was not taking over until September, so he was able to stick with big thoughts for the future rather than the daily agenda – and we also had a bit of fun going to watch the hockey, which is a sport he played as a teenager, and wandering through the crowds of the Olympic Park. I was proud to introduce him as our DG-designate to the sporting bigwigs and to our staff, without any hesitation about him being the right leader for the BBC after 2012. And everything went right for us: every day we got a sense of the marvellous legacy from leader Thompson and the gilded inheritance for leader Entwistle. The BBC game plan had worked. Our approval levels reached unimagined heights: more than 90 per cent of the population watched our coverage, and more than 90 per cent of those viewers said we had met or exceeded their expectations. The newspapers were universal in their praise. The sound of purring was to be heard from Broadcasting House.

I started in television headquarters on 20 August, just a week after the Olympics. I busied myself with familiarisation visits around the country, and I had occasional exchanges with George, who had taken his family to the United States on his final break before becoming DG in mid-September. During this period there was a steady reshaping at the top of the BBC: Caroline Thomson left with a large pay-off, to which she was contractually entitled and which was not seen at the time as controversial, and George thinned out the senior management team in the hope of making it less diffuse and more empowered than it had been under Mark.

With hindsight, this created gaps when the crisis hit us. At the time, it seemed like a sensible reorganisation, and the first meeting of George's management board was one of those heartening moments in the BBC when it felt like we had the right leadership, the right team and a determination to take the organisation forward.

The first warning we had in BBC television that something potentially nasty was about to break was when we received a request from ITV for the use of some footage of the BBC star Jimmy Savile for a documentary they were preparing. It was referred to television HQ because there was some question at a lower level about how any pictures might be used – a routine concern when content is being handed over to another broadcaster to use as they will. We decided to make available whatever ITV wanted because the approach appeared to be for a proper documentary programme, though we had no idea how serious it was going to be. The scale of what they had uncovered became apparent in the following days when the drumbeat of publicity for the programme signalled that they had a very important story indeed – and one that would rattle the foundations of the BBC.

As the transmission date for the ITV programme approached, the headlines agreed: Jimmy Savile would be revealed as a sex offender on a horrifying scale, and he had abused children, including ones he encountered during his work. But what brought the story up-to-date, and caused the crisis to centre around George and senior colleagues, was the revelation that *Newsnight* had been working on this story for the BBC in the autumn of 2011 – and it had failed to make the air. Worse still for our corporate reputation, we had broadcast tribute programmes to Jimmy Savile in the Christmas 2011 schedule. It was easy to write the narrative. Historically, the BBC had put a paedophile onto its most popular children's show. Recently, the BBC had blocked its own story revealing the true Savile in the interests of protecting his reputation and that of the corporation – and went ahead with tributes despite knowing the worst. Most acutely for George, he had been the director of television when the Christmas programmes were broadcast; and now here he was as DG.

That narrative did, indeed, seize hold of the press with a ferocious intensity. It was what the public came to believe too, for perfectly understandable reasons. But internally we knew the linkage was simply not right; and I never for one moment believed that George, as director of television, or Helen Boaden, as director of news, or any of the other contemporary figures, had done anything significantly wrong. I, like them, had been in the BBC for decades and had never had any knowledge that Jimmy Savile was a paedophile. Was it credible that those people would know for certain that Savile was involved in paedophilia and suppress it? From a television point of view, was an archive clip programme of Jimmy Savile at the BBC really a reason to kill a *Newsnight* investigation? The idea was ludicrous to me and others, which may explain why we were slow off the mark in rebutting it; and in any case the most likely true reason about the events of 2011 – that this was an enormous cock-up in which there was miscommunication and misunderstanding – was not exactly one you could roll out with aplomb on the *Today* programme.

For George himself, the dagger at his heart was the disclosure that Helen had told him, briefly, that *Newsnight* was investigating Savile. To me, the crucial thing here was always that there is a difference between 'we are investigating something' – which happens with dozens of stories at any one time, few of which make it to air – and 'we have discovered that Jimmy Savile was a paedophile'. For any broadcasting executive, there are hundreds of programme ideas floating around and lines from news stories in their heads, and spotting which one is the most toxic is not possible in a systematic way. I used to think as editor of the *Today* programme that it was almost never the 8 a.m. lead that 'got' you. It is the sweet little 6.50 a.m. filler, to which you pay little attention, that lands you in the dock of public opinion. However, George's personality – atypically in television – was the introspective type that induced him to rack his brains for ways in which he might be responsible even in situations where he patently wasn't, and I am certain that hobbled him through the whole of that dreadful autumn. Dealing with the crisis if he had not been personally dragged in might have been possible, but his own role made it a battle he was never going to win. He had some extraordinarily tough days.

We did try, though. The management board set up two inquiries into what had happened: the Pollard Review into the decisions around *Newsnight*, and the Dame Janet Smith investigation into past sexual misconduct in the BBC. As George said to me at the time, the Pollard Review was effectively set up by the DG to look at what the DG had done. What we did not realise in doing this was that we were creating processes that would preoccupy the BBC for literally years. Our aim with Pollard was to do something thorough and honest but on the lines of Will Wyatt's report into 'Queengate' – an exemplary review of the row about the editing of a trailer featuring the Queen. This was not, after all, the most complex of issues. Pollard needed to answer one main question: why had the *Newsnight* investigation into Savile been discontinued? This might have been because of a flawed editorial decision, or it could have been because of inappropriate corporate pressure. We thought that this approach had been agreed by the management board, but somewhere along the route through the lawyers and on to the BBC Trust, it became something very different. A trustee described what we actually got as 'quasi-judicial'. We never envisaged the courtroom-style interrogations, the indefensible strain put on individuals, or the fact that transcripts would be published. I and others were particularly upset by the treatment of the admirable Steve Mitchell. By contrast, Dame Janet's report was always intended to be much more thorough, and it was right that there should be an accounting for the misconduct of previous decades. It was expected in early 2013, but in May 2015 it was announced that its publication had been delayed again – this time at the request of the Metropolitan Police.

The inflation of the Pollard Inquiry was accompanied behind the scenes by a bureaucracy that was, on occasion, agonisingly slow. There were battles between the management and the Trust about who owned the investigations, and every time we wanted to move forward we found ourselves wading through the treacle of having the executive board and the Trust both trying to second-guess the DG. One Friday when George wanted to update the media on what was happening, we had everything ready by lunchtime and a press conference about to be called; but we had to wait hours longer for sign-off of his key messages by the non-executive directors and by the trustees. We never knew what position Chris Patten was taking on a given day. George was, of course, his appointed man and there were times when Patten was reassuring. Other times we held our heads in our hands as his comments intensified the crisis while we were still battling to discover the facts and the true sense of its scale. It was ironic that, a year later, Patten criticised newspapers for their overwrought headlines about the BBC when the single most lurid one of the Savile affair – 'a tsunami of filth' – was contributed to the nation by Patten himself.

It was also apparent how thin we were at the senior level, which was something of an irony given that over-heavy management was an article of faith among our critics. The organisation still keenly missed its former deputy director-general Mark Byford, and Caroline Thomson had just departed. Helen Boaden was wounded like George. It had been announced that the finance director Zarin Patel was planning to leave. I was only acting as director of television, which was a huge job in itself, and made more difficult by ambitious underlings positioning themselves for the substantive role. Graham Ellis was in a similar position, acting as director of radio, because Tim Davie had gone off to Worldwide and was out of the public service mainstream. It felt very lonely indeed, and I had the sense that we were tiptoeing along a plank with shoals of sharks in the waters below.

The lack of clarity about who was in charge of the corporation was exemplified by a disagreement about the hiring of an external crisis management company. The BBC press office was under immense strain because of the volume of enquiries they were receiving, the shifting information they were getting from internal sources, and often the uncertainty of the corporate line. Paul Mylrea, the head of communications, therefore discussed with me whether we needed some extra help. He proposed that we bring in Brunswick, the communications specialist, who, crucially, would be able to add a more strategic view of how we were to get out of the mess we were in – and ease the pressure on the internal teams who were being crushed into the ground. It was likely that David Yelland, the former editor of *The Sun* and now a Brunswick partner, would be involved, and he had experience of supporting people at the centre of a storm. George and I and the senior team thought we should give it a go. It was an extra resource at a time when we sensed we were in an existential crisis. The preparations were made and we were about to invite Brunswick on board when the idea was vetoed by Chris Patten. He later told the Pollard Inquiry:

> I thought to have David Yelland … being trooped through the newsroom at the BBC to brief the director-general … that seemed to me to be a seriously lousy story … While we were pressing him [George] to get a rather stronger team around him, the one thing we did suggest was that hiring Brunswick was not a very good idea.

Patten's concern, we gathered, was specifically around the appearance George was about to make before a Commons committee. As someone experienced in the ways of Westminster, Patten believed that MPs would immediately ask whether he had been prepared for the hearing by an external firm; and they would jump on him if he admitted that we had brought in help. This was doubtless true, though we did not exactly avoid an even more 'seriously lousy' story throughout the autumn, and George's appearance at the committee was a weak one, which might have been improved if he had had better coaching. But the wider point was about who was calling the shots. George was the chief executive, and in the view of the management team it was an operational decision, one that a CEO should have been able to take, if he wanted to bring in some communications advice. It was not, we believed, a function of the chairman of the Trust. He should have been allowed to castigate later if he felt a decision had been inappropriate, but he was not supposed immediately to overrule a decision taken in good faith.

Without the instant mechanism to create a stronger team around the DG, we failed to lift our heads from the daily struggle. During those dreadful weeks we were not able to reassert the values and the longer-term strategy of the BBC. Worse, we could not take on some of the more lurid media narratives because the detail of what had happened with the aborted *Newsnight* investigation was being dealt with by Nick Pollard's review. The kind of question the *Today* programme wanted to ask any BBC executive was 'What did Helen Boaden say to Peter Rippon, the editor of *Newsnight*?', and that was a question we had assigned to Pollard to answer. Those who did venture onto the media, like the estimable David Jordan, the director of editorial policy, found themselves dragged into the crisis by the lack of agreement inside BBC News about the basic facts; and those facts were so hard to discern because the people who might have established them were all about to be interrogated by Pollard.

A little way into the furore, George asked me to be 'Gold Commander' of the BBC crisis management team with my long-standing colleague Dominic Coles as my deputy. This was an industry standard model introduced to the BBC by Mark

Thompson, but understandably parodied as a title when the news emerged externally. It was not about second-guessing Pollard and trying to find out what had happened in the past. Rather, it was an attempt to keep the business of the corporation running. In this we were partly successful and partly not. The news about Savile had unleashed speculation about there possibly being a huge number of serious sex offenders within the BBC. The biggest nightmare was the one that did not happen: that we would discover paedophile activity from people currently working for the BBC in areas that gave them access to children. Every day, though, we received more and more allegations – some credible, some wildly implausible – that we had to review and decide how to process. All the serious ones went straight to the police, but we also had to navigate our way through potentially malicious accusations that would have destroyed the careers of innocent people. On the current evidence, I believe we got this right. However, any hope that launching the Pollard and Smith Inquiries would calm the crisis was misplaced. Every day something else went wrong: the wobbly performance by George at Westminster in front of a Commons select committee; discovering that the *Newsnight* editor's blog aimed at setting the story straight had inaccuracies; and the internal strains caused by *Panorama* investigating the behaviour of its own bosses. It was right for *Panorama* to do that, but the madness of that autumn was encapsulated by a subsequent call from *Newsnight* to television HQ saying they were minded to do something about why we had scheduled *Panorama* so late at 10.35 p.m. – presumably, they said, because we wanted to bury bad news. As it often does in the worst of times, the BBC was in danger of eating itself alive.

We also knew, because it is the first rule of crisis management, that the biggest problem would be if something else happened. The focus on Savile meant that management was over-stretched, stressed and dog-tired. Every day the press office dealt with dozens of hostile enquiries, and barely an hour went past without an MP firing in another long letter full of allegations – all of which the BBC was constitutionally obliged to take seriously. People like me were dealing with the day job, too: how to handle a drama with a violent episode that resembled a current news story, or pay negotiations with star presenters, or whatever the day threw at us. In BBC News, the elastic was most obviously at risk of snapping: the people running the division were being undermined daily by events, and the BBC was also having to create complex referral lines to avoid any conflict of interest between a manager and the reporting of their role in the Savile affair. This stemmed from a good instinct: fastidious respect for journalistic independence. But it had the result that the people in news who would have spotted something nasty looming were shut out of the room when it really mattered. I still can't quite believe that we somehow ended up with the directors in the nations – who were by definition hundreds of miles away from London – taking the editor-in-chief role on some days because everybody else was thought to be compromised.

I was on a brief holiday when *Newsnight* landed a second and fatal blow to the short career of George Entwistle as director-general. I had taken four days in Nice at the end of October as my first proper break since before the Olympics, in what seemed like a week's lull. It is worth noting that as director of television I would not, in any case, have been consulted about *Newsnight* because it sat managerially within the news division. Instead, I arrived back home on Friday 2 November to find emails from the BBC requesting that all my Savile-related correspondence be handed in; telling me that I might be required as a witness at the Pollard Inquiry; and, with a lack of finesse that is characteristic of Human Resources, warning me that any testimony might be regarded as part of a disciplinary process. The infuriating thing here, of course, was that my only involvement with the Savile affair had been in trying to help sort it out once the story had broken – which meant that the BBC had created a double jeopardy. Not only was it seeking to investigate the people who had allegedly botched the *Newsnight* Savile story in 2011; it was now threatening to investigate the people investigating the matters that had arisen.

So that day passed in a mix of unpacking, shopping for food – and increasing grumpiness. I was now leaning strongly towards leaving the BBC as quickly as possible, and all I could see before me was more weeks of corporate paranoia and hell for individuals. I wrote, but didn't send, a resignation letter. A colleague advised me, rightly, that this was not the time to abandon George. But I was simmering at the principle that trying to get stuck into the management of a crisis in itself made you vulnerable; and I had a night of lying awake until four in the morning with my mind trying to remember every email I had written in the past few weeks on the subject of Savile and also concocting unusual tortures for the folk in Legal and Personnel who were fuelling the investigation.

It turned out to be the wrong reason for a sleepless night. I was never called as a witness by Pollard, but just before bed I had seen the *Newsnight* report on a senior Conservative who had allegedly been associated with child abuse. I remember thinking it was a bit

thin as a report, plus there was the obvious risk of jigsaw identi-
fication – where information in different places, in this case TV
and the internet, can be added together in a way that identifies
an individual. But after what the BBC had gone through, and
after *Newsnight*'s particularly searing experiences, I never imagined that the story itself would be wrong – or that it would be so
easy to unravel it.

The following week back at work was a false calm between
two storms. At the senior management level, none of us heard
the time bomb ticking underneath Broadcasting House. Only
later did we find out that awareness was spreading in BBC News
that *Newsnight* had dropped an almighty clanger. George himself
was feeling more chipper, and a lot of the focus of his week was
giving a speech at an international broadcasting conference on
Friday 9 November. That was also the day I was in London hosting a board meeting of the European Broadcasting Union. And
it was the day *The Guardian* published as its front-page splash the
news that *Newsnight*'s big investigation was actually based on a
case of mistaken identity: it simply wasn't true. Lord McAlpine,
the senior Conservative who was the intended target of the report,
was blameless.

The initial fire-fighting – and the depressingly short quest to
find out whether *The Guardian* was right or not – was being
tackled by the DG's office and BBC News, with an increasingly
agitated BBC Trust demanding answers. I was deep in sopo-
rific EBU discussions about the future of public service media
in Europe with a series of directors-general, so I was unable to
join in any meetings or receive any calls; but as the day wore on
my mobile throbbed with messages from friends and colleagues

saying this looked very bad indeed and the BBC needed to take immediate and drastic action.

I extricated myself from the EBU and spoke to George around teatime. He was under no illusions about the gravity of what had happened, and he already had a list of actions he intended to take; but the Trust's fury had grown to the level that some of its members were demanding the management remove *Newsnight* from the airwaves – in an echo of the move News International had made against the *News of the World*. As we talked, George and I could see a small advantage in this. It was certainly shock and awe: what Murdoch does is one thing, but for a BBC director-general to shut a flagship programme would be a big play. It would also be the best thing for George to do in keeping the Trust on side. However, as we talked we also realised it would be barmy. The *News of the World* was riddled with systemic breaches of ethics and the law, whereas *Newsnight* had had one aborted investigation in December 2011 and one dreadful piece of reporting in November 2012. More to the point, as director of television I couldn't contemplate BBC Two not having a nightly news and current affairs programme – especially not at a time when *Newsnight* was itself a story. What would we have put on air on Monday at 10.30 p.m. where *Newsnight* had been?

George and I agreed that the best thing was to summon a meeting of the executive board. By this stage it was 7 p.m. on a Friday evening and people were scattered all over the place, which meant it had to be by phone. I myself had a commitment to a leaving dinner for my long-serving PA, Elaine Gold. In the event, Elaine and I had about twenty minutes of intermittent conversation while for the best part of two hours she was left on her own as I took part in conference calls in a courtyard just off Oxford Street. My pan-seared cod died in vain.

On the conference call, some of the board were attracted to the drama of axing *Newsnight*, but there was a trio of George, myself and David Jordan who argued it would be a short-term gain for long-term pain. That view won the day, but we still came up with a robust set of measures. *Newsnight* that night would apologise unreservedly. There would be a swift investigation of what had happened by a senior director. We would take disciplinary action against the people who had let down the BBC, and, if need be, heads would roll. We would suspend all further programmes involving the independent investigative journalism outfit who had worked on the McAlpine story – and overall this would be, in desperate circumstances, a chance for George to underline that he was in charge and was a fully functioning chief executive.

But we also knew that we were making his position with the Trust even more precarious. George called me after the board discussion in a calm and thoughtful mood but his conclusion was clear: 'Keeping *Newsnight* could cost me my job.' Given that he was uncertain of Lord Patten's support as the Savile crisis intensified, George was right that going against a number of trustees on *Newsnight* seemed unlikely to be a good career move. And that was probably why he chose to 'front up' the management response to the McAlpine catastrophe, and told the board that he would go on the *Today* programme the following morning to set out the actions he was taking.

Did this ring alarm bells? Yes and no. On the one hand, George had been in better shape in recent days – and he had been impressive in leading the discussions that evening. But I suppose those of us who supported him, and knew how much was at stake, also realised that this was double or quits. He had done the *Today* programme twice already in his short time as DG, and if he couldn't survive another *Today* interview as editor-in-chief about a major editorial issue, on which we'd got a clear and rational management response, then the game was up. He was right that, at this moment of BBC crisis, the leadership could come only from him. If he had disappeared and sent out a surrogate, the game would have been over too.

My last chat with him on the Friday night was just after ten o'clock, when a new mini-crisis erupted. I was called by network presentation because *Newsnight* were refusing to include the apology within their programme and were asking for it to be read before the show by a continuity announcer instead. Little did they know that the future of their entire programme was at stake that night. I made it clear to them, somewhat forcibly, that an apology within *Newsnight* meant within *Newsnight* not before *Newsnight*, and another small disaster was averted – which I told George about in a 'guess what the daft arses have tried to do now' fashion. I also agreed to take any calls for him late at night because he needed to get to his son's 18th birthday party, which was underway without him.

The next morning I listened, along with the rest of the chattering classes, to the car crash that was George's interview with John Humphrys. It was the first time I wasn't able to summon up an immediate text response to one of his media interviews. I could not think of anything helpful to say about it, and I therefore left it a couple of hours before sending a feeble 'How are things?' and expecting he would send his customary honest response when something had not gone to plan.

There was no reply. This was unusual but not unprecedented, and I had no idea that events were moving so rapidly to a conclusion – with the Trust's patience at an end because of the *Today* debacle compounding the disobeying of some of their views on *Newsnight*. It was also a Saturday, an unusual day for Trust activity; and I was due to go to a match at Arsenal, where I have season tickets, with Gabriel Walker, one of my godsons, fifteen at the time. This meant an afternoon of surrogate parenting: picking him up at Waterloo, feeding him, entertaining him through the highs and lows of Arsenal and then getting him home.

Bothered by George's silence, I texted him again on the way to the Emirates Stadium, asking if he wanted a chat. But by the time I had got there, and had bought Gabriel his favoured foot-long hot dog, there was an email from the DG's office saying that we should be on standby for another executive board conference call that afternoon – most likely at 4 p.m. This did not look good.

I calculated the place in the stadium concourse where I could take part in a call in relative privacy, and texted George once more to see if I could offer any help. By this stage I had no doubt, really, that it was all over. Piecing things together afterwards, I discovered there had been a phone conference involving George and the Trust in the late morning. It was, he told me later, apparent that he had lost the confidence of some, or even most, of the trustees, who argued that his package of measures was not enough. Some had pressed again for *Newsnight* to be scrapped. What followed was a one-to-one conversation, in which Patten's later public account is in harmony with George's recollection: that the chairman was not urging George to go, but he was also not urging him to stay. George then offered his resignation, and the discussions turned to his contractual entitlements – otherwise known as the pay-off. I blame him not one jot for seeking to protect his family and reputation to the best of his ability in dreadful personal circumstances, and I suspect almost everyone else in that situation would have had the same negotiations about the ending of their employment.

The conversations between lawyers continued. The emails to the rest of us kept pushing back the time of the executive board call, and I could see no better option than taking Gabriel back to his parents and going for a (large) drink with them on the South Bank. I had not intended to eat out, but Conrad and Annabel thought the best thing was to propel me into dinner with them and pour some more wine down me – which is why, when the executive board finally convened just before 9 p.m., again with people scattered all over the country, my own location was outside a branch of Brasserie Blanc with the phone on 'mute' to shut out the noise of Saturday-night revellers.

George made a brief, dignified statement that his resignation would be announced shortly, and a couple of us paid tribute to him. In doing so, the sadness flooded over me: George's decency and intelligence were sorely needed by the BBC, and it was the cruellest of outcomes that someone so full of promise for the future should have been destroyed by the evils of the past, which were none of his doing. Shortly afterwards I walked to the railway station, and on board the train home to Richmond I composed a tweet: 'I'm deeply, deeply sad that George Entwistle has resigned. He is a good, honourable man and I'm proud to call him a friend.' I am pleased I did that then, and I believe it even more now.

The next day it was a case of 'the King is dead; long live the temporary King'. Tim Davie was asked to act as director-general, which my kitchen cabinet and I had predicted. Also on that miserable Sunday morning, we spotted that there was an extra torment possible for me. If, as seemed likely, Helen Boaden would be sidelined from BBC News until the Pollard Inquiry was completed, they would need someone else to run news in the interim. As one of the tiny number of people left standing, and a former news executive, there was a finger pointing in my direction. I talked to a range of friends about 'what if…?' We all agreed: it would be the triple-strength poisoned chalice. To add to my temporary incumbency of television, with no full-time job on offer, I would be ushered into the lion's den of news without any long-term authority and with a director sitting unjustly in the wings. Head and heart came to the same conclusion: that the only sensible course was to dodge the lions and decline the chalice, though I also knew that, as a corporation man, it would be the first time I had said 'no' to a role that the top bosses wanted me to take.

The call came on my mobile around teatime as I trudged back from Richmond town centre with darkness falling. It was Lucy Adams, the likeable head of Human Resources, asking me to take on BBC News. I felt a bit sorry for her in retrospect but I was proud of myself that I came out with the direct answer: 'No.' I explained this was a combination of it being the wrong thing professionally, because a temping role would never have enough credibility to sort out news, and equally bad for me personally. I just didn't want to do it. She sounded taken aback, probably because the glad tidings of my move were about to be announced to an emergency meeting of the Trust, and we agreed that Tim would call me later. I said the same to him, and to his credit he took it with more magnanimity than I might have done if the roles had been reversed. Fran Unsworth was asked to do the job instead, which was a much better outcome given that she was already within BBC News and it was simply a case of stepping up from her existing role.

This was not quite the end of my BBC career. I didn't leave until September 2013, and there were occasional brighter interludes after the storms of that autumn. But as someone who had worked in the BBC for more than thirty years, and who had always believed in it as an organisation, there was a terrible sadness about seeing it so exposed and internally riven. The Savile crisis was first and foremost about a wicked man and his victims. What was uncovered about the past was deeply distressing. But it was also a crisis of the modern BBC.

There were many institutions tainted by Savile. The particular focus on the BBC was because it had created him as a national figure and sustained his popularity. It then had the additional misfortune of bringing the past evils into the present with the aborted *Newsnight* investigation. We handled that poorly, and we dealt with the consequences of that decision ineptly.

But in losing George as DG, and in the onslaught that many executives faced, it could hardly be argued that the old clichés applied: it was not 'assistant heads will roll'. Rather, it was a decapitation at the top of the organisation, and of someone who was later exonerated of the main charge against him. Helen Boaden was cleared too. The big question for Pollard was: 'Had there been improper conduct to suppress the *Newsnight* report on Savile?' and the answer was unequivocal. He concluded: 'The decision to drop the original investigation was flawed and the way it was taken was wrong but I believe it was done in good faith. It was not done to protect the Savile tribute programmes or for any improper reason.'

These events were a personal tragedy for George Entwistle. The irony is that when the process for appointing the DG was running, earlier than expected, the Savile documentary was in preparation over at ITV. It was a bomb primed to go off in the early autumn of 2012, and on the original timings it might have detonated in the closing months of Mark Thompson's director-generalship. Instead, it exploded in the face of the new man in the job. Someone who had been in the role for seven years might have been able to ride out the storm. George would have had a fighting chance if he had been a couple of years into his leader-ship of the BBC, but he had little protection when the biggest crisis in years landed just two weeks into his tenure.

You always hope that in adversity colleagues will come together to support each other, and that a corporation will throw its arms around the employees who are doing their jobs to the best of their ability. That did not happen with Savile, or with the Hutton Report eight years earlier, or in other bruising episodes that saw executives depart. This was sometimes for good reasons – public accountability has to come first – and sometimes for bad. When the stress tests have been at their most extreme, the corporation has tended to fracture rather than unite. There is an additional jeopardy in the BBC's structures, and in the separation between management and the governors or the Trust. This seems to have got worse, as the subsequent meltdown in management–Trust relations over pay-offs showed.

I reflected on some of this in my farewell interview with the BBC staff magazine, *Ariel*: 'The point is that the BBC is about a collective endeavour – most decisions are collective. Individuals do make mistakes, and there's accountability for that, but unless they've made completely bonkers, reckless decisions, they should be supported. For the most part, they are people doing the best they can.' I could have added that critics needed to take a wider view too. Many of the people at the heart of the Savile affair were the ones who, only weeks earlier, were part of the team that had successfully delivered the Olympic Games.

From this greater distance, it is easier to see that the BBC is, thankfully, a resilient organisation. Tony Hall immediately brought maturity to the DG's office, and the glories of the corporation's programme-making remain. I will always be grateful to the BBC for the opportunities it gave me. But the autumn of 2012 was a dreadful time; and I saw good people being added to the list of senior colleagues who had departed feeling battered by what had happened to them. Sometimes they might have been wrong to feel aggrieved. At other times it felt as if the difference between survival or resignation was whether you happened to have read a specific email or not. The sense that you could be next in line for the ducking stool of public opinion was not a pleasant feeling, and it was shared by many. I therefore feel lucky that I left on a relative high – that, after decades of doing some of the BBC's most scrutinised jobs, I got out alive.

CHAPTER 2

BRADFORD

I HAVE ALWAYS SAID I was born in Bradford in Yorkshire, but
that isn't true. I was born in a mothers-and-babies home in
Warrington, on the other side of the Pennines. Bradford came
six weeks later when I was adopted, and when I was issued with
a new birth certificate. My natural parents were from St Helens,
and they did something obvious and then something unusual for
the 1950s. My mother became pregnant – but her boyfriend, for
reasons we can only guess at, didn't do what boys usually did in
those times. He didn't marry her. And that's why she ended up

giving birth to me in secret and away from home, and why I was immediately put up for adoption.

My natural mother called me Stephen during the three weeks we were together in the January of 1958. 'Roger' came from my adoptive parents. Ending up with the surname 'Mosey' was a somewhat random process because my adoptive father wasn't born a Mosey: that was the name of his mother's second husband, who adopted my dad when he was ten or so.

It sounds like the recipe for an identity crisis, but in Yorkshire – which runs through my blood as surely as if I had been born there – you just get on with it. I was told when I was very young that I had been adopted, but until I was in my twenties I never talked about it outside the family and it was only in my late thirties that I asked to see my original birth certificate. This was accompanied by the social worker's report from 1958 with the few sketchy lines I know about my natural parents. But when I was interviewed for the role of Master of Selwyn College, I felt secure enough to tell them about my families' histories, and my relatives, blood and adopted, who were miners and train drivers and farmers and shop assistants. They would never have dreamed that their offspring would even get to university let alone make it to senior roles within the BBC and end up being head of a Cambridge college. 'Talk sense and I'll talk to you' would have been my grandfather's response to those kind of ideas.

What I regard as my real family – my life with the people who adopted me – was reasonably conventional. My parents ran a sub-post office in Bradford at the end of a terrace of Yorkshire stone houses halfway up the hill from the city centre to the suburb of Undercliffe. I was pushed in my pram around the nearby

Victorian cemetery with its spectacular mausoleums from the age when Bradford was the wool capital of the world. In our shop we sold tobacco and sweets and greetings cards, and a photograph of the time shows my mother displaying the calendars that were a special line for Christmas. My aunt and uncle ran a larger sub-post office, this time supplemented by a travel agency, a few hundred yards nearer the bottom of the hill. It was a poor, inner-city area with densely packed back-to-back houses, many of which were demolished in the late 1960s; within it, shopkeepers were the relative aristocracy. But we never had much money spare, and the working hours for my parents were long. On Saturday nights I was plonked in front of the TV to watch *Doctor Who* while the weekly accounts were calculated, with happiness if they all balanced and disaster if there was a missing pound or two.

Nowadays, Bradford's glories are its hills and valleys. In the early 1960s, you could seldom see them. My memories of the city's panoramas are of smoke from the mill chimneys mingling with the northern rain or fog to create a dispiriting murk, with only a windy and bright day opening up the views. I turned five during the brutal winter of 1962/63, which allowed daily sledging down the slopes of our local park but also brought ice on the inside of the house windows, and paraffin heaters struggling and failing to warm the bedrooms. I had bronchitis as a child, and no wonder, given the brew of pollution and bitter cold.

We explored Yorkshire on sunny, happier days. Along with the children of relatives and friends, I was loaded into a car – we had one of the early Minis – and we would go out for a 'motor-run': up into the Dales, with particular excitement about gated roads or crossing fords, across to see family friends in York, sometimes making it as far as Scarborough or Bridlington. The family photos show me as a blond-haired little fellow, carefully picking his way across the stepping stones of the River Wharfe at Bolton Abbey or looking alarmed by a hefty cow at the Bingley Show. We had a dog, a grumpy Corgi inaccurately called Chummy. Despite being an only child, I was never lonely – though I developed a reputation for being at my happiest when I was engrossed in a book without the need for any more company.

But I liked going along to sports events. My first football match was about as low-key as it gets, at the crumbling Bradford Park Avenue; we switched to Bradford City when Park Avenue went out of the league. However, my dad and family friends were promiscuous in their football tastes and we went to Leeds United during their Revie glory days and to Huddersfield Town when they were in the First Division. At Elland Road we had cheap tickets for behind the goal, and a small wooden stool was taken along for me to be able to see the pitch from the sunken terracing at the front of the stand. We watched cricket at Park Avenue and Harrogate and Headingley, and I was devoted to Geoffrey Boycott and the great Yorkshire sides of the 1960s. In Rugby League it was Bradford Northern, and my parents' badge of sporting pride was that they had been at Odsal Stadium for the Challenge Cup final replay in 1954, with its record crowd of more than 102,000.

My first school was Hanson Infants', just along the road from the lower post office. I made my own way there even at the age of five or six, taking the bus down the hill and then sometimes meeting my cousins Brenda and Lucy for the final part of the journey. There were journeys home on autumn nights when pea-souper fog, mixed with the city's trademark smoke and soot, meant you could barely see your own feet. The school was ethnically mixed because Bradford, a melting pot from the days of Irish immigration in the nineteenth century, had been one of the destinations for Pakistani migrants in the early 1960s. One of my friends was a boy called Tanvir Ashgar, whose parents were from Lahore and whose dad drove a city bus. His mother used to stroke my fair hair when I went to collect him on the way to school, and my family managed to be both personally courteous and interested in their different lifestyle while still disapproving of immigration in general. My granddad thought Alf Garnett was spot-on in his political views, and didn't regard *Till Death Us Do Part* as satirical in any sense, though he declared himself to be a Liberal all his life, as his generation of Yorkshire non-conformists traditionally did.

At the age of eight I sat the entrance exam for Bradford Grammar School, and later won a City of Bradford scholarship, which meant that my tuition was free. All the rest of my school education was there, but I would say I have a respect for BGS rather than a deep love. On the plus side, the school was academically strong in those days, and a few teachers were outstanding. When I was twelve, my English teacher gave me *The French Lieutenant's Woman* to read as an addition to the curriculum, and that and other novels that he suggested made me adventurous in literature. When I was sixteen, an exceptional teacher transformed history from learning by rote into something with academic rigour and the exciting exploration of sources, and set me up well for university. I made lifelong friendships there – notably my oldest friend Conrad Walker and the next-in-line Michael Forte (né Blackburn), who remain key members of my kitchen cabinet: the friends I rely on for advice and support. On the negative side, all-boys northern grammar schools of that age had their grim side and were not good at freeing up the mind: we were at risk of emerging with lots of O and A levels but not much creative energy. Music and art were for wimps; and for those not naturally talented at sport, like me, it seemed that 'Games' was a punitive and unpleasant part of the timetable. The school was divided, it seemed, between rugby players and non-rugby players, and I was firmly in the latter category.

In the sixth form I joined the national Young Liberals, then a byword for student radicalism, and earned myself a prim comment on my school report: 'I hope he will no longer bask on the wilder shores of Young Liberalism.' This naturally redoubled my commitment, and in the February 1974 general election I helped run the Liberal campaign in Bradford South, where we were operating in virgin territory but enthused by the national Liberal surge. I yomped around the streets after school, pushing leaflets through letter boxes and explaining as an earnest sixteen-year-old why the two-party system had failed. One evening I went to a Liberal rally in Pudsey, where the guest speakers were the party leader Jeremy Thorpe and the famously obese MP for Rochdale Cyril Smith. Quite a combination, given what we later found out about one officially innocent man and one who died without his alleged crimes being prosecuted.

By the time I was at Bradford Grammar, my parents had left the post office. My granddad, who had owned both shops, decided to sell up. My dad became a commercial sales rep, selling confectionery and moving between companies such as Batgers in London, Taveners in Liverpool and the Blue Bird toffee company. We had jars of sweets and lollies stacked up in the garage, which

fortunately – maybe inured by years of living in a shop – I never
found attractive. But it was a tough job for my dad, with thousands of miles of travelling each year and a constant fear about
not hitting his sales targets, and he never achieved stability in it.
He was made redundant twice, and I experienced through him
the blow to morale of unemployment and the worry about paying
the bills. His pride always made him believe that the worst option
would be for my mother to have to go back to work to support us,
so that never happened. But the two of them made astute invest-
ments in property when times were good, and we rose from the
terraced house in inner-city Bradford to a detached house in the
suburb of Heaton, which had trees and fields and even a nearby
bistro which used garlic in its cooking and was regarded as dar-
ingly avant-garde.

In these somewhat grey teenage years there was then an episode in transatlantic technicolor. At sixteen I had the chance to
go on an English-Speaking Union exchange visit to the United
States for part of a term at an absurdly low cost which included a
subsidy from Bradford Council. I was allocated to Farmington,
Missouri, which had probably been the original one-horse town in
the middle of nowhere. By 1974, it had seemingly more churches
for a population of 7,000 than Bradford had for a quarter of a
million, along with a single main street with shops that smelt of
citrus air freshener, and a drive-in cinema on the edge of town.
But teenagers had the benefit of the great American car culture
and were able to drive from the age of sixteen, so, as night fell in
the soggy heat of a Midwestern summer, they took to the streets
in their automobiles, tooted the horn at stop signs and urged pas-
sengers to jump from one vehicle to another before roaring off

again. We would then meet at the Dairy Queen for a malt and some fries to a soundtrack provided by the St Louis Top 40 radio station, KXOK.

This was impossibly exotic compared with the England of the 1970s. My host family was headed by a man called Homer, which was funny even then, but they did me proud. We went to the top of the Gateway Arch in St Louis, voyaged on a Mississippi paddle steamer, and went water-skiing on the Lake of the Ozarks, where I stayed upright for approximately three seconds and then sank inelegantly into its balmy waters. I ate pizza for the first time. I attended classes at Farmington High School which were some years behind Bradford Grammar School in their intellectual challenge, but the American students were socially confident and boundlessly optimistic in a manner that was unknown back home. When they graduated, with the school band playing *Pomp and Circumstance*, I felt an emotional commitment to their school and their town and their country that remained with me for years. I flew unwillingly home to Britain in a fit of teenage moroseness.

But the following year something transformational happened in Bradford: the city became the home of a commercial radio station. I had long been fixated by radio, starting with the discovery of *The World Tonight* on Radio 4 when I was twelve or so. At the risk of sounding like William Hague, I also used to listen in bed to *Today in Parliament*. But I liked music radio too, and in the analogue days of the 1970s – with little choice of listening – it was a thrill that Bradford was going to have its own station. In September 1975, Pennine Radio came on air, with a logo that included an ear affixed to nothing in particular and a jingle package that incorporated the refrain 'Pennine Two Thirty-Five. That's the sound going into your ear 'ole.' I was captivated by the programmes if not by the jingles. Pennine was part commercial operation and part community trust, which meant that it had a higher than usual speech content alongside the pop music that attracted its biggest audiences. I listened voraciously, even when I was doing my homework, and it was on Sunday night that I came across a programme called *Tops and Noils* presented by Austin Mitchell, who was then the star presenter on Yorkshire Television. It was a mix of folklore and brass band music, and featured within it old folk reminiscing about days gone by in a segment called 'How We Were Then'. I wrote to Austin professing a not entirely sincere admiration for the show, and he replied suggesting I could be a student volunteer collecting some of the material for him – which is how I made my first visit to that holy of holies, a proper radio station. It somehow added to the romance that it was located in the light-starved basement of a converted wool warehouse. After training that must have lasted fifteen minutes, I was sent out on my first assignment: interviewing an elderly man about his experience of the First World War.

Along with Austin, the big figure in my early experience of broadcasting was Dorothy Box. She was the community affairs producer at Pennine, and she took me under her wing: endlessly kind and patient with someone who was still a schoolboy, and willing to let me experiment with the medium with which I was falling ever more deeply in love. I made a half-hour documentary about Bradford Grammar School for the community access slot, and another programme about my German teachers, who had fled Austria in 1938 and made a new life here. Austin sent a letter in spidery handwriting on Yorkshire Television notepaper:

'Just a note, as all such letters begin, to say how much I enjoyed your Viennese interview. It was well done – apart from a dodgy first question – and the interest was very well kept up. Congrats.' Heartened by the mentoring I was getting, I knew with absolute certainty that this was the sort of thing I wanted to do in my working life.

But there was university still to come. The A-level factory did its stuff and I was considered good enough to apply for Oxford, so I did the entrance exam and on a misty December day I was interviewed by Wadham College and shortly afterwards offered a scholarship to read Modern History. When I started there in the autumn of 1976, I added German to my course for a reason that now seems odd: I had decided that I didn't like any history before the modern age, so studying Modern Languages allowed me to ditch the tiresome medieval stuff. It was quixotic too, because I was never an expert linguist and my eagerness to get out to work meant that I was determined to be away from Oxford after the minimum three years; I therefore didn't do the year living in Germany, which would have helped me enormously with my language skills.

I loved Oxford, while at the same time getting much less out of it than I should have. Wadham was a non-stuffy place, and it was conspicuous for its left-wing politics and its social liberalism. We had a Ho Chi Minh Quad in solidarity with the people of Vietnam. Despite thinking this was a silly gesture, even for 1970s students, I felt at home at Wadham. I adored living in a seventeenth-century building even though the plumbing had progressed little since its construction. We had to go down three flights of stairs and across the quadrangle to another staircase if we wanted to use the bathroom, and there was no heating in the bedrooms. In winter I sometimes slept in an unhygienic student fashion, with my pullover on top of sensible Yorkshire pyjamas, and the bed covered by the thickest duvet known to humankind. The more conventional images of Oxford turned out to be true, too. For two years running I had friends who rented a room from a don at New College, and the condition of tenancy was that they had to walk his three dogs each day. So I wandered miles with them, along the banks of the Cherwell and beyond, forming a particularly strong bond with a basset hound called Sally. I devoured what was on offer in the great libraries, wandered contemplatively across Christ Church Meadows on sunlit days, cheered our rowers from the banks of the river (always a position preferred to being in the boat itself) and debated political issues with my friends till dawn. By then, I had joined the Labour Party. I was probably one of a vanishingly small number of people to become a member because of the Lib–Lab pact, since I liked Jim Callaghan's centrist pragmatism and it was some years before I understood Mrs Thatcher's appeal.

In contrast to students of today, I also felt better off than at any time previously in my life. Tuition was free, and due to my parents' low income I received a grant towards my living costs from the City of Bradford. The teaching was, I suspect, patchier than it should have been. Like most students, I did best in the papers where I was inspired by my tutor and given no quarter when I was thinking sloppily – and not all my history sessions achieved those goals. In my German classes, I found I was fired up by the challenges of Goethe and Schiller and Grass and Thomas Mann, though my tutor sometimes accused me of taking too high an overview of the subjects. 'You write like a journalist', he said once, doubtless intending that to be a terrible insult. I, of course, regarded it as a compliment.

I know I spent too much time working at Pennine when I was back home in Bradford for the vacations. I used to do early shifts on the breakfast show co-ordinating the travel news and answering listeners' phone calls, and then I would persuade the programme controller to let me make a documentary or contribute to the station's magazine shows. I was unimpressed by people who did student media: I was doing the real thing. That should not, however, have included helping Pennine to cover the 1979 general election declaration in Skipton just six weeks ahead of my Finals.

My fascination with radio meant that I had a set with a powerful aerial that allowed me to pick up the London commercial radio stations – Capital and LBC – in Oxford. I supplemented this with a daily fix of news from the *PM* programme on Radio 4, though I never heard *Today*. It was on way too early for a student. The allure of the media was strengthened by appearing on *University Challenge* in the autumn of 1978. Wadham lost, and I wore a dreadful cardigan. There was a brief moment of pride when I broke into a question about ancient history and earned myself a 'well interrupted, Wadham' from the quizmaster Bamber Gascoigne, which made up for a number of wrong answers earlier in the show. But the main appeal was in seeing Granada Television, a shiny outpost of Television Land in the centre of Manchester, and being accommodated in dressing rooms used by the stars of *Coronation Street*. I concluded during the filming of the programme that I had no desire to be on television myself. The moment when I wrongly interrupted the first question was when I had a jolt of awareness that I was appearing on national television and this could be a route to glory or, more likely if I kept screwing things up, humiliation. What interested me most was what was happening behind the scenes: the mechanics of making the show, what the producers did – and how to set about getting a job there.

To my disappointment, a few months later Granada turned me down as a graduate recruit. So did the BBC news trainee scheme, without so much as an interview. But otherwise I did well: among my job offers was the Thomson Regional Newspaper traineeship in Newcastle and a researcher's job at London Weekend Television. What I did then was a case of heart overruling head. I turned down the big beasts of the media world and opted instead to take an initial six-month contract at Pennine Radio. My parents seemed phlegmatic at the time, but they later told me that they had received much 'sympathy' for having a son who had gone to Oxford and yet had chosen to return to Bradford and work in what its critics saw as a two-bit commercial radio station. All I felt at twenty-one was that, having had my life defined by high-pressure exams for almost as long as I could remember, I had the right to do what I wanted for once. Nowhere else would I have been trusted to do so much so young as at the place where they had known me for five years. I therefore set to work with a song in my heart on a starting salary of £3,750 per annum.

CHAPTER 3

LOCAL RADIO

W HEN I STARTED working full-time at Pennine Radio, just a week after I had finished at Oxford, I had a lesson drummed into me. If we sold commercials and made enough money, I was in a job. If we didn't, I would be out of one. It was most commonly articulated by our managing director, Mike Boothroyd, who had a Yorkshire attitude to financial prudence: never spend a pound if a penny will do. I knew that a community affairs producer, the role I was given, was a bit of a luxury even for a well-rooted local station like Pennine

– and our speech programming depended on us being successful as a business. I have therefore always appreciated an entrepreneurial spirit in media, even though my career ended up being overwhelmingly in the BBC. I also know that commercial radio can offer a public service.

As it happened, my first few months at Pennine coincided with the prolonged ITV strike that ran from August to October in 1979. This made it a lucky miss that I hadn't gone to London Weekend Television: I would have moved to London and promptly out onto a picket line. But it also meant swathes of the advertising displaced from ITV moved over to independent local radio, and Pennine was brimful with commercials – and not just the usual DIY warehouses and the Bradford Co-op. We had proper brands with decently produced ads, and real money coming into our tills. There was a sense of exhilaration among the sales team, and the sound of coins being counted could be heard from the boardroom. There was no talk of booting out the community affairs chap.

This was a golden time for commercial radio stations. There were not many of them, so they had local monopolies. Major personalities wanted to be on them, and Pennine often featured the Yorkshire miners' leader Arthur Scargill, while local MPs including Sir Keith Joseph would dutifully turn up for phone-ins. While he waited, Sir Keith read Proust in Pennine's reception area. The stations were popular enough to offer something for everyone, with Bradford's schedule including classical music, country music, a nightly Asian magazine programme, and a DJ called Julius K. Scragg who offered a late-night weekend show with 'dares' for guests including removing their clothes in his studio.

The stations could afford relatively large newsrooms: Pennine had between eight and ten journalists, and the main news programme of the day at 6 p.m. was an hour long. I produced 'The Community Show' twice a week within that, which gave me experience at the age of twenty-one of devising running orders and creating an appealing mix of speech items. I was also allowed to range across the daytime music programmes, booking guests and running campaigns on everything from getting fit to furnishing homes for Vietnamese boat people. It was what I had hoped for: the programme controller, Jeff Winston, gave me autonomy on a professional radio station. I learned a vast amount.

By contrast, the BBC at the time seemed like a somewhat grey and hierarchical place. We derided the output of our competition at BBC Radio Leeds because it was, to us, so yawn-inducingly dull. But I could tell that commercial radio would never offer me the opportunities in speech radio that there were at the BBC, so in the spring of 1980 I started applying for jobs at the corporation. I went for a role at Radio Sheffield and another one at Radio Lincolnshire, which was a new station scheduled to launch later in the year. My job at Pennine had been offered without competition and confirmed in a cheery letter from Jeff, but the BBC had a majestic appointments process that sent papers and projected salary charts and expense guidelines at every stage. After my preliminary interview in Lincolnshire, I was invited to London for a voice test followed by an appointment board, and candidates were offered a choice of subjects on which to speak: (a) Lincolnshire – the forgotten county; (b) Moscow or not – politics or sport?; (c) The problem of Doing-It-Yourself. Ever the sporting politician, I chose to advocate that Britain should take part in the 1980 Olympics. It was probably also a reflection of my youthful instinct that Mrs Thatcher was wrong about almost everything.

I was offered jobs by both stations. I had no hesitation in choosing Lincolnshire because it was about to pioneer radio in a county without any locally based broadcasting, and because Sheffield didn't seem much of a trade-up from Bradford. So on 14 July 1980, Bastille Day, I set off from my home city in a first class train carriage, since my reporter role qualified for such privilege. I presented myself as a new BBC employee at the Local Radio Training Unit in the Langham building in central London. It was the former grand hotel opposite Broadcasting House, and has since been converted back into a luxury hotel. Then, it was a decaying warren of BBC offices and studios for those not grand enough to inhabit BH itself. I began as a member of a new station training course, lasting five weeks, before we were transferred to our new patch and began preparing for an on-air date in November.

Lincolnshire, and BBC Radio Lincolnshire, will always mean a lot to me. I could not have had a better first manager than Roy Corlett, a swashbuckling Scouser who contrived to battle against the BBC and its dafter rules while also being a loyal servant of it. I made lifelong friendships, the strongest being with Les Sheehan, who became another key member of my kitchen cabinet – of the rank of Foreign Secretary, though given his love of television and radio he might have preferred to be Broadcasting Minister. He has been the brother I never had. I also became more attached to this 'forgotten' county than I ever thought possible as a Yorkshireman. My parents found Lincolnshire alluring, to the extent that they moved to the county as their retirement home and ended their days in a village just outside Lincoln, which gave them a peace and contentment they no longer found in Bradford.

Roy's recipe for team building on his radio station included plenty of alcohol and ribaldry. My memories of the training course are mainly about late nights in the Spaghetti House restaurant in Goodge Street, fuelled by gallons of cheap red wine. But he expected us to work hard too. When we arrived in Lincolnshire, he committed the staff to travelling along every road in the county with our radio car towing a giant transistor radio to show that local broadcasting was about to begin. As a nervous driver, the idea of being entrusted with the radio car and a trailer along the narrow B-roads of a rural county was unappealing, but fortunately there were some strong women who accepted the challenge and even managed to reverse accurately when we were blocked in by tractors. It was already apparent that we were welcome. One glorious day in the south of the county, where the Fens reveal that the sky is bigger than you ever imagined, my colleague Penny Bustin and I were waved down at the side of the road as we motored along with our giant radio. It was a farmer who had heard that Radio Lincolnshire was starting soon and was delighted to see us passing by – so he presented us with two Lincolnshire cauliflowers for good luck.

We had more formal outings across the county, too. Ahead of our launch, we held public meetings in Boston, Skegness and Horncastle and other significant centres of population. We discovered that most Lincolnshire towns had only one restaurant, which was Chinese and opened between 7 p.m. and 8.30 p.m. It would be closed most Wednesdays and every Sunday. The meetings were enlivened by Roy's irreverent introductions of his team, and he always defined me by two characteristics: (1) 'Roger is from commercial radio', and (2) 'He's a reporter but he's never even been a journalist before', which was true in the sense that I had never had any training, and Pennine was regarded by the BBC as being somewhat rock-and-roll and not at the required standard of the corporation. The star of the meetings, though, was our advisory committee chairwoman, an elderly gentlewoman farmer from Hykeham called Mary Large. Mary had little knowledge of broadcasting, but made up for it by limitless enthusiasm and a dose of eccentricity. When asked whether a particular location would be able to receive our signal, she would proclaim excitedly: 'Yes, the beams will get you. The beams will get you!'

Our test transmissions from the autumn of that year are like echoes from another age. We all spoke in a much posher way than we did after the onslaught of Estuary English and the rising inflections of *Neighbours*. Les Sheehan's announcements then sound rather like Prince Charles does today, with another colleague and friend Debbie Wilson as Princess Margaret. This reflected the voice training we had received during our course from David Dunhill, a former Home Service and Third Programme announcer, and Jimmy Kingsbury, one of the old-style brigade from Radio 2. We were taught to inflect appropriately: 'The stock market ended UP' (cheerful, rising voice) or 'The forecast is for more rain' (concerned tone, emphasis on 'rain'), with a precision of pronunciation that had never existed in commercial radio.

The beams began for real on 11 November 1980. We were buoyed by a message from the Prime Minister, who was, of course, a Lincolnshire girl. 'I am delighted to send my best wishes to Radio Lincolnshire on its opening day,' said the letter on Downing Street notepaper from Margaret Thatcher.

> The government attaches very great importance to the expan-
> sion of local radio. It can help to strengthen and develop that
> sense of community that is so essential a part of the fabric of
> our society. And it is particularly valuable in serving people
> who live in the country as well as those who live in towns. I
> am pleased there is now to be a BBC local radio station in my
> own home county and I wish it every success.

At the time we didn't appreciate the rarity value of Mrs Thatcher welcoming the expansion of the BBC.

The first news bulletin was read by Penny Bustin, who went on to a career in television, and the main local story was a report from me on the effect of fire fighters' strikes across the county. It was the first of hundreds of items I did in my year or so at Radio Lincolnshire, and we reporters were driven hard: sent off to the coast or the Fens or the Wolds to gather stories, assigned to council meetings where we were expected to report live and then produce more items for the following day's breakfast show, and despatched every Friday to talk to the county's football managers ahead of their weekend fixtures. This all sat within a radio station that had a friendliness and accessibility lacking in some other parts of the BBC local network of the time. There was an afternoon when, presenting the sports desk, I was confronted by a mountain of horseracing results that were supposed to be read out. I opted for interactivity. 'There are so many racing results that it's probably easiest if you phone in if you want to know any of them, and I'll give them to you direct,' I said. Nobody called, which shaped my attitude to the racing results on 5 Live some years later. Our breakfast show had a brief to play only instrumental music before

8 a.m. for fear of scaring off the opinion formers attracted to our news and current affairs items, but after that it became a station with a popular agenda. 'Super Trouper' by Abba is the record I forever associate with Radio Lincolnshire's early days, and it was deemed to be the perfect example of a pop single that wouldn't alienate the pensioners in our audience. The first set of listening figures confirmed we had the right formula: in our first couple of weeks of transmission we had overtaken Radio 4 in the Lincolnshire ratings, and we were only a whisker behind Radio 1.

We had a mixed reaction from the county's press. The Lincolnshire Standard Group, which ran weekly papers, had been friendly to us with preview articles ahead of our launch; but the *Lincolnshire Echo*, then published in three editions across the day, saw us as the enemy. Barely a word was printed about the new BBC station, until the day of our launch. Buried inside, with the headline in the tiniest font, were these words: 'On the air. Radio Lincolnshire started broadcasting today.' That was our last mention in print for months, but there was some collaboration across the battle lines. On the press bench at Lincoln City Council I sat alongside a reporter from the *Echo*, and in the way of the media we checked with each other after a meeting about what we thought the key decisions were and which stories we were going to file for our respective outlets. Sometimes there's safety in numbers if you want to escape a bollocking for missing a story. The reporter was called John Inverdale, and it soon became apparent that he was keener than he should have been on radio over print. After a drink one night, I took him round Radio Lincolnshire's HQ to see our studios and I could safely have predicted afterwards that he would end up in broadcast media – though not that he would achieve such eminence in national radio and television. Some years later, he reminisced about when we had first met. 'This was the 1980s,' he said, 'and I wanted to talk about Spandau Ballet and Lincoln City Football Club. Roger wanted to talk about politics. Central government, local government, the politics of the BBC. To me, he will always be the slightly rotund figure with a receding hairline with an obsessive interest in the workings of the Upper Witham Drainage Board.' Although there was significant truth in this – certainly in the rotund and receding bits – I had by this stage given up being a member of a political party, because I thought it was incompatible with journalism. I no longer believed in any single party's manifesto, and I realised it was more fun watching politics from the media than it was tramping the streets wearing a rosette. I therefore applied myself to watching the birth of the SDP from Lincoln – the home of Dick Taverne's Democratic Labour a decade earlier – presumably to the incomprehension of Inverdale. But we got on well, really, and he became my successor at Radio Lincolnshire, and later a top member of my 5 Live presentation team.

Thanks to my parents' move to Lincolnshire later in the decade, I never really left the county. Indeed, it now feels as much like home as Bradford ever did. That time at Radio Lincolnshire was a profoundly happy one. I still love walking round the Cathedral Close in uphill Lincoln and across the square to the castle with its view over the Trent Valley to Nottinghamshire and beyond; then down Steep Hill to the Wig and Mitre with memories of evenings of beer and chilli con carne with a dozen or more of us from the radio station. Skegness remains one of my favourite seaside resorts, though 'bracing' is the appropriate word when the wind comes in direct from the North Sea. I remember the impulse decisions to go to the coast when we were at a loose end, and to ride the Wild Mouse rollercoaster or fritter away 10p pieces in the slot machines before eating fish and chips late at night on a bench on the seafront. They are the kind of things you do in your early twenties and are too often lost when you become fully adult.

My next home was less romantic. I went to Northampton. This was partly because I was offered a promotion but also because I had so enjoyed launching one new radio station that I wanted to do another. I returned to the Langham for my second new station training course in two years. The manager of Radio Northampton, Mike Marsh, had a different recruitment policy to Roy Corlett's. I was a rarity at Lincolnshire in having a degree, and most of Roy's choices were, like him, from the University of Life. Mike went for graduates in pretty much every role, though his concept of the station was markedly more populist than in Lincolnshire. North-ampton had been transformed from a traditional market town by expansion zones with a young population, and the county included the steelworkers of Corby and the shoemakers of East Northants. Whereas Lincolnshire's recurrent stories were its agriculture and its coast, Northamptonshire was about industrial decline and the M1. Therefore we were set up as a bright pop station punctuated by a punchy local news service, and Lincolnshire's Abba was replaced by Adam and the Ants shrieking 'Stand and Deliver'.

I was chosen to read the first news bulletin on the day of the station's launch, with its opening headline 'General Galtieri tells the Argentine people – the Falkland Islands still belong to them' reflecting the end of the war in the South Atlantic. This was filmed by a crew from *Look East* and I was featured on their programme looking more confident than I felt and sporting an improbable haircut. But Radio Northampton, also in a county starved of local media, was an immediate hit, and it boosted the careers of many of its young team. Martin Stanford ended up as a Sky News presenter, Howard Stableford presented children's programmes and *Tomorrow's World*, and Lisa Ausden became one of BBC television's most respected executive producers on programmes including *Crimewatch* and *Watchdog*. My best friend on the station was Beverley Rigby, a fellow Oxford graduate and affectionately nicknamed 'the shrew' for her put-downs of annoying people, which has created a series of small furry animal jokes between us lasting more than thirty years. A clockwork mouse, given to me by Beverley on a recent visit to Cambridge, sits on my study desk.

I grabbed opportunities to report for television and network radio when they came along, because I hadn't yet fully realised that I was better as a producer behind the scenes than being on-air talent. An appearance I made as a reporter on *Look East*, wearing an anorak that looked like something from the C&A bargain bucket, should have been warning enough, but I had more luck with radio. The *Today* programme ran a report of mine on a new system in fire stations in Northamptonshire designed to switch off electrical appliances when the fire fighters were called out: the kind of piece I would have rejected instantly when I was myself a *Today* night editor. A rather better package about Northampton Town Football Club and its hopes of giant killing in the FA Cup ran on the BBC World Service, though the club's nickname of 'The Cobblers' is not one that travels well. Every so often there was a jab in the ribs about my relative inexperience. Commentary is a difficult art, and I felt that most keenly when I was assigned to Kettering

railway station at the start of the Queen's visit to Northamptonshire. When Her Majesty emerged, I began a sentence, 'There is
the Queen, greeted by cheering crowds, and…' – at which point,
and rather too late, I remembered that the sine qua non of a royal
commentary was to describe what the Queen was wearing. I hadn't
a clue. I had no sense of colour or style, either for myself or anyone else. Was she in red or cerise or maroon or what? 'And – she
is wearing a coat,' I revealed to the listeners at home.

There were two other highlights in my time at Radio Northampton. The first was on our Open Day when I was allowed to
present a music show while listeners were touring the station,
and the local paper ran a story about 'disc jockey Roger Mosey'
alongside a photo of me clutching a record album and preparing
to spin those tunes. I did not show that cutting to the Fellows of
Selwyn College during the Mastership election. But even more
exciting was the 1983 general election, when Northamptonshire's
concentration of marginal seats meant that we had our share of
the national spotlight; it was a thrilling time for a political animal
like me to be in charge of the station's coverage.

I sent myself off to report on Margaret Thatcher's campaigning
tour of the county, which featured a visit to the Weetabix factory
near Kettering. This was a reflection of the style of campaigning
that Mrs Thatcher had pioneered. There were photos to be had of
the PM in a white coat and hat, looking lovingly at lots of little
Weetabix as they whizzed off the production line, but, in the bus-
tle and din of a factory, she was completely inaccessible to the
journalists covering the event. Looking for the exclusive angle, I
bellowed at Denis Thatcher as he trudged along behind: 'Do you
like Weetabix, Mr Thatcher?' He grimaced at the noise, doubtless

of both the factory and me, and pointed to his ears in a gesture of 'can't hear'. The world was never to know what cereal he
preferred, and his wife avoided any pesky questions about local
issues. But I did interview other top politicians on their visits:
Norman Tebbit, who was charming, and Roy Jenkins, then Prime
Minister-designate for the Alliance, who wasn't. He struck me
then, and later, as one of those politicians who don't have much
time for courtesy for the people outside their social circle. Every
single candidate standing in a Northamptonshire seat was interviewed for constituency profiles, and we commissioned our own
election-day exit poll, which miraculously turned out to be right.
It was a wonderful opportunity for a 25-year-old, and it was to be
the perfect training for running campaign coverage on the *Today*
programme four years later.

The election over, I didn't feel much inclination to stay in Northamptonshire. I saw a television documentary in which one of the
county's former MPs said the happiest day of her life was seeing
the signpost for 'Northampton' in her rear-view mirror as she
escaped back to London, and, without quite reaching that level,
I was ready for a change. I had had the most wonderful time in
local radio, and, as commercial radio became blander and more
nationally programmed, I became ever more convinced that the
BBC should have an enduring role in the cities and counties of the
UK, reporting local issues and fostering community identity. But
for now I had done my bit for Lincolnshire and Northampton,
and I felt it was time to break the second of the vows I had made
when I left Oxford. I used to tell people that I never wanted to
work in news and I never wanted to work in London. The gravi-
tational pull was unavoidable, though, if I wanted to deepen my

involvement in current affairs broadcasting and to see what it was like having the canvas of a nation rather than a county. I started filling in applications for jobs in the capital.

CHAPTER 4

STARTING
IN LONDON

FROM MY TIME in Lincolnshire and Northamptonshire,
I had no idea how the BBC in London operated. It was
an article of faith in local radio that network people were
ignorant about life outside the capital, but we had little understanding about how the teams in Broadcasting House and Bush
House and Television Centre fitted together or what the jobs
there entailed. It was something of a lottery deciding which roles

to apply for, but I ended up in what was spectacularly the right place for me. I was given a six-month attachment to the Special Current Affairs Unit (SCAU, as it was known), which was the home on Radio 4 for political coverage. It was run by Anne Sloman, a formative influence on generations of young producers. She was a renowned producer of political documentaries as well as being in charge of regular output such as *The Week in Westminster* and *Inside Parliament*.

Initially, I was allocated to the departmental version of the salt mines. I had a few weeks as producer of *Yesterday in Parliament*, which had recently become part of the *Today* programme and was being encouraged to be wittier and more sketch-like in its approach. The producer's job was little more than monitoring hours of parliamentary debate and then, to the orders of the correspondent of the day, laboriously finding the clips for broadcast from a bank of recording machines. But this drudgery was incidental compared with my thrill at making it to Westminster, to walking down Whitehall and seeing the tower of Big Ben, and knowing that I had a pass that allowed me to see the great men and women of the day in the chamber of the House of Commons. This was before the collapse in faith in our institutions. It was only five years or so since Parliament had mattered enormously during the tail end of the Callaghan government, with its nightly crisis votes and ultimately a defeat on a motion of confidence. When I got there, it was at the height of Mrs Thatcher's dominance, with the Conservative back benches squashed full with the beneficiaries of her landslide victory earlier in the year. The Commons had the ideological chasms revealed during the 1983 campaign, with a Labour Party still dominated by the pro-nationalisation,

anti-Europe, anti-nuclear weapons left. It felt like politics was still
a battle that stirred the blood, and one that mattered.

I spent enough time on *Yesterday in Parliament* to pick up
another friend for life: David Kogan, who was a producer on
Today and seated alongside me in Westminster. David escaped
early from the BBC and later became the sports rights guru for the
Premier League, in which capacity he was to recur in my working
life but playing for the 'other side'. Now, though, it was time for
a dream role: Anne asked me to produce *The Week in Westminster*, the review programme that has been running on BBC radio
since 1929 and is therefore only slightly younger than the corporation itself. It offered a much greater opportunity for a producer
to make an impact than the obligation-heavy daily reporting, and
it required a good working relationship with the presenters, who
were some of the doyens (all men in those days) of Fleet Street.
Already starstruck by being in the same office as John Cole and
John Sergeant, I now had the chance to work with the political
heavyweights of the day: Hugo Young of the *Sunday Times*, Peter
Riddell of the *Financial Times* and Adam Raphael of *The Observer*.

The greatest mentor of all of them was Robert Carvel of the
London Evening Standard. Bob was in his mid-sixties when I met
him, so fully forty years older than me and with every reason to
be exasperated by a young chap from local radio trying to tell him
what to do. But his kindness and willingness to share his wisdom
set him apart. He would relate stories about the politicians, good
and bad, that he had encountered over the years. 'Never trust a
man who is rude to the servants', he once said, shaking his head at
the behaviour of a recent senior minister. But he loved the theatre
of Parliament and its conflicts, real or confected. One of his

favourite quotations was from Rab Butler: 'I believe the ferocity of the debate is a very great safeguard for our liberty, because out of the sparks you see liberty shining.' Many of his anecdotes were delivered from the middle of a cloud of pipe smoke as we sat in the parliamentary press gallery tea room planning the week's programme, and most weeks he would also take me off to the National Liberal Club for a lunchtime mix of ghastly food with wonderful political gossip. I learned such a lot from him, not just about the technicalities of Westminster but also about the values it should aspire to.

Bob indulged some, if not all, of my youthful enthusiasms. I was puzzled as to why *The Week in Westminster* came on air with the first sentence of the script, and without any words of welcome. In a revolutionary change of format, we negotiated that he would start by saying 'Good morning'. He allowed me to book for interview MPs whom I had read about and found interesting, hence the appearance of the newly elected Gordon Brown in a discussion about events in the Middle East. In return, and to hear it said in warm Scottish tones, I would occasionally sneak in a clip from George Foulkes MP so that Bob could say his favourite constituency name: 'Carrick, Cumnock and Doon Valley'. I am proud to this day that my first national *Radio Times* credit in December 1983 was thus: '*Week in Westminster*. Robert Carvel, Political Editor of the *London Standard*, views the past week. Producer Roger Mosey.'

The prospect of returning to Northampton at the end of this attachment was appalling. I therefore started applying for other jobs in network current affairs, and was lucky in that there was a vacancy on the *Today* programme. With some pre-interview help from David Kogan, I got the job – surviving a ferocious appointment board grilling from the programme editor, Julian Holland. He was another of the greats from the 1980s: a former features editor on the *Daily Mail*, and known universally as 'Jules'. He had very little sight, and wore the thickest-glassed spectacles we had ever seen. But behind the dishevelled appearance was an astonishing editorial brain. If you came up with a half-formed idea at a morning editorial, Jules would shoot you down without mercy – and the trick was to reformulate and persist until you came up with something that was intellectually and journalistically watertight. The words from him 'well done, lad' were magical because of the agony you had to go through to win them.

This was the era on *Today* of Timpson and Redhead, the best combination of presenters the programme has known. John Timpson was avuncular on air, representing southern suburban England, while Brian Redhead was northern and chippier. They covered most of the week, since there was then no Saturday programme. They seldom showed signs of liking each other off air, but on air they were brilliant: partly in their contrasting styles, but also in the way they had an understanding of the dynamics of dual presentation, and a generosity to each other when they came up with funny lines. Instead of the toe-curling attempts to out-talk and out-jest a colleague that many presenters think is clever, Timpson and Redhead would honour a joke by letting the listener savour it and then moving on, perhaps with a small chuckle of appreciation, to a new topic.

There was none of the indulgence towards new, young producers that I had found on *The Week in Westminster*. If you screwed up on *Today*, it was serious stuff – and Timpson and Redhead would take no prisoners. I made plenty of mistakes that were my fault, but one morning I simply obeyed the instructions of the output editor in changing the duration of an item and giving the presenters a little more time to fill. Brian was furious, and hurtled out of the studio into the control room to berate me: 'I will have you sacked,' he hissed, before running back into the studio and calmly reading the news headlines. By the end of the programme, he had forgotten that he had planned to have me sacked and was his usual chirpy self. It took time to earn his respect.

This kind of pressure was especially tough given the hours we worked. A night shift in that era started at 6 p.m. and finished at 9 a.m. the next day, with the intense concentration and adrenalin-surge of the programme's transmission at the end of the fifteen-hour stint. The air in the *Today* office was always full of smoke, with most of the programme team puffing away incessantly on cigarettes, and we drank instant coffee from a large catering pack of the cheapest Nescafé, which had a crust that must have been made up of equal parts of cigarette ash and London pollution. When we were released from this, we had just nine hours of rest before we had to do it again; though two night shifts comprised an entire working week when I began on *Today*, and it was impossible to complain about the amount of time we had off. Perhaps because of this, there was a strong drinking culture – exemplified by the bottle of Scotch opened by the editor at the end of a night shift and shared by the overnight programme team and presenters. We thought nothing of drinking a bottle or two of wine during our evening on-shift meal, which we consumed in one of the late-opening restaurants within walking distance of

Broadcasting House. Some producers supplemented the social drinking by stashing away spirits in their locker and surreptitiously glugging the booze during the early hours of the morning. We junior staff added to our experience by sometimes running a programme when our colleagues were not feeling quite well enough to do so. I discussed this recently with a former Radio 4 producer, who said I shouldn't convey the impression that the drinking was gentlemanly and benign. It wasn't: it could be unpleasant and unsettling. However, I was never aware of it leading to other kinds of disreputable behaviour, and we existed in our booze-suffused world of radio current affairs with little contact with the rest of the corporation.

When I began on *Today*, so did the miners' strike. For most of my first year there, the strike dominated the programme and almost every morning we tried to book Arthur Scargill for the union or Ian MacGregor for the Coal Board or Peter Walker, the Energy Secretary, to cover the latest developments in the story. Overall, though, *Today* was probably slightly less political than it became under my editorship ten years later. Breakfast television was still enough of a novelty to be favoured over radio for some major interviews, and *Newsnight* was a power in the land, offering more political exclusives. But this didn't bother us because one of the things we took pride in was 'light and shade': making sure that the heat of debate was tempered by a gentle feature or a sideways look at modern life. Julian Holland's *Daily Mail* background helped with that, and he built up a team of reporters who were able to turn in finely crafted pieces of radio. The mix was lightened further by amusing competitions, such as 'Mini Sagas': asking listeners to tell stories in fifty words, and reading the best of them on air. We producers would regard these as a chore to schedule and a bore to listen to, but the audience loved the warmth of the programme and the chemistry of its presentation team.

One of the great prizes for a Radio 4 producer in the 1980s was to be selected to be sent to New York for a six-month stint as American producer for all the radio current affairs programmes. David Kogan had done the job in 1985, and a year later I was asked if I would take it on – which was an invitation I thought about for no time whatsoever before saying yes. These were the days of BBC largesse to its foreign-based staff, before the chill of austerity had swept through the corporation. The producer was allocated an apartment in midtown Manhattan, on the ninth floor of a building on the corner of 1st Avenue and 54th Street. It had only two main rooms – a living room roughly the size of my entire flat in England, and an equally large bedroom – but it could sleep five or six with its combination of beds and sofas, and it was perfectly situated. If you stuck your neck out of the window, you could see the East River. Directly below was a stereotypical New York scene of an intersection jammed by illegally parked cars and cabs tooting their horns at all hours of the day, and streets lined with family restaurants and delis. It was a short walk to the BBC office, which was in Rockefeller Plaza near the NBC Network headquarters and the famous skating rink. We had space on two floors of a skyscraper, and for the first time in my career I had my own office with a nameplate on the door, along with a bank of televisions for me to monitor the American networks and make sure London was informed of significant developments. But amid all the buzz of Manhattan, it was hard work: the time difference meant that you were often woken up early in the morning if a lunchtime programme in the UK wanted some material. I was once roused at 4 a.m. by a phone call from Radio Ulster, and when I sleepily explained what time it was in America, they continued regardless: 'Well, since you're awake, we wondered if you could find us an interview for our morning show…' The American day continued with servicing the *PM* programme, all the news bulletins and *The World Tonight* – and then, by mid-afternoon, you had to start thinking about items for the next day's edition of *Today*. This meant staying in the office with a correspondent long into the evening, and playing the resultant reports across to London in what was for them the early hours of the morning.

Technology in those days wasn't necessarily a friend. We were issued with a radio pager, which was seen as thrillingly cutting edge before the introduction of mobile phones, but all it could do was signal that the office wanted you to call in about something. It bleeped when there was an urgent matter, and the drill was to phone the foreign duty editor in London to find out what was needed. One relaxed Sunday I met a new temporary correspondent for lunch, and we decided afterwards to take in the sights on one of the Circle Line cruises around Manhattan – only for both our radio pagers to shriek into life a couple of minutes after the boat had set off. We were scheduled to be on the boat for the next two hours and there was no means of calling London. Every half-hour or so the bleepers would sound again, and we spent our time praying that they didn't signify the assassination of the President or some other cataclysmic event. The disclosure that we had been drifting past the Statue of Liberty on a sightseeing tour would not have been a good alibi for the non-appearance of reports from America. When we were finally able to reach dry land and dial

London from a payphone, we found out that it was a minor story from the West Coast on which they wanted our guidance – and they had lost interest when we failed to report in. But it was the beginning of the age in which everyone was supposed to be 'on' all the time, and there was to be no escape from the electronic call to attention.

Amid the regular duties, there was a special responsibility. The New York producer was in charge of Alistair Cooke's *Letter from America*, and it was close to the stature of a royal visit when Alistair came into the studio to record the broadcast. He was not always in New York: he still made trips to the UK, and he spent part of the year in California, which meant that sometimes he appeared only as a disembodied voice from a remote studio. But Alistair, then in his late seventies, was a veteran who turned out to be a man of considerable grace. He had to put up with a regular turn-over of producers jetting in from London, but mitigated this by having his favourite engineers to keep him company as well as look after the technical side of things. This was one assignment that you did not give to the trainee sound guy. The engineers gave me a tip early on. When Alistair had a funny line or an out-and-out joke in the script, he would look up from his papers and glance through the glass to check that we in the control room found it funny. So the engineers would prompt anyone watching to react as conspicuously as possible. 'OK, you guys, laugh!' they would say, as Alistair reached his punchline. It guaranteed a happy presenter at the end of the talk, though the recording invariably took a lot longer than the fifteen minutes of his regular slot. Alistair was a smoker, and there were prodigious numbers of coughs in most of his studio sessions, all of which had to be excised before broadcast. I got on well enough with him to receive one of his honours: an invitation to tea in his apartment, overlooking Central Park. When I left, he gave me a signed copy of his book *The Americans* with an inscription reflecting my job back home. 'Gratefully and with good wishes, for the world Today and tomorrow – and on and on. Alistair.'

The New York producer had the freedom to travel across the United States. I frequently caught the Amtrak train to Washington to work with our correspondents in DC, who were then preoccupied with the Iran-Contra affair. With the radio bureau chief David McNeil, I flew to swing states for the 1986 mid-term elections and we found ourselves at the State Fair in North Carolina and, by a bit of personal planning, tracking Senate leaders on a campaign trip to my old haunts in Missouri. It was in a small town there that David, a wine buff, came up against the limited ambitions of the Midwest. 'Do you have a wine list?' he asked the waitress, over-optimistically, in a homely diner. 'No, we don't,' was the reply, 'but we got red (she pronounced it 'ray-ud') and we got white.' David said he would have the red, earning the approving response, 'Red – that's mah favourite!'

I flew back from New York to London at the beginning of 1987 and went to the family home in Lincolnshire. That January it snowed heavily in the east of England and the temperatures were below freezing for days, which meant that after the neon-lit razzamatazz of Manhattan I was confined by a snowdrift to a bungalow on the outskirts of Lincoln. I was not happy. But by then I knew that I had another pleasurable assignment ahead of me. After the retirement of Julian Holland, Jenny Abramsky had become editor of *Today*; and she was to become the dominant figure in my professional life for the next ten years. I would end up doing five of the jobs that Jenny herself had done, and she entered *Today* – as she did all her roles – with breathtaking energy. She was unable to pass a news agency ticker service without ripping the latest story from the printer, brandishing it in the air and demanding that we do something about it immediately. But my first big assignment was Jenny asking me to take command of the programme's election coverage. Mrs Thatcher was expected to go to the country in the summer of that year, and the two *Today* political producers were to be Peter Burdin and myself. This initiated a deep friendship, and I became godfather to Peter's son Julien when he was born the following year.

The two of us cooked up our master plan. We had a stellar set of reporters on *Today*, so we decided to make them the centrepiece of the coverage by allocating them each to a nation or region of the UK. Thus Justin Webb, who rose to become a *Today* presenter, was sent to the battlegrounds of the Midlands, while Bill Turnbull, now the host of BBC Breakfast, was put in the south of England. The full team of six gave listeners a lively account of the campaign on the ground, while also offering us the flexibility to track senior politicians across the country. But we knew we needed the set-piece interviews, too, and in trying to attract the party leaders onto the programme we promised them something a little different. Ours would be longer, more reflective conversations – not the standard knockabout political interview, but something that would allow the leaders to think aloud and have more time to set out their views.

These encounters were to be near the end of the campaign. Peter Hobday duly did a gently probing interview on the

Thursday morning with the two Davids (Steel and Owen) who were representing the Liberal/SDP Alliance; and on Friday it was Brian Redhead who sought light rather than heat from Neil Kinnock. But the biggest moment was to be on the Saturday when John Humphrys, the rather feistier replacement for John Timpson, was going to interview Margaret Thatcher. This caused a surge of excitement because she was planning to come into the studio, which was an extremely rare event in those days. Prime Ministers were far less accessible than they are now, and they tended to be interviewed in the grandeur of Downing Street rather than in the grubby studio 4A in Broadcasting House. But the BBC Premises team had some thoughts about that grubbiness: to our astonishment, the *Today* green room was repainted overnight in honour of the Thatcher visit and flowers were put in locations that she might visit. Peter Burdin and I satirically sketched a design for a fountain that might be installed in our office, so Mrs Thatcher could watch the calming waters while she waited.

The Prime Minister was due on air in the prestige 8.10 a.m. slot, but she arrived extremely early – only just after Jenny Abramsky and me. We therefore had more than half an hour of trying to entertain someone who probably did not want to be entertained at all, and she certainly did not indulge in the free-ranging and indiscreet conversations favoured by some politicians in green rooms. I mentioned that, as I had driven through her constituency of Finchley that morning, I had seen a particularly high number of posters. This earned us a five-minute monologue on the cost of printing and the economics of publicity material. We also tried to find out whether she listened to our programme in the way ministers thought she did. Geoffrey Howe was famous for always wanting to go into the 7.50 a.m. slot, because it allowed him to filibuster up to the start of the weather forecast at 7.55, and it was rumoured that 7.50 was the radio-listening slot within the Thatcher household's breakfast routine. 'I listen to the news at 6 a.m.,' she said, 'and then I turn the radio off. At seven o'clock I hear the news, and then I'm often working. But I sometimes listen again to the news at eight, and that is it.' We were duly put in our place.

It was then through to the studio for the intended reflective conversation with John. Within the first minute I knew with certainty that this was not going to plan. John asked a reasonable first question, to which Mrs Thatcher gave a robust answer, but then he used the word 'uncaring' in a description of her prime ministerial style and got this blunderbuss reply:

And look who is charging me with being uncaring, the people who supported a coal strike, who didn't support the miners who went to work, but supported those who conducted that strike through intimidation, the object of which was to bring to a stop the whole of manufacturing industry which was to deprive the household and the pensioner of heat and light; and now they want to bring back secondary picketing, that was the party which votes against the prevention of terrorism, the party who in 1979 jolly nearly closed cancer wards. If you look under the health service, if you look at the headlines, then there was a strike in the health service, there was a strike in the ambulance service, the party which supports the teachers in striking against children. No, we care deeply, that's why I have gone through so much, Mr Humphrys, to restore Britain's reputation as a reliable ally and a trusted friend, that's why I went through so much in fighting strikes and that's why I'll continue to go through a great deal in standing up for Britain, and might I just say one further thing, the standard of living in this country, including the standard of care, is higher than it has ever been. We don't talk, we deliver.

She barely paused for breath, and the interview remained as combative for its full duration. She repeated the words 'Mr Humphrys' a number of times, with the warmth with which you might say 'bubonic plague'. It was, at the time, like watching a train careering out of control down a mountain track with Mrs Thatcher and Mr Humphrys grappling for control in the driver's compartment. Afterwards, I steeled myself for the task of escorting the Prime Minister to the doors of Broadcasting House. As we descended to the ground floor in the lift, an aide to the Prime Minister started to apologise to her that the interview had not turned out to be the kind of conversation that had been expected. Mrs Thatcher looked into the eyes of the BBC contingent, and said simply, 'We get what we expect from the BBC.' To make sure we'd got the message, she repeated, more slowly: 'We get what we expect.' We bade her a polite farewell, and the prime ministerial car swept her back onto the campaign trail and, within a few days, to celebrations of another landslide victory.

Today's campaign coverage was seen as a success. In the following weeks, Jenny Abramsky was identified as one of the leaders of the revolutionary change that was about to be unleashed in BBC News, courtesy of the arrival of John Birt as deputy director-general. Jenny, who was by this stage a friend as well as my boss, told a group of us over drinks in our regular wine bar that she was never going to be in favour with the new regime. She was promptly given a sizeable promotion to become editor of news and current affairs radio. When this happened, I never thought there would be any consequences for me. I had only been a senior producer on *Today* for a year, promoted just after Jenny's arrival. I had thrived on the election coverage, and now I wanted to become better at the most interesting job in radio: being a regular output editor on *Today*. But the Birt revolution was sweeping away the old guard, creating a raft of vacancies, and I was encouraged to apply for the role of editor on the *PM* programme. The people choosing the successful candidate were Ron Neil, who had been promoted to running all television and radio news, and Jenny, in her grand new role, and I regarded myself as such an outsider that I did one of the most relaxed and free-thinking interviews I have ever done.

That must be a good tactic. I was at home a couple of days later when Jenny phoned me, with the opening words, 'Hello – I'm speaking to the editor of the *PM* programme.'

Thinking she had kindly rung to tell me who had been appointed, and they were sitting alongside her, I replied, 'Oh, who is it?'

'It's you, you dope,' she said. And so at the age of twenty-nine, only three years after starting in network radio, I was put in charge of one of the flagship daily programmes. It turned out to be the start of the best part of a decade as a Radio 4 editor, in which I gradually moved backwards through the schedule, though upwards in terms of prestige – from *PM* to *The World at One* and then back to my original home on *Today*.

CHAPTER 5

THE AFTERNOON SEQUENCES

M Y FIRST VISIT to the *PM* office after I had been announced as the new editor was a nervous one. *The World at One* – *WATO* ('what-o') as it is known by its staff – and *PM* worked together in the same third-floor area of Broadcasting House. It has been managerially fashionable to marry and divorce them, and then remarry them, over the years; and I was inheriting *PM* as newly divorced from what had been called, quaintly, 'the afternoon sequences'. But the teams were still in the same office, and they included some redoubtable BBC veterans: the presenters Gordon Clough and Bob Williams, and long-established output editors like Carole Lacey, the partner of Julian Holland. As someone in my twenties, I was about to run a team with people in their fifties, and Gordon had been present-ing on Radio 4 when I was still in short trousers. They peered at their new editor from a fug of cigarette smoke that was even thicker than in the *Today* office, and a glass or two of Valpolicella was seldom far away. Until recently, a bottle of whisky and a bot-tle of gin had been delivered to the *PM* office every afternoon for 'hospitality' ahead of the presenters' stint on air. There were often no mixers, and the spirits were consumed – as on *Today* – from paper cups.

Most striking was that I was now the editor responsible for Valerie Singleton. Valerie had been the most famous television face of my childhood. She was the presenter of *Blue Peter* throughout my formative years, and forever associated with Petra the dog, Jason the cat and things made with a cut-up detergent bottle. She had escaped from children's television to grown-up programmes like *Nationwide* and *The Money Programme*, but it is hard to over-state how iconic she was to my generation. She still turned heads in restaurants where there was any accumulation of thirty-some-things or their parents. I had never met her before my arrival on *PM*, but within minutes she had invited me to a cup of tea in the BBC's eighth-floor restaurant looking out over the London rooftops. 'I bet you never thought when you were watching me on *Blue Peter*', she began, 'that you would one day be my boss.' I confirmed to her that this was true. When I was entranced by children's television on the flickering black-and-white set in our living room in Bradford, I did not muse during the duller episodes of *Bleep and Booster* that I would one day become Valerie Singleton's editor.

The difference between being the overall editor of a programme and being a senior producer, as I had been on *Today*, was a significant one. I was now in command of the budget, of staffing and of handling the requests for information and data that were a growing part of BBC life. When I had duty-edited an edition of the *Today* programme, I could go home and forget about work. Now I discovered what it was like managerially to be 'always on' – concerned about the programme and its people and its reputation even when I was on holiday. I was given not one scintilla of training. It was assumed that we could appoint staff and look after money based on the ability that had got us the job; this was an age before the Fair Selection courses or Producer Choice seminars that burnished our non-editorial skills. I was fortunate to have Jenny as my boss and the wise Martin Cox as my opposite number on *The World at One*, who were there to offer advice when the BBC management systems left me perplexed.

In any case, I saw my main task as editorial. *PM* was rather different in the late '80s to what it became with Eddie Mair a couple of decades later. For a start, we had two presenters every night, usually from a pool comprising Gordon, Bob, Val and Frances Coverdale. There was a signature tune, which prompted my one order from Ron Neil. He didn't like the old one at all, so I was despatched to the composer George Fenton, who had written the *Newsnight* theme, to get a better one. And this was the analogue era, as far away from today's digital technology as were the gramophone recordings of the 1940s and '50s. When I arrived at *PM*, almost every item was on tape; and, as was the case throughout radio in that era, the tape was manually edited by producers. They sliced it in two with a razor blade, removed a section they didn't want and stuck it back together with a sliver of sticky editing tape. This was burdensome enough on a *Today* night shift, but it was masochistic in the extreme for a fast-moving high-item show like *PM*. At half past four and quarter to five you would find presenters and producers running in and out of studios recording down-the-line interviews with correspondents, and then frantically removing retakes or stumbles on the tape machines in the office. It was sometimes known as 'de-umming', as interviewees' 'ums' were cut out of the tape.

There were two reasons for doing it this way. The first was that, if you got it right, it did sound slicker when the bulk of the programme was on tape. You could cut out hesitations, repetitions and deviations. The second was that producers had doubts about Val in particular on live interviews. She was an actress by training and a children's presenter for most of her career, and some felt it was risky to let her loose on a breaking story. There were examples of correspondents being left almost speechless by a Val question zooming onto the airwaves from the non-journalist segment of her brain. But I thought this was wrong on both counts. Live broadcasting has a charge and an excitement that you do not get from a bunch of tapes; and the point about *PM* was that it was on air when a lot of news was breaking. As for Val, I was sure that she could take a brief and I have always had a consistent view of presenters: they need to be produced. This can be synonymous with 'being told what to do', but so be it. They need to be listened to and handled sensitively, but ultimately editors should edit. I admired a deputy editor of *Today* who once wrote the word 'OBEY' in mirror writing on the glass between the control room and the presenters, to remind them of what was what. Val always had a wonderful, commanding presence on the radio; and with the right handling her performance became even better.

So we increased the number of items in the programme that went out live. We upped the story count, too, and sometimes a correspondent would pop onto the airwaves for less than a minute to update a breaking story. I was pleased when the Bradford *Telegraph & Argus* came to visit their local lad made good and headlined the report: 'Roger's Radio Rush Hour'. The copy began: 'In one of the control rooms at Broadcasting House, the atmosphere was so highly charged with adrenalin that even an observer like me, tucked away in a corner with notebook in hand, began to get high on it.' And the writer concluded: 'I left the studio appreciating why broadcasting is regarded as a branch of the media to which people need to be recruited young to learn its demanding ways, and wondering how on earth the *PM* team can do that job day after day without ending up either mad or dead.' But that was what we enjoyed, of course: the rollercoaster ride of never being quite sure what was going to happen next, which produced an engaging listen for people travelling home in their cars or having their tea.

We had relatively little interest in political interviews, which were regarded as the fiefdom of *Today* or *The World at One*. But I wanted the programme to have the occasional interlude from the rush of daily news, and we were lucky to have on our staff Roger Harrabin – who was then, and is now, one of the best reporters on environmental issues. With a bit of nagging from him, and a sense in the editorial team that green politics was going to be one of the themes of the future, we carved out a role for ourselves as environment specialists. In October 1988, we launched a feature called 'World Watch' which used BBC correspondents, and Roger when he could persuade me to pay for an air ticket, to report on some of the challenges the globe was facing beyond the usual headlines. From Lake Baikal, in what was then the Soviet Union, we examined irrigation and its effects; we took to the highways of California to see how they were trying to reduce lead in petrol. Roger visited Switzerland, conducting interviews about the integrated public transport systems there, which never seem to have made it back to Britain. This initiative drew an approving article from the arbiter of all issues in radio, Gillian Reynolds of the *Daily Telegraph*. She quoted me as asserting, in Birtist-approved fashion, that radio still had to choose 'important' over 'popular' as a criterion for inclusion in a news programme. 'With the environment,' she concluded, 'he may well have hit both targets at once.'

Encouraged by the first nice thing ever said about me in a national newspaper, we launched a competition to show how deeply green we were. I confess that this happened partly because we were able to secure a partnership with *The Times*, and for the lowest-profile of the daily news magazines it was a boost to see our name emblazoned across a distinguished broadsheet's pages. Hence 'The *Times/PM* Environment Award', which was brought into the world without any of the editorial compliance or competition rules that are mandatory today. It was, however, a lovely source of stories. We invited readers and listeners to tell us about people who had made a difference to their locality by putting the environment first, and the final shortlist showed the quality of what was being done. There was a New Forest keeper who was preserving hornets; a miner in Nottinghamshire who had created a wildflower meadow; a wildlife trust from Radnor; the Orkney Field Club, who were looking after the most northerly woodland in Britain; and a primary school from Reading trying, *The Times* wrote, 'to instil in its pupils a lasting reverence for the earth'. They were heart-warming tales, and also met another wish: that *PM* should get around the country and not be as metropolitan as it had been in former incarnations. It was the miner from Nottinghamshire who came out on top, helped by a background story that involved his working countless hours of overtime to fund the meadow. He was duly awarded £5,000 of *The Times*'s money, and invited to a celebration lunch at Broadcasting House, where he received his award from Princess Alexandra.

As someone who celebrated his 30th birthday while being editor of *PM*, I was still somewhat callow about the way BBC headquarters' politics operated. I had only a hazy grasp of the hierarchies beyond Jenny as my immediate boss. What I did know was that Radio 4 had little responsibility for us: our line management had moved fully into the news empire of John Birt and Ron Neil. This was deemed necessary to stop non-news specialists interfering in editorial decisions, and to safeguard television news in particular from any pressures from a ratings-minded controller of BBC One. As part of the shutting out of network influence, the controller of Radio 4 had not even been on my appointment board. I took this division rather too much to heart when I was invited by the controller, Michael Green, to be one of the speakers at the Radio AGM, a session at which all the genres of the network came together to share their ideas and plans. In my allocated slot, I said what I really thought. I argued that Radio 4 needed news programmes much more than news needed Radio 4. The network was given its biggest audiences by *Today*, *The World at One*, *PM* and *The World Tonight* – so why did we need the drama and the comedy and the documentaries, which were just a drag on the ratings? We could stand alone. They could not. This was, to say the least, not a tactful case to make to an audience of producers from drama, comedy and documentaries. When I reported back to Jenny what I had said, she went pale.

'Oh, Roger – how could you?' she asked, as someone who adored almost everything Radio 4 did.

'Well, it's true,' I replied. I thought it was generous of Michael Green to send me, along with other speakers, a bottle of champagne for my efforts to sabotage his network. But I never took to much of Radio 4 outside of the news sequences, and I used to pride myself on being able to run across the *WATO/PM* office to switch off *The Archers* before the signature tune had stopped playing.

PM was a wonderful programme for the cutting of editorial teeth. But in the middle of 1989, a vacancy arose 'next door' on *The World at One* when Martin Cox moved to become a managing editor alongside Jenny in her management team. It was a move made many times before: to slip from *PM* to *WATO* into what was seen as the more prestigious daily programme – with the editorship bolstered by *The World This Weekend* as radio's Sunday flagship. I moved at a fortunate time. *WATO* was in excellent health thanks to the output skills of its deputy editor, Kevin Marsh. He had transformed the programme from being often a disconnected set of individual interviews into a format that told stories much more coherently, using clips – short extracts from interviews – and well-crafted scripts. Interviewees would then have to respond to the evidence presented to them; I learned more about how to make daily current affairs programmes from Kevin than from anyone else. *WATO* had also relatively recently acquired a new presenter in James Naughtie – invariably known as Jim – who had previously been a newspaper journalist on *The Scotsman* and *The Guardian*. He had started promisingly, and he was much more of my generation than Gordon and Bob on *PM*. Almost immediately we developed one of the most intense and enjoyable professional relationships of my career. Jim was backed up by the talented Nick Clarke, making a team that was close to perfect.

The World at One is a deeply satisfying programme for a presenter and an editor. We would start the day at 7.30 in the morning, scrutinising the newspapers almost line by line, and being rude about *Today* and the stories we believed they had missed or got wrong. The morning editorial meeting had intellectual rigour: everyone from presenter to production secretary was invited to contribute their ideas, but woe betide them if they were half-formed or something that had been done elsewhere. This forum, sometimes brutal but often humorous, was an excellent training ground; and I am proud that so many *WATO/PM* alumni from the time that Kevin and I were editors went on to become editors themselves. From 9.15 we were firming up stories or hunting down interviewees, and it was a typical *WATO* gag that one of our producers was so adept at getting people out from hiding to face the microphone that his catchphrase became 'come on out, I know you're in there'. The tight deadlines meant that you could move from an idea at the morning meeting to a fully realised story in four hours flat, and there was none of the risk that *Today* has of a day team's conception being strangled by the night team or completely misunderstood by the presenters at 6 a.m. Additionally, the flexibility of radio allowed you to change course if something wasn't working. There were some days when I would look at the running order at half past twelve, decide I was not enthused by it, and throw it up in the air in the hope of transmitting something utterly different at one o'clock.

Doing this is much easier if an editor has a close relationship with the presenter. There has to be a mutual trust. Jim and I had that, even though at times we succumbed to bickering like an old married couple. Still firm in my belief that presenters are best if they are produced, I would supervise Jim minutely. He called me 'old mother hen' by way of thanks, so I named him 'wayward chicken'. Jim would sometimes ad lib from his scripts, and if he stumbled I would immediately say into his ear, 'Make it up, cock it up.' I so annoyed him one day, giving last-minute instructions through his headphones during the news bulletin, that he threw all his scripts into the air in the studio. They floated gently downwards across the presenter's table and onto the studio floor, while the announcer carried on reading the news in his best Radio 4 manner. But Jim and I were the closest of friends, and when we were out of the office we would socialise together or be endlessly on the phone or chatting about stories for the next programme. I became godfather to Jim and Ellie Naughtie's younger daughter. She is one of two 1991 goddaughters I have who are called Flora, the other one being the child of Bill and Sesi Turnbull, who both worked with me on *Today*.

My editorship of *The World at One* coincided with the most extraordinary time for global news stories. The first edition of *The World This Weekend* that I edited started with the breaking news of the massacre in Tiananmen Square in Beijing. We then had a segment devoted to the death, announced overnight, of Iran's revolutionary leader Ayatollah Khomeini. Finally, we just had time to squeeze in the news that the Eastern Bloc's first non-communist government had been elected in Poland. Throughout the second half of 1989, Sundays were particularly frantic for news because they always seemed to have astonishing developments in the collapse of Soviet-imposed communism, and after the fall of the Berlin Wall in November, we were still putting on special programmes on 24 December as the Ceauşescu regime came to an inglorious end in Romania. I was so tired by the end of that year that I fell asleep at the wheel of my car when driving home for Christmas. I ended up in a muddy field in Lincolnshire, too exhausted even to be shocked. I spun the car back onto the road and drove on, only realising a few miles later that I could easily have hit a stone wall and killed myself.

In the following year, Nelson Mandela was released from prison and Saddam Hussein invaded Kuwait. The first Gulf War continued into 1991, followed by the abolition of apartheid in South Africa and the end of the Soviet Union. In the Balkans, Yugoslavia was breaking up. The transformation in communications brought all this vividly to British listeners. For the first time, radio had satellite-quality foreign reporting, and there was more chance than ever before that the key participants would be available down the line or even in Broadcasting House. The Serb nationalist leader Radovan Karadzic was interviewed face to face by Jim in our studio 3B during a visit to London before the world knew about the full horror of what he had unleashed in Bosnia.

It was a period of seismic change in British politics, too. The foundations of Mrs Thatcher's prime ministership were increasingly shaky. We loved nothing more than giving the political pot a good stir, and it was easy to get backbench Conservatives to be disobliging about their leader after a misstep by the government or a bad by-election result. We liked the humorous newspaper claim that Sir Marcus Fox, the plain-speaking MP for Shipley, had been knighted for 'services to *The World at One*' – and we would most certainly have recommended him. He had a unique ability to start an interview loyally and then bring up complaints which guaranteed bad headlines the next day for Mrs Thatcher, along with an attribution in the newspapers as 'speaking on *The World at One*', which delighted us. He was not alone. The ill-discipline of the Conservative Party was a gift to political journalists throughout the time I was a programme editor. Initially on *WATO*, the loyal government response to these claims would often come from Sir Geoffrey Howe, then leader of the House of Commons. After his resignation, he was equally willing to appear on our airwaves as one of the government's critics – to the extent that when I left *WATO*, my gifts included a model of a dead sheep in recognition of Sir Geoffrey's ubiquity.

I would confess that on quiet days we sometimes overdid the internal disputes of the Conservative Party. But it was unquestionably the big theme of 1989/90. Jim and I were in Brighton for the Conservative conference in the autumn of 1990, which turned out to be the last for Mrs Thatcher. Despite our best efforts, paradoxically it was not one of the events where *WATO* was awash with dissent. The conspiracies were being conducted out of sight. Indeed, my strongest memory of that conference was of the hostility towards the BBC – exemplified by the fact that a motion attacking the corporation was selected by representatives for debate on the final day. There was a conspicuous act of bravery by David Mellor, then the broadcasting minister, in facing down the BBC's critics, but it was inescapable that we were not popular with many ministers, nor with the Tory rank and file. Political support for the corporation felt in doubt. In the weeks that followed, though, it became clear that the skids were under the Prime Minister, and speculation built that Michael Heseltine would stand against her for the leadership of the party. One morning in the *WATO* office we listened with particular pleasure to the *Today* programme waffling away again on this theme to no particular purpose – when Jim and I knew that Heseltine was definitely going to declare his candidacy. We had clandestinely agreed to go to Heseltine's house at 11 a.m. to record an interview for that day's programme in which the gloves would come off: Mrs Thatcher was to face a fight for her political life. The public announcement would be made just before lunchtime.

When Jim and I got to Michael Heseltine's house, few were aware of the secret. There were no crews outside and we walked up the pathway without anyone observing us. Inside, Heseltine and his wife seemed, understandably, to be nervous. This was an enormous moment in their lives: after all the thinking and the political plotting, one of the best politicians of his day was about to challenge Britain's first woman Prime Minister, a three-time election winner, for the crown he had always wanted. While we recorded the interview, a lengthy one at twenty minutes or more, word spread that Heseltine was about to announce his candidacy. By the time we opened the front door, photographers and crews were crowding the pavement to the extent that Jim and I had to crawl our way out on hands and knees through a maze of snappers' ladders and television wires and journalists' feet.

This is only one example of the 'backstage' view of politics that *The World at One* offered. Each year at a party conference I would be fascinated as the 'minister under fire', whoever that happened to be, would finish his platform speech and then hotfoot it to our studio. He would listen intently to the way the news was reporting what he had said, and to our collection of immediate reaction. Often with a wife and special advisers watching from our control room, during the live broadcast he would then try to spin himself out of disaster or bask in an unexpected triumph. It brought home the brutality and the relentlessness of politics, sometimes distilled into a career trajectory being decided by twenty minutes of platform oratory and an interrogation on *WATO* straight afterwards.

We were nicknamed 'Westminster at One', a title we accepted with equanimity. Our political instincts sometimes caused bafflement in the radio newsroom, who supplied our news bulletin, when we said we were planning to lead the programme with fifteen minutes on Qualified Majority Voting in Europe or whatever party crisis we could see looming. They preferred their headlines to be about things that had actually happened, like court cases or motorway accidents. But we took pride in working our contacts, and that often put us ahead of the game. On the day after Mrs Thatcher's inconclusive leadership ballot against Michael Heseltine, the lunchtime television outlets focused on her pledge to fight on and to win the second round. We led with a much more pessimistic outlook for the Prime Minister, based on dozens of phone calls and a senior MP telling us in a pre-recorded interview: 'I don't think you can stop an avalanche halfway.'

The truth of that was revealed the next morning when Margaret Thatcher resigned shortly after the *Today* programme went off air. There was enormous frustration for *The World at One* team because Radio 4 turned down our offer of a special live programme at the next available junction, 10 a.m., saying they would like something 'more polished' a little later. So at 10 a.m. they stuck with their published schedule and broadcast *The Natural World*. The billing was: 'Small mammals can use hedgerows as roads, connecting many lanes of bramble together into one large habitat.'

Television, meanwhile, was covering one of the biggest political moments of the century. We were only allowed on air in suitably polished form at 11 a.m., and this became used as a compelling example of why radio needed a rolling news network to bypass such ridiculous decisions. For our regular slot at 1 p.m., John Birt slipped into the back of the studio to watch – one of those gestures that increases the pressure on the studio team, but is nonetheless appreciated as a sign that the bosses care about what you are doing. We knew by then that Douglas Hurd and John Major would stand against Heseltine in the next phase of the contest, and their champions were interviewed live on the programme. On major news days, Jim Naughtie would wave his arms in the air like a prizefighter who had just won a bout. There was much arm-waving that lunchtime.

John Major was considerably more accessible as Prime Minister than his predecessor. There had been a lapsed tradition that the PM would give a radio interview to mark the New Year, and we decided to try to revive that. This was both to cement

WATO's role as the leading political programme of its day, and to fill the gaping forty-minute hole that was otherwise looming on 1 January. Downing Street liked the idea, so on a dank New Year's Eve Jim and I and our engineer presented ourselves at the Majors' home near Huntingdon to record the broadcast. We were greeted by the normality of family life: dad John open-necked and in a comfy pullover, some banter between him and their teenage children, and the Majors preparing to go to see the neighbours later on for a 'pot-luck supper'. I recall Norma Major was supplying the dessert. Only the red box in the study confirmed that this was actually the Prime Minister's residence. Major showed us the file marked 'action this day', and Jim attempted to squint at its contents as proof that he was still a hack at heart. The Prime Minister gently but swiftly removed it from sight.

The interview itself was a success: robust questioning from Jim, and enough news lines to dominate the television bulletins and the newspaper headlines. We maintained the New Year tradition for some years, taking it with us to *Today*. Major was always the most courteous of interviewees. Snobs would regard this as inappropriate, but he sent thank-you letters in response to thank-you letters. With a handwritten salutation and sign-off, he replied to my thanks:

> Thank you very much for your letter which I received today and for taking the trouble to write to me. I was delighted to be able to help 'The World at One' by recording an interview for transmission on New Year's Day and shall be happy to do what I can to assist you on future occasions. With all good wishes to you and to everyone on 'The World at One' and 'The World This Weekend'.

He nonetheless maintained a robust operation at Conservative Central Office under Chris Patten, and the 1992 election was notable for the toughness of both Tories and Labour in dealing with the media. This was partly because it was such a tightly fought campaign and there were daily skirmishes for control of the agenda, with Labour refusing to put up speakers on subjects they didn't care to talk about and the Conservatives doing the same. We would threaten the 'empty chair': 'X refused to put up a speaker on this topic today', to the hysteria of press officers who wanted us to opt for their story instead. We would routinely be scolded for falling for their opponents' agenda or for disrespectful questions to their star performers, in a way that we hadn't experienced on anything like the same scale in 1987 – nor in most later elections.

We tried to subvert this by presenting the programme each day from a location outside London, with Jim or Nick taking it in turns to be on the road and as far away from the spin doctors as possible. This also permitted us to stage another event that created pictures across many of the front pages. When we were planning the programme from Northern Ireland, we realised that an election campaign overrode the broadcasting ban in force at the time that kept Sinn Fein representatives off the airwaves. Only in the UK could it be the case that banned spokesmen were actually required to be allowed to take part in programmes once an election had been called. Nick Clarke therefore hosted a feisty debate in Broadcasting House in Belfast, unprecedented at the time, between Gerry Adams of Sinn Fein and John Hume of the SDLP, which was genuinely illuminating and showed the absurdity of trying to ban people from making a political case.

As well as the deluge of foreign news and the seismic events in politics, this was a time when the royal family was in a tumult too. The BBC has always been a somewhat nervous purveyor of royal news, but in the Birt era we were particularly cautious about the sources and provenance of a story. This meant we had no problem with the formal announcements – we did a Radio 4 'Charles and Diana to separate' special – but there was corporate anxiety about speculation in newspapers and any items broadcast by the BBC that appeared to be derived from that. Andrew Morton's sensational book about Diana therefore posed a dilemma. *Diana, Her True Story* was serialised in the *Sunday Times*, and detailed an account of her marriage that we now know to have been supplied by the Princess herself. But, at the time, barely a word made the BBC bulletins outside the newspaper reviews. At *WATO* we enjoyed the thrill of chasing a story, but we were also not averse to winding up the people in news management that we thought of as 'the Thought Police' – and the best way of doing that was to pop a few provocative stories into our draft running order. Our computerised systems meant that the *WATO* provisional schedule could be read over in Television Centre, so we would gaily write in 'Diana – the story – Morton interview' and 'Diana – reaction – bid for Charles' and then wait for the phone to ring.

It invariably did: 'Roger, I just wondered whether you were thinking about doing anything about the Morton book? Doesn't look much in it to me ... but just checking...' The often-benign nature of the BBC bureaucracy meant that, on a day when we decided the story was genuine enough to tackle it properly, we did so without recriminations – and with full credit to BBC News, it was they who got the ultimate scoop of the Diana interview for *Panorama*. But we were conscious that we had a chairman in Duke

Hussey, who was married to one of the Queen's ladies-in-waiting, and if we made a misstep on a royal story then the management would get an earful from Dukey.

Against this background, I was pleased that we had a royal scoop ourselves on *WATO*. One day in March 1992, on a relatively quiet day in that year's election campaign, I received a phone call not long before 1 p.m. from Paul Reynolds, the BBC's royal correspondent. This was just after it had been confirmed that the Duke and Duchess of York were to split up, after years of gossip about the state of their marriage and some lurid behaviour by the duchess, Sarah Ferguson. Paul had been to a briefing at the Palace and he was, by his gentlemanly standards, very excited indeed. The Palace had laid into the duchess, he told me, and there was an unprecedentedly strong briefing against her. He had this exclusively for *The World at One*, and it would make headlines without any doubt at all. Paul is a correspondent I would have trusted with my life, so after a swift consultation with Jim we opted for what we used to call 'busting the bulletin': dropping the news summary down the programme, and starting with a presenter interview on a breaking story.

Paul delivered in spades. 'The knives are out for Fergie at the Palace,' he told us live on air. 'I have rarely heard Palace officials talking in such terms about someone. They are talking about her unsuitability for public life, royal life – her behaviour in being photographed for *Hello!* magazine, fooling around, putting paper bags on her head on an aircraft while she was being watched by reporters…' He added that the Palace believed Sarah had hired a public relations company to leak news of the separation to the *Daily Mail*.

This was incredible stuff to be coming from Buckingham Palace about a royal duchess, and officials had, it was claimed, made it plain to Paul that some of the anger was coming from the Queen herself. The story the next day in *The Sun* compressed it into 'Queen Puts Knife Into Fergie'. In her autobiography some years later, the duchess described it as 'the royal story of the year', with what she called a 'somewhat breathless' Reynolds making a 'bombshell allegation' on *The World at One*. Why had Palace officials behaved in that way, she asked?

> They needed to cut me off at the knees, abort my future options, destroy my standing with the Queen. They also needed to send a warning to Diana, to keep her in the fold and shore up the monarchy. My public vivisection would be a reminder: this is what happens if you cross us.

I doubt that the founding fathers of *The World at One* quite had this role in mind for the programme. But we sat there with open mouths, before ploughing dutifully through the rest of the day's agenda.

Inevitably, the phone call came in shortly afterwards from BBC News HQ. 'Great story. Where did it come from? And, er, are we sure it's true?' Other phone calls rained in from rival broadcasters seeking a copy of the tape for their own output, and from newspapers and agencies wanting a transcript. The truth of it was that this was a case where you put your trust in a correspondent, and you have to exercise a judgement on his or her record and the plausibility of what you are being told. In a fast-moving daily news programme, you can take a decision to make the item your main story, or play it somewhere down the running order, or drop it altogether. There was a manifest danger in giving such prominence to the Fergie story that day, as subsequent – and more substantive – scoops broken in a correspondent 'two-way' have shown. But there is also a journalistic risk if you have a story like that and fail to trumpet it. By no means did we – or I – get this right every time; and I always have the greatest fellow feeling for any editor who has to make a call at short notice and stand by it. There is no scientific way of being right 100 per cent of the time in the content and weight of a story, and belief in standards has to be tempered by an understanding of the pressures of daily journalism. You cannot hand over all the big decisions to a management board or a regulatory review panel.

By contrast with the breathless rush of *The World at One*, *The World This Weekend* ('*TW2*') was a more considered weekly current affairs programme run largely by the same team. I was fortunate to have support from two deputy editors who did the planning for *TW2*: first Rod Liddle, who would have been surprised at that time to know that he would one day feature in television's *Pointless Celebrities*, and Anne Koch. Rod was a formidable journalist. He was on best display at a party conference where, with his long, tousled hair and a cigarette never far from his hands, he would sidle up to politicians with a genial 'Hello, mate, what's going on?' He almost always came away with a story and he was effective at digging away for the longer-form journalism that *TW2* needed.

The programme was an hour long in those days, and that gave us room to experiment. We introduced 'signed features' – reports by people in the news expressing their personal points of view. One of the early ones tried to illuminate the issues in the ambulance drivers' dispute by giving airtime to Kenneth Clarke, as Health Secretary, and Roger Poole for the ambulance workers.

Somewhat to type, I produced the Clarke report and Rod worked with Poole. I was amazed by the access Clarke let me have to the government meetings working out how to keep services running and win the dispute. Even more impressive, he never said 'this is highly confidential' but simply trusted us to behave properly. It was hard work to get these kinds of features by public figures to the standard expected of a professional broadcast. Yet they were illuminating because they broke out of the routine 'X said this, Y said that' approach, and they allowed time for an argument to be developed.

This did prove a trial, though, when we asked Tony Benn to do a report. I had a jolly breakfast with him at his home in Notting Hill, where he made delicious wholemeal toast and was in his more attractive 'grandfather of the nation' mode. But when it came to conducting interviews, and more particularly writing a script, he had revolutionary ideas. 'I think working people are never allowed to have their say,' he told us, 'so I don't want to filter their views and offer mine. We should just hear them as they are.' This is, of course, a rational argument, though at the time we wanted more Benn and fewer unknown interviewees. We therefore tried to persuade him that a radio report in which he said only 'here's Joe Bloggs' and 'here's Mary Bloggs', with a lengthy extract from what they had said, was possibly not going to be as interesting as if he made a case. But he was not to be persuaded. It was a big enough wrench that he had to edit his interviewees in any way. I could not claim that the end result was the finest piece of broadcasting, but Benn himself was happy. He wrote to say he had enjoyed it and volunteered himself for further duty. 'I would really like to do an alternative news bulletin – dealing with some issues that never seem to surface in the official news.' Rightly or wrongly, we decided the world was not yet ready for *News at Benn*.

Norman Tebbit was more amenable. He was invited to give us his view of Europe, and I still have his handwritten script.

What will be the effect of the Maastricht Treaty? Will Britain as a self-governing nation be like a salami sausage on the slicer – disappearing bit by bit into a new Euro state? Or has the Treaty, as John Major claims, reversed the slicer and begun to put the sausage back together again?

This seemed to us to be claiming improbable things for slicer-reversal, but that was what the signed features were for. They were a modest commitment to plurality in public service broadcasting.

There were more conventional political set pieces on *TW2*. I enjoyed bringing together Ted Heath, Roy Jenkins and Denis Healey for their one and only joint broadcast. The significance was that they had all been students at Balliol College, Oxford. They had fought in the Second World War. They had risen to positions of political eminence, but had never been interviewed together because Healey and Jenkins had spent most of their time in the same party, and Heath had been Prime Minister, which meant he did not take part in the run-of-the-mill broadcasting debates.

It was, I thought at the time, one for the archive, and elder statesmen are invariably more relaxed and revelatory than those in power. Hence another rarity: Heath in discussion with James Callaghan, as two former Prime Ministers. This got off to a bad start. We were scheduled to do the recording in a basement studio in Broadcasting House, only to find that the key had gone missing. With no hospitality area, and only a gloomy corridor to wait in, we had fifteen minutes of anguished time-filling while the Premises team searched for a spare. For two men who had been served in their high office by the machinery of the state, they bore the inefficiency of Broadcasting House with surprising equanimity. I always found Heath, contrary to his reputation, to be easy to deal with. He would answer his own phone when we called him at home, and give a speedy answer on whether he would take part in a programme or not. It was usually 'yes' if there was an opportunity to be disobliging about Mrs Thatcher.

The rogue factor among these veteran politicians was Denis Healey. He liked to be playful. A *WATO* producer once came across a quavering falsetto on the end of the line, with someone claiming to be the Healeys' cleaning lady. After some minutes of this becoming ever less convincing, the producer challenged the char: 'Is that actually Mr Healey I'm talking to?' 'Oh dear, I've been rumbled. Yes it is,' he replied.

During this period, the BBC gave us a lot of autonomy. One of my friends, who had been on *The World at One* a little before me, described her time there thus:

> My *WATO* days were balmy – almost no competitors, a news cycle that didn't start up until the *Today* programme was off the air, no management interference, no budget awareness (we were actually forbidden to know the details lest it affected our editorial judgement) and compulsory alcohol in terrifying quantities (no one minded what that did to our editorial judgement).

In my period on the afternoon sequences in the more controlled

Birtist days, radio was still less front-of-mind than television for the news division management, and in any case Jenny Abramsky was a doughty defender of her medium against any encroachment. Our faults were seldom, I believe, in political balance: the somewhat leftish tinge of some of our producers was balanced by the mildly rightist instincts of some of the editors, and everyone accepted the idea of impartiality. If there was a fault, it was that we were all rather alike: youngish, university-educated, metropolitan. I am unable to remember ever doing an item about rural affairs, unless it had a Common Agricultural Policy dimension.

But *The World at One* and *PM* years were marked by an extraordinary camaraderie among the staff. In the early '90s, with Kevin Marsh editing *PM* and me on *WATO*, there was sparring between the editors, but friendship and respect too. Our teams would breakfast together, lunch together and then go to the pub together after work. We would repair en masse to the Dover Castle and stand outside in the mews on warm days in summer, and we had a softball team that played, badly, in Regent's Park. The programmes we produced each day had a journalistic swagger that made radio punch above its weight, which is what the founders of *The World at One* wanted. But the shows were also the most tremendous pleasure to work on. When I left the BBC, in my interview with the staff newspaper, *Ariel*, I was reported thus: 'Mosey regards his years as *World at One* editor, working with presenter James Naughtie and a "fantastic" team of producers, as the "purest" BBC job for a news hack like him. "I love the big TV moments, but as a practitioner, I think radio is fantastically creative."' I had no itch at all to move into television at that stage, and there was about to be an even bigger radio challenge.

CHAPTER 6

BACK TO *TODAY*

I REALLY DID NOT want to leave *The World at One*. It had got into my bloodstream, and on my wall in Cambridge I have a cartoon that I was given as a leaving present. 'Why are you so glum today?' asks one character. 'I got the job I was going for,' answers the other. The job I got in 1993 was editor of the *Today* programme; and it was terrific, once I became established, to return to the place where I had had my first full network job. But the pressure of being overall editor, and the antisocial hours of the duty-editing roles, meant that I was less able to be hands-on than

I had been on *WATO*. *Today* is divided into day and night teams, with the day team, under its duty editor, planning the next day's programme, and then the night team, also with a duty editor, supplementing what they have been given and turning the items into a running order. Both are long stints, since they cover a 24-hour period between them, though the day shifts were longer and the nights were shorter than when I had been a producer. I made occasional appearances as a duty editor myself, but ran into the inevitable problem after a tiring night shift of having to cope with issues that emerged during the daylight hours. It was also a shock to the system to discover how much higher-profile is the editorship of *Today*: within a week of arriving I was being denounced in the House of Commons for some transgression on the programme, and the scrutiny was of a different order to the quieter life of Radio 4's afternoon programmes. Two of my successors, Rod Liddle and Kevin Marsh, would undoubtedly confirm that.

I had set out my manifesto for *Today* in my application. It began:

> *Today's* strength is range and diversity, and it should be seeking to broaden its agenda. The single most important task is to report Britain to itself. Government and society are becoming complex, and this must be reflected and explained by programme makers. We should focus on the day-to-day concerns of our listeners in areas such as health, education, crime, the economy, Europe, science and leisure. Reporting from the grassroots is vital in presenting the big picture.

All pretty obvious, I accept. I proposed appointing at least one reporter to be based permanently outside London. This became two: one in north-east England, and the other in the Midlands. 'New technology', I wrote, 'should allow increasing use of live reporter injects from across the UK.'

I went on to spell out the immediate priorities: improving planning, being better at set-piece events and, I noted, '*Today* has to win the battle for the big interviews and generate more publicity.' This was a reflection of the belief within the *WATO* team that we regularly beat *Today* in getting the main newsmakers onto our airwaves, and *WATO* was more often quoted in the following day's papers. We also believed that *Today*'s interviews sometimes missed the point, hence my pledge of 'higher standards in briefings and in writing scripts'. But potentially the most contentious point was number 5: 'The Presenters', which said baldly, 'John Humphrys should be The Voice of *Today*.'

I inherited John as an established *Today* presenter along with Brian Redhead, Sue MacGregor and Peter Hobday. As a producer on *Today* in the 1980s I had got along increasingly well with Brian, once he had stopped trying to have me fired, and he was an advocate for my return as editor. I also rated Sue: I used to say 'when you return from a foreign holiday, you simply need to hear Sue MacGregor on the radio and you know you're home and all is well' – such was the warmth and authority of her presentation. I liked Hobday personally, but I had never been keen on him on air. He was not as charismatic as the others, and in a decade on the programme he had not risen above being 'the nice bloke on a Monday, or when the others are on holiday'. However, Humphrys seemed to me to be in a league of his own: outstanding in confrontational political interviews, incisive on the issues of the day and also increasingly good at human interest stories. If it had been possible, I would have had him presenting six days a week.

The looming problem was what to do about Brian. It is always a tricky issue when the broadcasting greats are not quite as good as they used to be, because producers wish that they would go out at the top with appreciative applause from the audience. As a listener to *Today*, I could tell that Brian was no longer at the peak of his form, and my early days back on the programme confirmed that impression. There is a narrow borderline between 'charmingly tangential' and 'off-topic', and Brian was edging too much to the latter. One morning he was supposed to be interviewing a leading politician about a breaking political story, but instead his first question was about the previous day's *Afternoon Play*, which he had heard and found fascinating. The politician sounded bemused, and the studio team were holding their heads in their hands. This was the kind of episode that used to produce much yelling at the radio in the news-hungry *World at One* office, even if for many Radio 4 listeners it was part of Brian's appeal. But as the incoming editor I was awash with views from colleagues, managerial and journalistic, that we needed to have a new presentation strategy.

Happily, the resolution came with extraordinary grace from Brian himself. I had a catch-up with him over a cup of tea when my appointment was announced. But after I had taken over in the spring of 1993 we arranged to go over to the Langham Hotel, site of my local radio training, for a post-programme breakfast. I had prepared myself to ask the question about his plans, and I had also rehearsed my response. If he said that he wanted to go on and on, which is the default position of almost every presenter, I was going to ask him whether that was wise in his early sixties and with the ghastly hours on the programme, and suggest that we had a number of proposals we could make to him about other broadcasting roles in the BBC. I am embarrassed only by thinking in those days that early sixties was quite old. But none of this was necessary. As we set to work on the vastly expensive scrambled egg, Brian told me he had decided to go. He needed a hip operation within the next year and he just didn't fancy having the time off and all the recovery period – and then having to go back to early starts. He was apologetic: he said he would have loved to work with me for longer, but his health and his love of living in the north of England made him feel that this was the right thing to do. I was already fond of Brian, but this made me even fonder of him. Gentle waves of relief were filling my head. He did, after all, turn out to be one of the rare breed who knows the time at which it is right to quit, and he had done so in a way that meant we could honour, rather than be embarrassed about, one of the giants of radio. If only every transition could be like that.

I had been asked during my appointment board who I would seek to bring into *Today* if Brian left, and it cannot have been a surprise that my answer had always been Jim Naughtie. It was known that we were personally close, and my Naughtie goddaughter was not a state secret, but my preference was endorsed, with due process, by Radio 4 and by news management. Jim had become loved by the audience on *WATO*, and we liked the idea of his warm Scottish tones on *Today* – complementing the harder-edged Welshness of Humphrys and the perfect English of MacGregor. (It is one of the more surprising facts that she was brought up in South Africa.) It was not the toughest of negotiations to get Jim to come to *Today*, and we duly announced that

Brian would be leaving and that Jim would be joining, with the switchover planned for the summer of 1994. There was a press announcement and a photo call on the steps of All Souls in Langham Place, with Redhead, Humphrys and Naughtie sporting the forced grins that presenters have when they are not quite sure who is top dog.

Sadly, Brian's planned transition was not to be. It became increasingly obvious that he was not well. He would limp his way into the office at 4.30 in the morning, singing tunelessly as he always did, but unmistakably in pain. He often looked awful – though there was never a flicker of that in his voice on the radio. By the time we despatched him to the Conservative Party conference that autumn, I was seriously worried. It was at Blackpool, always his sentimental favourite, but he spent most of the day in the hotel and avoided the winds and lashing rain of the seafront. We would amuse him by bringing him pieces of political gossip from the fringe meetings, which he would retail on air next day as if he had been there. But apart from a fish-and-chip supper at Harry Ramsden's, which seemed to bring him back to his old self, there was little of the Redhead ebullience that made him such a splendid companion.

On 7 December 1993, Brian presented what was to be his last programme. He was taken ill shortly afterwards and found to have a perforated appendix. I spoke to him by phone on the afternoon of 22 December and found him sounding surprisingly cheerful. He was amused by receiving a 'get well' card from Virginia Bottomley, then Health Secretary, and he told me he was itching to return to the programme. But that evening he was operated on, and in the aftermath faced ever more serious medical crises. He

died in January 1994, aged sixty-four. The Archbishop of Canterbury, George Carey, wrote to me when the death was announced:

> The loss of such a brilliant and warm personality must leave
> you all feeling bereft and very sad … The tributes flowing in
> for Brian should make you all feel some pride, as well as sad-
> ness, and it matters very much to me, as to millions of others,
> that the splendid traditions of the programme should continue
> to play an honoured part in our national life.

He was right about our sadness, and also correct about the death
of a radio presenter having such an impact on so many. Margaret
Thatcher led the on-air tributes to Brian, and his memorial service was held in St Paul's Cathedral. As someone who had seen
himself as an outsider – the non-metropolitan, former Labour
man – we knew he would have absolutely loved both those
things.

Jim Naughtie transferred from *The World at One* earlier than in
the original plan, and by that stage we had also added Anna Ford to
the presenter roster. There had been acres of speculative newsprint
since my arrival at *Today* about the future presenter line-up, and a
number of well-known broadcasting figures had quietly expressed
an interest. We had also tried out some promising young talent,
including a programme reporter in his twenties called Jeremy
Vine. Anna's name had been suggested to me by Tony Hall, and
she was the only one of the famous folk who agreed to do what
was effectively an on-air audition. I will always give her credit for
being willing to stick her neck out. She told Paul Donovan for
his book about *Today*: 'What they wanted to do at the time was

try out a number of people, and I know they approached some people who said, not on your nelly. And they approached other, braver, folk like me who said, yes, I'll have a go.'

When Anna did her initial couple of mornings on *Today*, I liked what I heard. She had a lovely radio voice, accompanied by some of the television charisma that she had accumulated at ITN, TV-am and the BBC. It was also a counterbalance to the blokeish nature of some of the John-and-Jim political axis to have two strong women – Anna and Sue – in the team. Unfortunately, this meant there was even less room for Peter Hobday and we came to a parting of the ways.

Tony Hall put this to Paul Donovan a couple of years later more sharply than I articulated it at the time. Tony said: 'If you asked me to rank the five of them [Ford, Hobday, Humphrys, MacGregor, Naughtie], I would put Peter at the bottom and that's the way it is. You're picking and choosing, trying to work out the winning team.' It was because that is something you seek not to articulate in public that a whole set of different reasons for Peter's departure took hold of the press, principally that he had been let go because he was too polite. This erroneous view was later summed up by John Timpson: 'The reason he [Peter] fell out with them is because he is not part of the new aggressive knock 'em down and kick 'em brigade.' Peter himself was quoted by Donovan as saying:

> A fat middle-aged hack like me didn't really square with the lean, mean interview machine. Nobody ever said to me, 'You're crap.' But when people say my interviewing wasn't as 'sharp' as it could be, perhaps what they mean is that it wasn't invasive and I didn't feel the need to scream and shout.

I nonetheless felt content with the screaming and shouting of John, Jim, Sue and Anna. But some of the newspaper campaigning for Hobday did create a chilly air in the office first thing in the morning. *The Times* ran a daily campaign: 'Don't sack Hobday, sack X', with X being a presenter each day that they proposed for the chop instead. They carefully set out all the things that were terrible about the people we had kept on, which was not the best start at 4 a.m. for whoever was target of the day.

I became the firmest of friends with John, as I was with Jim, and I socialised with Anna and Sue too. Sue used to regard me more warily than the others. We had a friendly early tussle when, during a pre-recorded interview, I had followed my usual practice of suggesting a question through her headphones. She smiled through the glass, took the headphones off and put them to one side so she could no longer hear me. This is a technique a number of presenters have tried over the years, and I have never let them get away with it: editors must be able to edit, and interviews should be produced.

In her book, written after I had left *Today*, Sue berated me for giving her fewer of the big 8.10 a.m. political interviews than John and Jim. I am unrepentant about that. John was the consummate political interviewer of his generation, a questioner who could spot a weaselly nuanced answer at fifty paces. The man met his time as the Conservative government helpfully fell apart live on *Today*'s airwaves; and, without any intervention from BBC bosses or any evident sexism, the programme's night editors would almost always choose John for the latest joust at 8.10. It did not mean any lack of respect for Sue. She did brilliant interviews with Nelson Mandela and with the Duchess of York, and was sent on assignments like the

Copenhagen European summit, where she interviewed the Prime Minister. She also had guts: if you gave her a brief to battle away on a line of questioning, she was fearless in pursuing her quarry. But on breaking domestic political stories, I am not sure I can think of many occasions when I wish we had sidelined John in Sue's favour.

I would admit that I was very hands-on during my time as editor of *Today*. 'Obsessive' or 'a control freak' are the other words that would have been used by my colleagues. Some of this was done by tricks of the trade. If I was up late, I would sometimes call the night team at two or three in the morning, and word got around that I was always awake at that time and monitoring the news wires. Most of the time I was sleeping soundly through the night. But I never minded if the night team called me with a problem. I perfected the art of waking immediately, sounding wide awake, making whatever sense I could and then falling asleep again.

Most programme days I would be up by 5.30 a.m. at the latest, scanning the running orders by what was then new technology – a laptop with a phone connection – installed in my house in south-west London. Night editors in the *Today* office would relate stories about seeing a running order mysteriously rearranging itself on their screens, as I changed it from my study. I would then drive into the office to help, as I would see it, or interfere, as they saw it, in person. Some years later, when I left television news, Anna Ford noted that she had enjoyed working with me as an editor 'even when you used to tinker with my scripts from your home at four o'clock in the morning. Obsessive, or what?'

But, as on *WATO*, I had a brilliant team around me – including, once again as my deputy editor, Rod Liddle. Rod was particularly adept at changing a programme round to throw everything at a tale that took his fancy. One morning he pursued a story about a prisoner who was being let out on day release to run a marathon. Outrage poured out of the radio for the best part of two hours, before the Home Office issued a statement saying he would not be allowed out after all. Over a post-programme coffee, Rod ruefully considered the trade-off: a great edition of the programme with further evidence we could set the agenda – on the other hand, some poor bloke, near release anyway, was going to be locked back in his cell because of the controversy we had generated.

Complementary to Rod, though never one of his bosom buddies, was the formidably competitive ex-ITN journalist Chris Rybczynski. She was the exemplar of the night editor who would relentlessly pursue stories and cajole interviewees onto the air with a mixture of charm and bludgeoning. Beating BBC Television and 5 Live on a breaking news story was a badge of honour for her. She is another colleague who has become an enduring friend.

As on *WATO*, I would defend *Today* against any charge of intentional political bias. Two output editors, Rod Liddle and Tim Luckhurst, had previously worked for the Labour Party but were scrupulously fair in their judgements. My other deputy editor, Francis Halewood, ended up helping to run the Conservatives' 1997 election campaign, and senior producer David Vigar went to work for the Liberal Democrats. It is true that we had almost no voices on air calling for Britain's withdrawal from Europe, but this was a time when UKIP came eighth in the 1994 European elections with only 150,000 votes. It was also not for want of trying. During the *WATO* and *Today* years it was my hobby to attempt to get Tory Eurosceptics to admit that the logic of their position was to get out of Europe, and they would never say so. But our airwaves were awash with them criticising the European project and John Major's handling of it: Bill Cash and Iain Duncan Smith and all the rebels against the Maastricht Treaty would pop up to goad the government, and No. 10, duly goaded, would provide a minister to reply to them and create a few more headlines. This was a sharp contrast with the New Labour opposition, who were conspicuously more united around policy than the Conservatives, and also ran a much more robust media operation. They clamped down on dissent within their ranks on the rare occasions it flared up, making it harder for a negative story to run for long. But this reflected a greater truth: they were the best-organised opposition in modern political history, campaigning against a government that suspected it had lost the next election from Black Wednesday onwards.

It is, of course, the responsibility of programmes to try to set the agenda, rather than the job of politicians. This line of argument always used to irritate Michael Howard in particular, who seemed to believe – in both government and opposition – that there was a duty for broadcasters to allow politicians airtime even if it was principally for an attack on their opponents. We attempted to set the higher threshold of 'Is what they are saying interesting?' We liked to take a contrary approach to conventional wisdom, too. One morning, Howard was scheduled to appear as Home Secretary with a string of tough measures including longer prison sentences, and he probably expected the standard interviewer's challenge from the left: was this not too draconian, and what about civil liberties? Instead, we briefed Humphrys to come at him from the right. If he wanted to be tough, and do what the public wanted, why would he not bring back capital punishment?

He had, after all, voted for it in the past. This was a much more discomfiting line of questioning. Similarly, we challenged New Labour's agenda by a series of reports on what we termed 'fecklessness': people who, no matter what help they had from the state, would not conform to the values of the rest of society, and frittered away whatever resources they were given. We fostered independent thinking, and Rod Liddle remembers one morning meeting when a producer said disparagingly, 'The Eurosceptics believe Germany is going to dominate Europe!' This generated laughter from bien-pensant colleagues about the ridiculousness of that idea. 'But what if that is true?' was the response from the editor, and he set the team thinking about items that would examine whether Euroscepticism had some well-founded beliefs.

One reporter in particular might be cited as a defence against the BBC being relentlessly left-wing. We hired a bright young chap from the television current affairs programme *On the Record* to bolster our coverage of politics. He was a Scot, interested particularly in the Conservative Party, and he was preparing a biography of Michael Portillo. His name was Michael Gove. Gove was actually the second future Cabinet minister that I recruited to network radio, with the first being Ben Bradshaw – later a Labour Culture Secretary – on *The World at One*. I would not have guessed that Gove would become as eminent a politician as he became. He was effortlessly charming and polite, which made it a surprise when he showed his steeliness as Education Secretary. But he was a fine reporter. His best moment came when the Tory leadership contest was underway in 1995, triggered by John Major's resignation of his party role while staying on as Prime Minister. Breakfast television and most of the papers were predicting that Major would run with little or no opposition, but Gove's sources told him that John Redwood, a serving Cabinet minister, would declare himself as a challenger. This was another call where you either back your reporter or not, and we trusted Gove. We went on air saying that Redwood would challenge Major, with confirmation gratefully received later in the day that the story was true.

This balance within our team and in our journalism did not stop storms emerging in all parts of the political sphere. One of the more destabilising came from Jonathan Aitken, then a Tory Cabinet minister and later an inmate of Her Majesty. He accused Humphrys of 'poisoning the well of democratic debate' in his conduct of the *Today* programme, with the example cited of his interrupting Kenneth Clarke thirty-two times in one broadcast – and, allegedly, showing partisanship in chairing a meeting of government opponents. John told *Desert Island Discs* in 2008 about the moment I called him to tell him about Aitken's attack and the proliferation of headlines it generated:

> I was terrified at the time. I was phoned at home. I can remember it ever so clearly, as you can with important moments in your life. My then boss phoned and said, 'Look, he's made this speech and we think this is potentially rather serious', and of course he was right. I actually thought my career, such as it was, had come to an end at the *Today* programme. Because if others in the Cabinet had taken the same view, and did not want to be interviewed by me – and that was the implied threat, a stated threat in the Aitken speech – I couldn't continue to present the *Today* programme. That would be the end of it.

I would not say I was terrified, and I have never really known John be terrified. But it was certainly a deeply uncomfortable few days. Other Cabinet ministers joined in the criticism: Home Secretary Michael Howard, Welsh Secretary John Redwood and Conservative chairman Jeremy Hanley. And it was not clear to us that we had the support of the BBC. There had been persistent murmuring from along the executive corridor about the alleged aggression of Humphrys on *Today* and Jeremy Paxman on *Newsnight*, and in the immediate aftermath of the Aitken attack I received only the support of my immediate boss, the excellent Steve Mitchell. No word was heard from on high.

Deciding that if we did not defend ourselves, nobody would, I used an awards ceremony lunch to fight back. I told reporters that a number of other Cabinet members had told us they supported *Today*'s journalism. Of these, the main one – predictably, though I didn't name him – was Kenneth Clarke. He had arrived for an interview and been greeted by Humphrys bearing a pocket calculator and inviting him to count the number of interruptions as he went along. The Chancellor had laughed uproariously. As I collected our award, I slipped in a joke. I thanked Aitken for 'helping to publicise the programme. Other people have Saatchi & Saatchi, we have Aitken & Aitken.' It was a couple of days before we found out we had no need to worry about our internal position. Humphrys bumped into the director-general, John Birt, in the toilets at an external event. Birt breezily told John that he and the programme had the support of the executive – and of the governors, who had discussed the affair at a meeting. It might have been less of a strain if we had known this more immediately and more formally than via a chance conversation in the lavatories.

But this reflects one of the curiosities of being editor of *Today*. On the one hand, it was to many people, including most opinion formers, the BBC's most important programme. On the other hand, we were left to run it largely as we saw fit, with almost no top-level intervention. I would have lunch with newspaper editors who, used to their meddling proprietors, assumed that John Birt exercised at least some influence over the 8.10 interviews or the major themes we chose to cover. Absolutely not: he never interfered. The only threat to our distinctive voice was a structural one that came from within the news division. There was an attempt to split *Today* managerially from the rest of the Radio 4 sequence programmes and to put us into a group with breakfast television and the TV *One O'Clock News*. It was floated to me that I might become executive editor of both television and radio breakfast output in a fashionable commitment to bi-media working, but I rejected the idea immediately. It was bizarre to imagine that you could edit *Today* and a television programme at the same time, and it was loopy to try to cut off *Today* from the spine of daily radio current affairs.

There was just one time that I can recall a significant executive-level presence during a programme. It was when the Tory MP Stephen Milligan died – being found naked, an inquest heard later, apart from stockings, with a plastic bag over his head and a cord around his neck. A piece of satsuma was found in his mouth. Some details appeared in the papers the morning after the news broke, but we were not able to report them on air because – under Birtian rules – we could not ourselves substantiate the story. The authorities had leaked to the tabloids but not to us. That morning, as a sign of the seriousness with which the rules were being taken, the director of news, Tony Hall, stood with me in the *Today* studio as we put out a programme in which something significant appeared to have happened in connection with the death of an MP, but we were unable to tell the audience what it was. At ten past eight we did a solemn interview with a leading Conservative about there being an apparently significant factor in Mr Milligan's demise, again with not a flicker of what might have been out of the ordinary. We could not even do our usual ruse of revealing what the papers were saying as a way of getting an unsourced story on the air, because it was deemed the risk was too high that we would introduce the satsuma via this unauthorised route. It was without doubt the most incomprehensible programme for which I was ever responsible.

So there was no row over auto-erotic asphyxiation, but I was the direct cause of another furore. One morning in the April of 1996 I was coming into Broadcasting House a little later than usual, walking up Regent Street listening to Sue MacGregor interviewing Brian Mawhinney, the chairman of the Conservative Party. He was doing the standard defence of the government ahead of the local elections, arguing that the party had been down in the polls before, as in the late 1980s, but had bounced back in the subsequent general election. 'But you only did that by getting rid of Margaret Thatcher,' I muttered to myself as I went through the doors of the building. By this stage of my editorship, presenters were reconciled to me dropping ideas for questions and comments into their ears via their headphones as they were conducting interviews. So by the time I got to the studio, and Mawhinney was still pursuing the same line, I spoke a suggested question into Sue's headphones: 'But you got rid of Mrs Thatcher,' I said to her. The question came out on air shortly afterwards: 'In 1990, you did something dramatic. You got rid of the poll tax, you also got rid of Mrs Thatcher – aren't you going to have to do something as dramatic as that not to lose a lot more seats?'

By the time the question was put, I had walked the short distance along the corridor to the *Today* office. I listened transfixed to what happened next.

Mawhinney: Oh come on, Sue, let's stay in the real world, can we?

MacGregor: Well, I hope I'm talking about the real world.

Mawhinney: What you have just suggested to me, in front of the nation, is that we should dump the Prime Minister. Don't be ridiculous, Sue, that isn't even worthy of an answer.

MacGregor: I wasn't suggesting you should dump the Prime Minister. I was saying dramatic gestures sometimes work.

Mawhinney: On the contrary, you drew the parallel with Mrs Thatcher, and that is a ludicrous and indefensible question and if you think I'm annoyed with you it is because that is the kind of smeary question by *Today* programme presenters which so annoys people who listen to this programme up and down the country.

Reading the transcript two decades on, I am struck by how well Sue handled what was a raw and angry outburst from a party chairman. But on the morning it happened I had a swirl of emotions: first, guilt at landing Sue in what was bound to be another media storm; second, pride that it was a perfectly good question that would now get lots of publicity for the programme; and third, some doubt about quite how I would explain this to the uncomprehending official complaints apparatus if any process began. 'That question wasn't in the briefing notes, no, it was something I thought of in Regent Street.'

Relations with Conservative ministers otherwise remained civilised. We had a particularly entertaining time whenever Ken Clarke came into our orbit. He would think up good lines during his car journey to the studio from Whitehall, and deliver them on air with professional spontaneity. The Prime Minister, John Major, never showed any antagonism towards us, and the New Year's Day interview successfully transferred with Jim from *WATO* to *Today*. One thing we learned about John Major was that, unlike Mrs Thatcher, he liked to cut things fine. There was none of Mrs Thatcher's arriving half an hour early and chatting in the green room. Sometimes for live 8.10 interviews, when we were nervous that the eight o'clock pips had gone and there was no sign of the PM, we would discover from Downing Street that he had only just set off. It is true that prime ministerial convoys can move faster than normal traffic, but even so it was risky getting from SW1 to Broadcasting House during the course of the news bulletin. After a number of these episodes, with Major walking into the studio just as the newsreader finished their final story, we decided it must be deliberate to keep the presenter on the edge of his seat. This was confirmed when Humphrys was interviewing Major in Downing Street itself, with me producing, and the Prime Minister strolled into the Cabinet Room while John was reading the introduction to the item. That morning was memorable for underlining just how much in harmony Humphrys and I were about interviews. I was sitting in the radio car in Downing Street, talking as usual into John's headphones while he did the interview inside the building. 'Move on,' I would say, and he went to the next topic; or 'Ask him that again,' and John obediently put the question once more to the PM. Afterwards, I complimented John on a good job done with all instructions followed. 'Actually,' he said, 'the link from the radio car was distorted. I couldn't make out a word you said, so I had to guess.' Years of working together, and coming to trust each other, are what produced those best guesses.

For the New Year's Day interviews, we had a couple that were pre-recorded in Downing Street, but at the end of 1995 Jim Naughtie and I were back on the train to Huntingdon for another visit to the Major residence. It was with some flicker of nervousness, because we knew something was up politically. I had bumped into Paddy Ashdown, leader of the Liberal Democrats, outside the studio that morning. I told him we were recording a Major interview later that day, and his diary recounts our subsequent conversation. 'Look, I can't tell you why', he told me, 'and I cannot give any details, so do not ask me and do not go beating the bushes. But I will share a very private confidence with you. If you interview the Prime Minister today it will look exceedingly silly by tomorrow, because something is going to happen that will change everything. So here's a tip for you. If you do him today, make sure you get a commitment for him to return if anything big breaks.' Paddy concluded in his diary: 'Mosey tried to drag more out of me, but he didn't succeed.'

This was, of course, largely useless information and wasn't a very private confidence at all. I could see no sensible route to beating the bushes, as Paddy had brilliantly put it. You cannot just move a prime ministerial interview or force the PM to come back and do another one. But Jim and I speculated about what the Lib Dems might be up to, and we did try to persuade a puzzled Downing Street that we might seek to add a section to the interview if a new significant story broke, though we had no idea whether anything would.

Paddy's bombshell turned out to be the defection to the Liberal Democrats of the senior Conservative MP Emma Nicholson. It was announced just as we arrived back in London clutching our tape of the Major interview. This is not an event where the public will remember what they were doing when they heard the news, but in 1996 it was a damn good story and Paddy was right that it instantly made the Major interview out-of-date. For the first time, the Prime Minister's New Year interview was bumped from pride of place right after the news into the much less prestigious 8.30 slot – and Ms Nicholson and a live response from a senior Conservative dominated the programme instead. We had made another attempt to get Downing Street to give us a soundbite or two from the PM, but he understandably decided to keep his counsel in Huntingdon even if Paddy had succeeded in making his interview look 'exceedingly silly'.

My relationship with Paddy Ashdown was one of the strangest with any politician. He was perpetually cross with us because he didn't think we gave the Liberal Democrats enough airtime. As an early adopter of email, he would send tirades to me about how unfair it had been that Labour or Conservatives had been on air on a particular subject but his party had not. Many mornings there would be phone calls too, usually from the Liberal Democrats' chief media handler, Olly Grender. But Saturday mornings were special. If my phone rang at home round about 8.30 I knew it would be Paddy, incensed about the sequence after eight o'clock and either the absence of, or the disrespect towards, the Liberal Democrats. The oddity was that he would usually begin by saying 'Don't tell Olly I've called you!' because she, I now know, had instructed him not to do anything unofficially or anything beneath his dignity as party leader. But Paddy ignored that if he was sufficiently irritated by us, and I would get my ten minutes of being told off – or of being implored: 'Roger, what can we do to get your programme to take us seriously?' I came to like Paddy, and I missed our Saturday morning chats when I left *Today*.

But it was with Labour that we had the close-up view of the people who were about to move into government. Rod Liddle and I had lunch with a casual Tony Blair in Islington about a month before the death of John Smith in 1994. On the way back to Broadcasting House, Rod said he was worried about trusting a man who, like Blair that day, wore white jeans. When Blair became party leader, *Today* had his closely guarded bedside phone number – so if there was a major breaking story we could go to him immediately for comment. Most contact was still done through the press office, and via Alastair Campbell, and Blair would come into the studio with Campbell almost weekly during the early part of his leadership. I have never seen a closer relationship between a politician and a spin doctor, or one in which the spin doctor was so obviously an equal. Many press officers fade into the background when their principal is on parade, but that was the last thing that Alastair would do: he was never less than a commanding presence.

We sometimes had a glimpse of the difficulty of managing personalities in Labour. One morning when Blair was due in at 8.10 we had also booked Robin Cook, the shadow Foreign Secretary, for an 8.30 slot from an overseas visit he was making. But there was a breaking foreign story that morning that needed to be put to the Leader of the Opposition, given that he was in the studio. We told Blair that we would do that, and he looked bothered. 'Haven't you got Robin on later? Can't you put that to him?' We explained that we would have to ask both of them, and Blair reluctantly agreed to take one question. Within a minute or so of that being broadcast, the phone in the office rang with an incandescent Robin Cook shouting about why we had trampled all over his foreign affairs brief by putting 'his' key question to Tony Blair.

We used to find John Prescott difficult sometimes, too, and less full of bonhomie than the image he sometimes projects. I recall one morning when he arrived in the studio straight from the train from Hull and discovered that his shaving foam had exploded inside his suitcase. He stood in our office, face like thunder, case open, scraping foam off his best shirts. We thought it best not to make a joke about the froth of politics.

But it was the Labour spin machine that caused us the real bother. In the 1992 general election there had been a broad balance between the Conservative and Labour press operations. Both were very tough, and it had been as unpleasant being on the wrong end of Chris Patten's Conservative Central Office as it was being upbraided by Kinnock's Labour. During the subsequent Major government, there was a wild imbalance. Neither the government nor Conservative Central Office could get a grip on discipline, and the people running both tended to be nice rather than feared. At one point, *Today* was given its own Conservative spin doctor in the form of Alan Duncan MP, and for a while he would ring the night team at midnight – emulating what was believed to happen with Labour – and demand to know what was in our programme. Our editors would tell him we were not in the business of sharing our running order with anyone at that stage, and he would ring off. Alan subsequently went out for dinner with some senior editors and me, and we had a riotous night of political gossip in Orso's restaurant that conspicuously failed to increase our fear level of him and his colleagues.

Labour remained a different matter. I would come in some mornings to find night editors close to tears after a series of unpleasant conversations with junior spin doctors. If Labour thought we were doing a story they didn't like, they would phone and try to get us to change it. If we had a balance of guests they disapproved of, they began by talking to the output editor, and then sometimes the call would be escalated to me. The threat was often that they would complain to Tony Hall or John Birt or the chairman because of the incompetence or intransigence of the *Today* team. I would like to think that we never changed anything at their insistence, but it was unpleasant and wearing: the attempt to control, and the inclination to bully, was greater than anything I had experienced before or since. Dealing with a relatively new phenomenon, on this scale at least, we did make mistakes. On occasions, calls from parties – almost always Labour – would end up getting put through to the control room and direct to an editor. They would find themselves being harangued by a party apparatchik while trying to edit a live programme. We soon put a stop to this, and insisted that calls came to me only; often a complaint faded away if the output editor was safeguarded from the ear-bashing.

The pattern, then, was of lower-level vicious skirmishing but higher-level charm from New Labour, and one memorable weekend encapsulated the latter. I used to socialise with politicians from all parties, and over the years I have been to sport events with Conservatives, Liberal Democrats, Labour, SNP and Plaid Cymru – with the latter a disastrous invitation to watch Wales being hammered at Twickenham by England. On this occasion in 1996, it was Gordon Brown who invited me to go with a crew of people to watch England play Scotland at Wembley in the European Football Championships.

The night before, we were asked along to a party that Gordon's wealthy friend Geoffrey Robinson was giving at his flat in Park Lane, and I stood on the terrace, clutching a glass of white wine and overlooking a summery Hyde Park, with some of the folk who would, in a year's time, be running the country: Gordon himself, John Prescott, and Ed Balls, Gordon's chief adviser, who brought along his girlfriend, Yvette Cooper, for the match. We met to go to Wembley at a pub near Marylebone, and then the future Chancellor caught a packed train with us up to the stadium, standing in the middle of a bunch of England fans chanting 'Gordon Brown, Gordon Brown, Gordon Brown'.

It was an extraordinary opportunity to see these people close up, and especially in the heightened circumstances of the run-up to a general election. As a boy in Bradford, I would have thought I had died and gone to heaven if I had had this degree of contact with prime ministers and chancellors and foreign secretaries. Of course, seeing John Prescott's exploded shaving foam, or being told off for the eighteenth time by Michael Howard or Paddy Ashdown, tempered this – as did the unpleasantness of some of the encounters with spin doctors. But when the time came to leave *Today*, my leaving tape – the compilation of kind wishes from friends and colleagues – included recorded contributions from John Major, Paddy Ashdown and Gordon Brown. I was never less than exhausted by the hours that the programme demanded, but the excitement of it always thrilled me and gave me a fresh kick of energy. I'm delighted that *Today* remains in such good form, and continues to captivate the chattering classes and perform its civic duties, two decades later.

CHAPTER 7

RADIO 5 LIVE

O N 26 OCTOBER 1996 my transfer from *Today* to become
controller of Radio 5 Live was noted in the editorial column of *The Independent*, edited at the time by Andrew
Marr. 'To those unversed in the way the corporation gives ever larger
amounts of money and status to those moving further and further
away from the cutting edge of programme production, his is an odd
move,' it said. And there were certainly some Radio 4 aficionados who
thought I had gone crackers by leaving the *Today* programme, especially just before an election, for what was then known as Radio Bloke.

I had been sounded out about becoming controller of 5 Live earlier in the summer by Tony Hall over a relaxed lunch in Marylebone. Jenny Abramsky had launched the station brilliantly, but was being moved into the role of director of continuous news to create BBC News Online and a television news channel. I didn't think the idea of moving to 5 Live was terrible – it was intriguing to contemplate running a whole radio service and to add sport to my professional skills, especially after reigniting my love of football during Euro '96. But the election loomed large in *Today* thinking, and even though 5 Live had its commitment to news, it was sport that defined it and won the biggest audiences. There was a risk of journalistic marginalisation. I had also been part of a team that saw 5 Live as the competition, and may well have been guilty of saying the odd disobliging thing myself about the upstart channel. I therefore said no to Tony's overtures, and repeated that to Jenny when she asked me directly whether I would enter the selection process – and I meant it, rather than trying to play the traditional 'chase me, chase me' game favoured by job applicants.

What changed my mind was a brilliant bit of psychological warfare by Jenny. Just before the final interviews she casually dropped into our conversation that she had mentioned my decision to Will Wyatt, then the all-powerful head of BBC Broadcast. 'Silly boy,' she reported him as saying, 'nobody should turn down a controllership.' That pulled me up short. Yes, it was a controllership – which was still a venerated thing in the BBC. And I had spent nine years as an editor within Radio 4 so there was a question about what I would do next, and I had thoughts about moving on after the election. I could see that 5 Live was one of the best things on offer, and if I didn't take it when it was vacant then it would be daft afterwards to wish I had.

So I put in a late application – and, given that Tony and Jenny had wanted me to do the job, it was not entirely a surprise when I became the recommended candidate. Predictably for someone from news, my pitch was to increase the profile and ambition of its news coverage, but I also wanted to give it a more unified style and tone across the schedule. There were some very odd juxtapositions of content, so at one point the network went from live football into a discussion programme on foreign affairs hosted by the cerebral Paul Reynolds – and Jenny, who had always wanted to be controller of Radio 4, had a somewhat loftier view of Radio Bloke's speech programming than I did. The editors on the channel still talked of her noisy despair about a programme in the early days of the network that had not given enough attention to the election results of a former Soviet republic.

John Birt was helpful in unlocking this dilemma. I was only the recommendation of the interview panel, so I had to go and see him for a one-to-one chat to be confirmed. It was not the toughest of grillings. 'Do you *like* sport?' he asked. 'Yes,' I replied, and it was clear the discussion was going in the right direction. But when I had a chance to ask the DG what he thought about the station, rather than going for the macro view I asked him a specific question about that day's news agenda. There had been a small and relatively dull development in the Northern Ireland peace process, and England had won a key World Cup qualifier. 5 Live's news had dutifully led on Ireland, but I suggested to John that a coherent news and sport network might put the football first as a way of attracting people into the station's news programming while still paying Northern Ireland due attention a little lower down the running order. He thought for a moment, then said he agreed – which I felt gave me permission in the coming months to refresh the editorial thinking and make the station speak with one voice.

Jenny was still my ultimate boss on 5 Live since we were part of her continuous news empire, and she tolerated my murdering of some of her beloved programmes in the interests of a more fluid, contemporary station. The template was already there in the sparky breakfast show with Peter Allen and Jane Garvey, edited by Bill Rogers, but on the fringes of the schedule there had been a black programme, an Asian programme, a gay programme, a series on popular protest songs, a history of agony aunts and all sorts of worthy 'built' programmes. I stabbed them one by one. I discovered, though, that commissioning was a much slower process than editing a programme. I turned up at my desk on Day 1 and said we should have a sports magazine programme on Sunday mornings, and I was discomfited to find that it would take months to do. We had to wind down the contract of the existing programme in the desired slot; go to a tender process for the new one; and fit it all within our budget cycle. This was a different world from the instant hits of daily journalism, but one that became more satisfying. The sports magazine programme – *Sportsweek* – is still running, and doing what we hoped it would in finding the newsmakers and creating headlines for the Monday morning newspapers. It illustrates the different scope of a controllership compared with an editorship. You become responsible for the range and tone of everything on the station, twenty-four hours a day, seven days a week. You allocate budgets across news and sport and independent companies, and at times you run competitive processes to decide which programmes or teams will occupy a particular part of the schedule. For instance, we replaced a flabby in-house news magazine on a Sunday morning with *The Sunday Service*, produced by an outside independent company. It brought Fi Glover into a prime slot on the network, with a regular pundit team of the journalist Andrew Pierce and the spin doctor Charlie Whelan.

What you do less of as a controller is intervene in the running orders of individual programmes, although I did take an interest in what the subject was for the hour-long phone-in each morning at 9 a.m. My *Today* instincts would take over if I heard a trail for what I thought was a poor topic, and I would call the office – doubtless making hearts sink on the production team – and 'suggest' they might opt for something different.

It was essential that 5 Live was credible in its news coverage. At the time I went there, it was the only continuous news service in the BBC apart from Ceefax. We therefore made some grand gestures to signify that we mattered, including hiring David Dimbleby to present a special current affairs debate at the height of the Kosovo conflict. I'm not sure he had ever even heard 5 Live before, but he coped valiantly with jingles and sports news bulletins.

In former days, major breaking stories would have been the responsibility of the radio newsroom and the Radio 4 sequence programmes. When Princess Diana's car crashed in a tunnel in Paris in August 1997, 5 Live was the only BBC news service broadcasting as the information started to emerge in the early hours of the morning. Woken at home, I changed the schedules to take off the Birmingham-based discussion programme that was on air and replace it with news output from London. But, perhaps thanks to my fuddled, just-awoken state, I was initially unable to shake off the feeling that this was like a vivid version of the royal obituary rehearsals we had done so many times in the past. In the early hours there was the erroneous eyewitness account on American television claiming that Diana had walked away from the crash, while some reports of her death emerged out of Manila, where the Foreign Secretary Robin Cook happened to be. It was uncannily like a scenario devised as a test of our obituary procedures when, based on fragmentary and contradictory wire reports, Prince Charles was said to have been trampled to death during a polo match in the Middle East. Only this time it was real, and the journalistic challenge was made even tougher by the shock we were feeling about the tragedy unfolding in Paris.

Since it was a bank holiday weekend – as with the death of the Queen Mother five years later – presenters were initially hard to come by when we hit the phones to put together on-air teams. We realised, somewhat too late, that a rota which had some people off one week and a different set off the next had the flaw of potentially having everyone unavailable on the weekend in between. One presenter gamely came in straight from a dinner party but had consumed so much wine that we put her back in a cab and sent her home. Eddie Mair answered his mobile promptly but was abroad. In particular, we needed to put together a breakfast programme, when the nation would be waking up to the most shattering news in a generation. We were relieved to find Jim Naughtie available to be the Radio 4 voice, in combination with Peter Allen for 5 Live. I stood in the corner of the familiar *Today* studio watching them open the programme, while still in disbelief about the words coming out of the speakers.

After the first-ever combined Radio 4 and 5 Live breakfast programme went off air, we had 'scratch' combinations of presenters from the two networks providing a continuing news service through the day on the conjoined channels. The odd rough edge in presentation was disguised by the quality of the guests, as world leaders including Nelson Mandela responded to our requests for live interviews. We had extraordinary moments of live broadcasting, such as Tony Blair's eulogy to 'the People's Princess'. At one of our stock-taking meetings during the day, John Birt materialised at the back of the room in a pleasing show of DG solidarity, and the only curiosity, looking back at it, is that we were so reluctant on that day to open the phone lines and get the audience's reaction to such a momentous event. Radio 5 Live was built around phone-ins and they were not unknown to Radio 4, but the fear of creating the wrong tone – of having a caller who might have said they didn't care about Diana – meant that we waited over twenty-four hours before Brian Hayes was allowed to solicit Britain's views on air.

It was, candidly, something of a relief that the day of Diana's death also happened to be the day of the US Open Tennis final featuring Britain's Greg Rusedski, so our fourteen hours of obituary programming had a logical end in the early evening as 5 Live reasserted its sporting identity. Our specialisms stood us in good stead for the funeral, too. Many of the best commentators on sport are gifted wordsmiths who can apply themselves to any event. For the radio coverage of Diana's funeral, we therefore used sport commentators to be out with the crowds and to commentate as the procession moved by, supplementing the more traditional voices of Radio 4.

I was fortunate on 5 Live to have the space to bring in new

regular news presenters, with Nicky Campbell the highest-profile. He was introduced to me by the fabulously assertive agent Jon Thoday, with the statement that Nicky had had enough of doing Radio 1 and wanted to move into speech radio – which in those days was extremely unusual, even though he had the reputation of being Radio 1's intellectual. This was only slightly undermined by his hosting of ITV's *Wheel of Fortune*. But I leapt at the offer. Something about Nicky made me think he was perfect for the next stage of 5 Live, and it was only when I heard him on his new morning show that I realised precisely what it was: the ability to create one of the better pub conversations in which you move from high politics and sport to ethics and entertainment – all with intelligence, but in an engaging and non-pompous way.

Nicky had one of the classic presenter–editor relationships with his boss Mark Sandell, and they rightly won a Sony Award in the first year of the show. But Nicky was also adept at managing me. There was one day when I was listening in my office with increasing irritation to what I thought was a wayward and irrelevant discussion. At precisely the moment when I was itching to tell the studio to move on to something better, a computer message flashed up from Nicky. 'Yes, I know. This isn't right. Moving on.' Those instincts serve presenters well.

I was also certain about the talents of Victoria Derbyshire, who was found by our commissioning editor Steve Kyte. She had done some guest-presenting on our *Media Show* from Manchester, and hearing her voice coming out of the radio I thought she had the perfect combination: warmth and just enough of a northern accent to be distinctive without sounding too much like Radio Lancashire. I read an article by Victoria some years later when she described the meeting in which I asked her to stand in on the 5 Live breakfast show: 'I recall thinking I had to be really cool in the way I reacted in case he thought I was too northern or common, so I expressed my gratitude, ran down Regent Street to All Bar One and ordered half a lager and lime. I wanted to scream with happiness.'

When I made a contribution to the taped tributes the BBC collected when she left 5 Live, I retold the story and joked that she fitted the bill because we *wanted* someone who sounded northern and common. But she is a broadcaster with conspicuous talent and especially in her interviewing – which can range from the empathetic to the tiger-like, with the latter deployed especially when confronting a BBC boss. I went onto her show years later as director of London 2012, and she mercilessly challenged me about staff numbers and costs, to the fury of my BBC press officer in attendance. It may be strange to outsiders that a BBC station covering the Olympics challenges the resourcing of the BBC's coverage of the Olympics, but I would rather that than a Stalinist silence about internal issues.

It was more of a gamble taking on Edwina Currie. The cynical reason for doing so was that we had late shows on Saturday and Sunday nights which had low audiences and no profile. We also had a commitment to doing the programmes from Birmingham. We always had floods of demo tapes from would-be presenters but, unsurprisingly, few were anxious to be in Pebble Mill after midnight at a weekend. It was hard to think of anyone who would put that part of the schedule on the map – unless you had someone who really was 'love her or hate her', with a probability of the latter. I had bumped into Edwina on Radio 4 over the years, and I liked her feistiness. She had lost her seat in the Labour landslide of 1997 and was therefore available, indeed very available, plus her former Derbyshire constituency gave her enough of a link with the Midlands for a Birmingham posting to be credible.

I am not sure how aware she was of these not entirely flattering calculations, but full credit to her for taking on the role and for being the person who was incarcerated in Pebble Mill until the early hours. She even lived with us calling the show *Late Night Currie*. To describe her early programmes as 'rough' would be accurate, but she became a decent presenter who got the BBC way of doing things – proudly announcing that her own views had been surgically removed. I admired her pluck in doing something new and delivering us increasingly impressive audience figures, while also being relieved that her Birmingham location meant that she was one presenter fewer on my doorstep.

But inevitably for BBC bosses, on Radio 5 Live as much as *Today*, it is the departure of presenters that makes the headlines – and my moment in the spotlight as controller was when I fired Danny Baker as a 5 Live football phone-in presenter. This was painful because I loved Danny's style as one of the brightest and most articulate radio hosts, as well as someone who clocked up the ratings. We were bothered, though, that his behaviour on air seemed to be getting ever more unpredictable: he urged Spurs fans to throw their programmes onto the pitch (illegal) and he routinely wished ill will on specific football club directors. But this was just building up to a programme where any executive listening would have had to hide behind the sofa with his hands over his ears. It followed a controversial refereeing decision by Mike

Reed in a cup tie between Chelsea and Leicester, and Danny let rip: 'Football has a maggot at its golden core, and that maggot is referees,' he said. 'Most of them need a good slap round the face. Hacks should doorstep this man like he's a member of Oasis … That worm should be on the phone now, Radio 5 should be knocking down that ref's dressing room and asking do you know on behalf of all referees how bad you are.'

Then, when a caller defending referees ill-advisedly suggested Danny should shut up, he turned on his producer behind the glass and yelled: 'Keith – will you take him off? Seriously. What is the matter with you? What is the matter with you in there? I'm not a confrontational shock-jock. I'm not like this. Will you stop putting through smart-arses who just want to be contrary? Give me back my old producer, someone.'

I went into work the next day knowing we would have to take the programme off because for a BBC programme to suggest referees needed 'a good slap round the face' is not on – and it compounded the previous offences for which he had been given a warning. When I arrived in my office, Bob Shennan, then the head of radio sport, was waiting there grim-faced; for him there was the extra factor of the on-air haranguing of one of his producers.

It was a rather muted sacking in that we only asked Danny to leave his Wednesday night phone-in; we wanted him to stay on *Baker & Kelly Upfront*, which was a more amiable pre-match show with Danny Kelly on a Saturday lunchtime. Baker, understandably, thought you could not be half sacked from a radio station – so he quit, creating lots of headlines, and jumped ship with the other Danny to our rivals, Talk Radio. There he had the satisfaction of going head to head with his arch-enemy David Mellor. I often thought Danny delivered the more entertaining show but it was Mellor who won the ratings war.

The immediate problem was how to replace Danny, and an astute agent made a call while Mr Baker's 5 Live body was still warm. How about Richard Littlejohn, he asked? And a quick debate in the office led us to the view that that was rather a good idea: Richard was an experienced broadcaster, a high-profile columnist on *The Sun*, a football nut and also agreeably outside the usual BBC presenter gene pool. So Littlejohn was hired within twenty-four hours. I had been interviewed on 5 Live about Danny's departure and I went back on the station to announce the arrival of Littlejohn, only to be sandbagged by a characteristic Eddie Mair question: 'You've been on your own station twice in two days,' he noted. 'Do you think that's how Robert Maxwell started?'

Leaving any hint of media mogul self-aggrandisement aside, though, Littlejohn was a popular signing and within a couple of years he had displaced Mellor from the flagship 6-0-6 phone-in. Some years later Bob Shennan rehired Danny Baker for 5 Live.

On the sport side of the station, I had the guidance of my experienced deputy Mike Lewis and I came to enjoy the poker-playing side of sports rights negotiations. This was a time when competition was starting to bite in radio, with Talk Radio a fully-fledged commercial speech network keen on the success that 5 Live had acquired through live sport – and, as sign of that, rebranded as Talk Sport after the arrival of Kelvin MacKenzie at its helm.

Kelvin ran the BBC awfully close on snatching *Test Match Special* and at one point he was bidding for anything that moved in a sporting arena. With hindsight I suspect the BBC was initially too defensive in response and there was no problem for either side when we shared some events, as with the FA Cup contract from 1999, but we relished the adrenalin rush of the competition with Kelvin even if some of his activities gave us disturbed nights.

The papers never cared when we retained a set of sports rights. Television was going through a rocky period of losing cricket and Formula 1, so the only story for the press was further losses. I was amusingly stitched up by the *Evening Standard* when I noted this in an interview on our *Sportsweek* programme. 'All it needs is the opening of a bid process', I said, 'such as Open Golf, and you get headlines like "BBC could lose Open Golf".' The next day the *Standard* duly obliged with the headline 'BBC could lose Open Golf'. But we realised this reflected how crucial sport was to the corporation.

Astonishing effort went into the bid to keep Wimbledon across television and radio, and we radio folk watched open-mouthed as the TV presentation to the All-England Club included constructing a special television gallery within a Wimbledon auditorium, which revolved into sight on the click of an executive's fingers, to show how keen we were to retain the rights. Some years later, when I was director of sport, Mark Thompson mused that losing Wimbledon from the BBC would be like the ravens leaving the Tower of London – and he was right, even though there was the occasional rumble from Corporate HQ about how sustainable it was going to be to stay in sport in an age of hyperinflation of rights fees.

Kelvin was brilliant in attack. In one magazine interview he accused us of being state monopolists.

Twenty years ago it would have been called British Steel. When

I wake up in the morning I think how I can earn revenue and grow our business. When the BBC guy wakes up it's 11 a.m. and he's trying to work out whether it was the Rioja or the port that caused his stomach upset. He has a couple of meetings and is home for tea … Buying sports rights shouldn't be the role of the BBC. A public service broadcaster should be doing programmes about sparrows in Serbia and the lower-crested rhubarb-hunter.

This gave us a laugh but reinforced our determination to win. Given how important football in particular was, Mike Lewis and I set ourselves the task of meeting every Premier League chairman for lunch or dinner before the next rights negotiation was due. We discovered that Chelsea's Ken Bates really did hand the keys of his Bentley to the maître'd and ask him to look after it while he ate. Afterwards, Bates sent me a typed note of thanks that referred to our conversation about the BBC being on another corporate economy drive: 'I hope we can work together to our mutual benefit. Meanwhile, keep up the savings.' He then added by hand: 'So that you can pay us more!'

At Southampton, Rupert Lowe greeted us in a towering bad mood because of rude things said about him on 5 Live by David Mellor, and said he could spare us a meagre forty-five minutes, only to relax considerably and spend more than two hours with us. There followed invitations for a number of visits to the Dell and then St Mary's, which showed the benefit of personal contacts.

The lurking nightmare on 5 Live was that a new Premier League deal, inevitably negotiated well under the radar, might be threatened by some of the news and sport journalism on the station.

This was not because the Premier League was over-sensitive but because some club chairmen were. It was, and always has been for me, a matter of faith that we would never curtail our journalism because of rights considerations. I was proud of Rob Bonnet's tough weekly magazine *Inside Edge* calling the sport administrators to account, and I had introduced *Sportsweek* to bolster the journalism further. However, on the day that we knew a contract was going for approval to a rights holder, there was always some relief if that was not a day chosen by our breakfast programme to duff up their chief executive. Experience shows that the Chinese walls between the journalism and the corporate interests of the BBC are widely understood and supported inside the organisation – but they almost never convince outsiders, especially in sport, who would naturally choose the promotion of their wares over scrutiny.

I also never had any doubt that some sporting bodies might be tempted to put commercial gain over sentiment. The best ones do consider the quality of the broadcaster, and in television they think about getting the big audiences that only free-to-air channels can deliver. But it is a remarkable chief executive who tells his governing body that they will turn down an offer that may be double or treble the BBC's in order to stay in their traditional home. So I developed a wariness that also stood me in good stead when I became director of sport, though I would pay tribute to the good guys like Ian Ritchie at Wimbledon and Richard Scudamore at the Premier League who were tough but trustworthy in negotiations – as opposed to a few who were in the 'tough and would sell their granny twice over' category.

Towards the end of my time at 5 Live, I was delighted when

Kelvin MacKenzie paid me a compliment, telling *The Guardian* I had done 'a bang-up job' – though I had to look up the phrase in a dictionary of slang to check it was as complimentary as I hoped it was.

Certainly, I was proud of my time at the station: we became the Sony Station of the Year; audiences rose to over six million; the sport side remained in glowing health; and news programmes had improved in listening figures and range. Most of all, it was stimulating working with a great management team and pretty much doing what we wanted with a radio station. It was nothing like as much the place for networking with the political establishment as Radio 4, though the more astute politicians were beginning to engage with it. It offered a different audience – 'real people' rather than the chattering classes – and it encouraged politicians to take a more open and conversational approach to interviews. John Major recognised this by agreeing, as Prime Minister, to a phone-in from Downing Street, and some of my *Today* contacts kept in touch with me in my new home: most notably, the man who had become Chancellor of the Exchequer – Gordon Brown.

The episode that stands out was a visit with him to Rome to watch the England football team play a crucial game against Italy. The Chancellor had government meetings to attend, but the idea had been developed during the previous months that business would be combined with pleasure, and a party of journalists would accompany him to watch the football. As a dutiful BBC apparatchik, I checked with my bosses and advisers that this was acceptable, and they sensibly took the view that contact with the new Chancellor was a valuable thing. I was cleared for take-off. The experience began with a reception at the British ambassador's residence, and then a hair-raisingly fast journey through the streets of Rome on which our foreign VIPs' coach was accompanied by police outriders. This felt more, rather than less, dangerous in the narrow streets. At the match, Gordon was seated with the true VIPs, while we journalists were with rank-and-file England supporters. This had the unfortunate consequence that, owing to crowd trouble, we were detained within the stadium after the game and not allowed out for the best part of an hour. We tried in vain, and in pidgin Italian, to convince the security people that the British finance minister was waiting for us and we must be released, but they were unrelenting. We finally made it back to the bus to find Gordon waiting with surprising patience. However, by the time we got back to our hotel, its restaurant had closed and there seemed to be nowhere nearby to eat, either. At this point, Geoffrey Robinson, who was in the travelling party, had an idea: Harry's Bar was not too far away! After a phone call to persuade them to accept a late booking – in every sense, because it was getting close to midnight – we set off to the Via Vittorio Veneto. As pinch-yourself moments go, a night watching England in the Olympic Stadium in Rome, followed by eating lobster in Harry's Bar with the Chancellor is definitely up there.

That may have led, during my last few months on 5 Live, to the most extraordinary job offer of my life, which started on a nippy January day during an awayday meeting of the station's editors. I took a call on my mobile from Gordon Brown's office, asking if I wanted to pop around for tea at the end of the working day. This was not unusual, because I still got calls from the Chancellor's office if he fancied a chat, and I had once had the pleasure (for a political anorak like myself) of eating a sandwich with Gordon while watching a televised speech by William Hague – with Gordon expertly dissecting what he was getting right and what he was getting wrong.

I was naïve about the agenda for the January tea. Just before Christmas, Charlie Whelan had been forced to resign as Gordon's press spokesman and fixer in a nasty meltdown for the Labour government that had also included the (first) resignation of Peter Mandelson. When I arrived at the Treasury, Gordon made small talk while the tea was poured but then gradually edged into a conversation in which it became apparent that he was asking me if I wanted to step into the role of being his special adviser.

I remember a number of things from the conversation. First, Gordon was playing the unity ticket with the Prime Minister: he emphasised that they both wanted to put the disaster of the past month behind them and start with a clean sheet of paper. They wanted to raise the tone after the spin accusations that had beset the Whelan incumbency. And here was I, just the man for the job.

While listening to this, and smiling as calmly as I could as I stirred my tea, I had a shuddering clash of emotions. On the one hand, it was incredibly flattering to be sitting in Whitehall being offered a job by the Chancellor. There was a big hint that if I did the role well in the coming months then I would be helped to find a seat at the next general election, and my family had always suspected that one day I would become an MP. On the other hand, much as I liked Charlie Whelan, I thought the role was one in which I would be highly likely to be eaten alive by the internal politics of the government and by the ravening press. I also hadn't voted Labour in twenty years, and becoming one of its advocates was an improbable step. I was therefore resolutely non-committal, while Gordon was unstoppable: 'Come for lunch on Sunday!' he said. 'Let's talk about it more!'

As I got the Tube home I was in turmoil, though I don't think I ever came close to accepting. The first thing I did the next day was to tell Tony Hall and Jenny Abramsky because ethically I couldn't keep this as a secret to myself. They told me later they had both believed I would take the job. But I let Gordon know via Ed Balls, who was involved in the discussions, that I was too busy to have lunch on Sunday, while thinking to myself that it was an odd state of affairs for a boy from Bradford to be telling the Chancellor of the Exchequer that he didn't fancy sharing a plate of roast beef at the weekend.

Most of my kitchen cabinet thought I would take the job too, and my hesitation about joining Team Gordon prompted a very serious love-bombing. Gordon asked me to go out for supper instead if I was unable to make Sunday lunch, and I accepted because I couldn't plausibly be busy every night for a year. I therefore found myself in a Chinese restaurant down the Horseferry Road with Gordon, his then unknown girlfriend Sarah, and Ed Balls. I knew that associates talked of 'Good Gordon' and 'Bad Gordon', but I have only ever seen Good Gordon, and he was charming, persuasive and non-factional in all our discussions. The brief was to build bridges with No. 10, not blow them up. The latter order presumably came if you got the job.

For moral support I was driven to and from the restaurant by my friend Chris Rybczynski, who was the only one of my circle to be consistently against the offer. She had diagnosed that working for Gordon when I was used to running my own show would be a nasty jolt to the system, even leaving aside the sharks that patrolled the political waters. But the incentives kept coming, including the one added to many job offers: foreign flights. I could travel around Europe as one of the Chancellor's personal emissaries, assessing the lie of the land on the Euro, which was the knottiest political challenge facing the government.

By this stage, my heart was shouting 'no' even while my head still entertained subversive thoughts of 'yes'. I liked Gordon, but I knew definitively in these exceptional circumstances that politics was not for me. There was more I wanted to do in broadcasting, and I had had signals that a senior job in television might be on offer soon. I was also not sure I could take the financial risk of a special adviser's post with zero security, against the more cushioned BBC. On a Sunday night I sent a fax to Ed Balls:

> I've thought about this for much of the time since we last spoke
> – and I've come to the conclusion, with great sadness, that we
> shouldn't take our discussions any further … The sadness is,
> of course, because I'm aware that chances like this don't recur.
> Without wanting to sound too pious, I'm honoured that it
> happened at all.

Even at the time, I think 'sadness' was stretching it a bit. 'Relief' might have been a more honest word. I knew with absolute clarity that this was a once-in-a-lifetime offer and I got it that it was a momentous decision one way or another; but I never really had any doubt about what was right for me, and subsequent stories about the TB–GBs have confirmed that view. Indeed, a few years later at a programme recording, I met Ed Balls and Ed Miliband, who had been aware of the discussions, and they fondly recollected life within Team Gordon while also giving me a distinct sense that I had had a lucky escape.

There were no hard feelings from Gordon. I was invited to his wedding reception when he married Sarah, and he came to Twickenham as my guest when I was director of sport. I admire a politician who can both enjoy the sport and talk about his favourite books during the breaks in play, and he was amused to be offered a pint of Guinness by the fan sitting directly in front of us. However, ever the cautious politician, he only sipped it before gently manoeuvring it under his seat, and the Chancellor's glass was left half-full.

I never pass through Westminster without a flicker of wondering what might have been if I had made a different choice, but I cannot pretend to have any regret. For all that John Inverdale said about my obsession with politics, I prefer to be an observer rather than a participant; and the Brown episode was useful in confirming that.

CHAPTER 8

TELEVISION

I N THE AUTUMN of 1999 the plan for me to move to television became a reality. I had always loved radio, but I had a feeling about working in television of 'if not now, then never'. I didn't want to exclude myself completely from the most powerful medium of our age. I had spent part of the year being acting director of continuous news, the pantomime horse department with which Jenny Abramsky had been saddled. It included the recently launched BBC News 24 and BBC News Online as well as 5 Live, but it also had within it Ceefax and the Travel Unit. This meant that management meetings sometimes underwent conversational detours about roadworks and the need to service multiple outlets with traffic news. It was the last manifestation of John Birt's bi-media, or even tri-media, approach: the idea that television and radio and then online should work together – which was sensible in principle but had led to curious forced marriages, of which continuous news was probably the oddest.

Now, though, Tony Hall was proposing to do something more sensible. One of the problems in his news division was that the programmes department included the flagship BBC One bulletins at 1 p.m., 6 p.m. and 9 p.m. – while the 24-hour television operations, domestic and international, sat in continuous news. There was a similar barrier in radio with *Today* and *The World at One* in programmes, and 5 Live in continuous. It was obvious that all those beloved management concepts such as synergies and efficiencies would be far better delivered by re-creating a television department and a radio department. In particular there was an urgent need to add some of the TV bulletins' credibility to the struggling News 24. So that is what Tony did, and I was asked to run television news while Steve Mitchell ran radio news.

I will always be grateful to Tony for taking the gamble of putting someone who had never worked in television into running the biggest TV news operation in the UK. I had it on good authority that, a few years earlier, senior figures in BBC Television had wanted me to edit *Newsnight* – but the move had been vetoed by BBC News because I wasn't a television animal. Now here I was running the whole lot. I believe that, in reality, editing is editing: if you know a story in newspapers or radio then you know it in television too, and running orders have a lot in common with each other even if the technology is different. But there was still a lot to learn, and sometimes I yearned for the simplicity of radio, where you could pop a few phone interviews on the air on a breaking story and not have to worry about satellite trucks or the pictures still being stuck in the edit suite. I know in the early days I would sometimes question a *Newsnight* running order late in the afternoon, and suggest they did something different, which would have been easy for *The World at One* but was close to impossible for a programme that has sent out its cameras and outside broadcast vans to far-flung parts of the country.

The new structure generated the predictable headline 'Here is the BBC News: Birtism is dead' with the journalist Maggie Brown writing of my new job: 'The appointment in itself is an indication of the end of Birtism and the birth of fresh thinking.' She added that abandoning the old structure 'is clearly an acknowledgment that it didn't work'.

What certainly had not worked was creating two heavy and competing management teams for one medium, and my immediate problem was sorting out a mini-mountain of managing editors and commissioning editors from the old regimes. It was a grisly process, reducing nine managers to just three. I hated having to do it and it caused a permanent rift with some of those affected; but that kind of decision is unavoidable as you become more senior, and it felt right to protect jobs in the newsroom by streamlining the management. When I started at 5 Live, a newspaper profile said: 'The saintly image has taken firm hold ... It is hard to find anyone at Broadcasting House with a harsh word to say about [him].' However, that would not have been the case at Television Centre four years later.

Television news was often a bumpy ride because it was so much bigger and more multi-tentacled than anything else I had done, and whereas people have an intimate relationship with *Today* and find 5 Live likeable, in TV news there is a harsh spotlight from which few emerge unscathed. An immediate lesson I learned was that emails sent to television staff other than my most senior colleagues could swiftly appear on Media Guardian or in *Broadcast* magazine. I empathised with Will Wyatt's account of turning down the job of controller of news and current affairs because previous senior figures in that area had variously been rubbished by official reports, been exiled to the regions, cracked under pressure, taken endless flak or hit the bottle. That was without having to deal with two continuous news channels, bulletins on four different television networks, the death of the Queen Mother, 9/11, 7/7, another war in Iraq, a tsunami and two general election campaigns.

But in my first year we had an exhilarating flurry when Greg Dyke, as the new DG, showed just how different his BBC was from John Birt's. There had long been a view inside the corporation that our main news should be at 10 p.m. not 9 p.m., because it was both a better time for the bulletin – taking in parliamentary votes and a flavour of the next day's papers – and also kinder to the BBC One schedulers in their battle with ITV. There was a convenient gap left by ITV's daft decision to move out of the 10 p.m. slot. Greg correctly diagnosed that the old BBC would have taken years to make this kind of decision, if ever, but by August 2000 he proclaimed it would happen in 2001. There was a general caterwauling from politicians about the BBC moving news from the middle of the evening and being too competitive, and the *Daily Telegraph* said bizarrely that the DG was 'yielding to the forces of Philistinism at the corporation … A philistine BBC is a supine BBC; a nation kept in ignorance is a nation easily led.' Delighted by the heat being turned on the BBC, ITV retaliated by saying it was going to move its news back to 10 p.m. early the next year – which prompted Greg, characteristically, to escalate the arms race by asking us if we could move to 10 p.m. that autumn at three weeks' notice.

This was a big ask. It was toughest on the network television service, headed at the time by Mark Thompson, because many of their programmes were the wrong length for the newly freed-up 9–10 p.m. slot. A lot of documentary and drama programmes were fifty minutes long, as was common for the old 9.30 p.m. placings, and our early liaison meetings had to kick around ideas for padding the slot or for bringing forward programmes planned for later in the season that were audience-winners and, crucially, the right duration.

It was not simple within BBC News, either. I had surreptitiously tipped off our graphics team as early as I could that we might need a title sequence with a '10' in it rather than a '9', but we also had to change shift patterns, incorporate the newly extended Nations and Regions slot within the programme and alter a generation of planning assumptions about Outside Broadcast (OB) trucks and satellite bookings. But it was stimulating. Our staff responded brilliantly to the challenge, and we loved the way the BBC under Dyke and our chairman Christopher Bland smacked away the competitive and political challenges – helped, of course, by the belief that what we were doing was right for the news audience as well as for our main TV channel.

That said, I was horribly nervous on 16 October 2000 when the first BBC *Ten O'Clock News* was about to go on air. We were still being assailed for rushing the changes, and as I got into the glass lift in the News Centre to go down to the editorial floor I had a clear notion in my head: 'If this goes wrong now, it will be very, very bad.' All it needed was a tape to be missing or a satellite link to go down, which are always possibilities in a live news programme, and our critics' case would be proven: it was a botched job. I also could not quite imagine how the news division would explain itself to Greg if it screwed up the launch in any way.

My recollection is that the programme was editorially rather dull that night, but to the relief of all of us it was technically 'clean' – and the next day we discovered it had healthy ratings, too. Those continued. It was an article of faith among the media chattering classes that when ITV moved back against us, even if only for their peculiar pattern of three nights a week, we would lose the war for audiences. Initially, that was the case – but we went on to confound those expectations, and some years later the BBC was even able to appropriate the 'News at Ten' moniker that had been the proud badge of ITN when it owned the ten o'clock spot in its heyday.

Huw Edwards has been the under-appreciated hero of this long-term victory. The *Ten* was launched by the established and authoritative pairing of Peter Sissons and Michael Buerk. When it became time for them to move on, it was a strongly contested battle about who would take their place. It was arbitrated by Jana Bennett and Lorraine Heggessey for network television with my boss Richard Sambrook and me from news, and we had three people who clearly could be great *Ten* anchors: Huw, George Alagiah and Fiona Bruce. We argued it every way round, but opted for Huw because he had done a terrific job on the *Six* and because he shaded the others as a presenter on a live breaking story. It was one of our better decisions, with his authority on the *Ten* building over the years and his move into the iconic television events. By the time it came to planning the Olympic opening ceremony in London 2012, I would have no hesitation in wanting Huw to lead the commentary team.

The longer-term task facing television news was bringing the news bulletins and News 24 closer together. News 24 was continually being slated in its early days, and the Commons media committee had recently concluded: 'We find it difficult to discern the justification for News 24 in view of its huge cost and small audience.' Predictably, since they were in completely different departments, editors in bulletins and the channels saw each other as the enemy. Giving resources to one, they believed, took something away from the other – and our first combined editors' awayday felt like it was composed of two opposing armed camps. It was a worryingly big culture change to get people on the bulletins to see that it was not good for BBC News to have an underperforming news channel.

My deputy, Rachel Attwell, set about transforming the look and feel of News 24 so that it was more in harmony with the rest of our operation, rather than the somewhat wacky initial incarnation with bright made-up flags and male presenters in their shirt sleeves. But what helped the credibility of the news channel more than anything else was the volume of huge stories. The first time we put News 24 onto BBC One for a breaking story was the crash of Concorde in Paris, and television controllers came to trust the channel, in a way they hadn't before, as a source of coverage for the news they wanted on the main networks. In particular, Alison Sharman, the controller of BBC Daytime, saw that news was often good for ratings as well as for her editorial mix

– so we cheerfully did snow and flood and crime specials for her alongside the 'must do' agenda of wars and terrorism. One day in September 2001, when we were at a staff lunch with the TV on in the background, we saw the traumatic pictures of a plane crashing into the World Trade Center; having News 24 meant all it took was a phone call to the network for us to be able to switch the coverage immediately onto BBC One.

Alison's instincts sometimes overcame my journalistic caution, but she was almost always right. Just before Christmas in 2003 she phoned me at home on a Sunday morning about the rumours we were picking up that Saddam Hussein had been captured. I did the usual news division caveats: 'At the moment these are only rumours; we haven't got any official verification; we don't want to build this up by putting rolling news on BBC One if it turns out not to be true.' At which she responded politely but firmly: 'It's a story either way and it's a darn sight more interesting than what we're currently transmitting – so let's go on air in five minutes.' By then, the breaking news was about to be confirmed and we were broadcasting it on our main channel well before the competition. This increased profile for News 24 on the networks helped it become stronger in its own right, too. By the end of 2004, we had drawn level in viewing figures with Sky News after years of lagging behind.

Not every breaking story was quite so smoothly handled. One weekend, in March 2005, the former Prime Minister James Callaghan died. I took the view that the death of a former PM was something that should be noted in a brief news report on BBC One, pointing those interested to fuller coverage on News 24. I hadn't reckoned with another venerable figure from the '60s and

'70s. It was the night that *Doctor Who* was being brought back to network television after a long break, and the channel wanted to give it the best possible lead-in from the previous programme to get the audience hooked on the return of the Doctor. I thought Lorraine Heggessey was a splendid controller of One, but that night she was immoveable. I argued for a one-minute Callaghan news report in the next programme junction. 'But Roger,' she said, 'it's *Doctor Who*!' 'I know', I replied, 'but we're talking about a former Prime Minister.' Her voice took on an increased edge of determination: 'It's *Doctor Who*!' Viewers wanting to know about Callaghan's demise had to wait until after the Doctor's reincarnation.

Throughout this period, the traditional programmes were in robust health. There was an amazing set of editors, including stars of the future like Jay Hunt on the *Six O'Clock News*, who went on to become controller of BBC One and then chief creative officer for Channel 4; Kevin Bakhurst on the *Ten*, who became deputy director-general at RTE in Ireland; and George Entwistle, who was so strong as a deputy editor that, when there was a vacancy, we handed him the role of *Newsnight* editor without an appointment process. He was exceptional in his editorship of the programme, too, bringing the best out of Jeremy Paxman and creating some memorable encounters with Tony Blair in the days when prime ministers thought it worth their while appearing at length on *Newsnight*. I was now the boss of the likes of Paxman and Sir David Frost, both of whom were, in their own ways, thoroughly charming. One of Frost's greetings when I met him for lunch was characteristic: 'Roger! This is the perfect day! Lunch with you and dinner with George Bush Senior!'

Paxman was a more formidable presence when I turned up at

Newsnight team meetings. He would lurk towards the back of the room with the kind of look he reserved on air for ministers who were on a sticky wicket. BBC managers like me were juicy items on his menu, and he would apply himself to deconstructing the case we were trying to make. However, he was a pleasure to deal with one-to-one, and he was capable of discarding the conventions of the presenters' rule book. There was one night when I was massively irritated by *Newsnight*'s editorial line on a story, which seemed to me wilfully divergent from some facts that had been set out on the *Ten O'Clock News*. Unusually, I called the duty editor at the end of the programme and made my displeasure plain. It was a surprise the next morning to read an email to me from Jeremy in which he sought to absolve the output team and take the responsibility himself. I have never known such willingness to take the blame from any presenter before or since.

It was largely unnoticed, which is as it should be, that we had rather a good balance of age and gender and ethnicity in our presentation team. Anna Ford was expertly steering the *One O'Clock News*, and Moira Stuart was reading the bulletins on Breakfast. Both departed from those roles after I left television news. Having two presenters on one programme is always controversial, but I was pleased we promoted Sophie Raworth to co-host the *Six O'Clock News* with George Alagiah. Darren Jordan, who had an intriguing past as a member of the Jamaica Regiment that had invaded Grenada, moved into network bulletin presentation and deputised for Anna on the *One*. Mishal Husain was introduced to domestic audiences on Breakfast after I'd seen her skills on BBC World, and some years later I persuaded her to take a major role in the 2012 Olympics.

It is an iron rule, though, that an organisation never gets credit for what it does right. The thousands of daily programmes and the dozens of breaking news specials that are sure-footed fade into nothing compared with the time you make a mistake, and the BBC is rightly judged by a higher standard than the rest. I have the utmost respect for Sky News, but the internal News 24 joke slogan about it was 'never wrong for long', based on its alleged ability to break a story and then break a different one if the first one turned out not to be entirely true. I recall Mark Byford's reaction when Sky announced the death of Yasser Arafat a few days before he actually died: 'If that had been us, Roger, I'd have had to go,' he said. 'I would have had to go!' I hope that would not have been the case, but we could all see the point – and by then, of course, we had been through the row around the death of the Queen Mother.

Someone said wisely at the time that in the same way that the BBC had been rehearsing major royal obituaries for decades, so some of our critics in the newspapers had been rehearsing their coverage of the BBC's coverage of the Queen Mother. We had a foretaste of that when Princess Margaret died earlier in the year, and our press office received calls from newspapers about our 'disrespectful' coverage of her love life in our obit – only for the same papers to go much, much further in their editions the next morning. But we unquestionably had a shaky start to our reporting of the death of the Queen Mother. If the death of a 101-year-old can be unexpected, it was unexpected: we had no warning signals, and the first I knew was a call on the Saturday afternoon of Easter weekend saying the announcement was imminent. By a horrible mischance, we had rehearsed major obituaries the previous week, which meant that everyone who had been part of that was now on days off, and rounding people up on a holiday weekend, as we had found when Princess Diana died, is tougher than when a death occurs in the middle of a weekday and the building is full.

The conceptual mistake we made in the first couple of hours of coverage was to think that, in an era of rolling news channels, this was 'breaking news'. It was not. It was the death of a much-loved and very elderly lady, and once the announcement had been made we should have played the long-ago commissioned tapes about the Queen Mother's love of horses or her Scottish roots – instead of which, we sought reaction on the phone and went live to hastily arranged outside broadcasts. It was only when we went to structured bulletins and the full obituary programme that we did justice to the Queen Mother's life.

Crucially, too, Mark Damazer and I, as the senior news managers who had hurried into the building, were occupied not with what we were putting on air at that time but with the scheduling of the rest of the evening – complicated by the fact that almost all the other BBC bosses were away for Easter, and there was interim management in television because Mark Thompson had departed for Channel 4. Lorraine Heggessey was on a skiing holiday in Canada. We were trying to work out with her via a crackly mobile what to do mid-evening on BBC One, rather than being at the back of the gallery.

In the middle of this was Peter Sissons, who was the duty presenter that day. His burgundy tie became notorious as the emblem of the BBC's disrespect, rather as if we had dressed him up in a bright pink bow-tie and made it revolve when he was on camera. The reason we stayed with the burgundy was that in our rehearsals we had always assumed that we would have some advance notice of the Queen Mother's final illness. We would typically have Nick Witchell outside a hospital saying things were looking serious, and then the formal announcement would come from the Palace. This gave an odd challenge in that the presenters on air for the hospital watch would not be wearing black, but when the news broke they had to change – to a black tie for men and black suits for women – in about sixty seconds flat under the most pressured circumstances. This was strange because when the presenters came back into vision, the most conspicuous thing to some observers was that they had changed clothes, rather than that they were announcing an historic event – so we loosened the rules a little to say it was acceptable not to change if they were wearing sombre apparel. A bright frock or floral tie, no; but if they were unobjectionable in their turn-out they did not need to rush into black during the early part of the coverage.

In retrospect, that was the wrong call. But it would have been equally remiss not to have refreshed the guidelines. In the early part of my career, a royal death would have been marked by the tolling for one hour of the Croydon Bell across all our networks, and only when the Countess of Wessex was taken ill in the late 1990s did we realise that she was still within the top category of royals who would have required the bringing together of every single network for a major obituary – which I suspect even she, as a former public relations officer for Capital Radio, might have found something of an over-reaction.

What there emphatically wasn't was an anti-royal agenda, as the days of reverential and polished coverage of the Queen Mother's lying-in-state and funeral showed: the BBC has never been in the vanguard of republicanism. I wrote in 2002, and I still believe, that the BBC can do two things simultaneously. First, it can provide the platform on which the people of this country can share national experiences such as the big royal events. But, second, there is no compromise in the journalism because BBC News is free to report the failures as well as the successes of the monarchy – and certainly did during the crises of the 1990s and the Queen's annus horribilis.

In my time in television news, the greater challenges about bias sat elsewhere. I believe most people in the BBC are fair-minded individuals, and journalists in particular have a professionalism that means they steer well clear of any party political bias. I have never had the problem of an editor who skewed an agenda in favour of Conservatives, Labour or any other party. But there can be a default to 'groupthink' – a set of assumptions that seem reasonable to everyone they know. We had an editorial debate around the time of the election of the new Pope in 2005, for instance, in which it was apparent that some of our output editors thought the correct positioning for a Pontiff would be pro-women priests, pro-gay rights and generally the kind of agreeable ecclesiastical liberal who would be at home in a north London Church of England parish. The idea that the cardinals might elect a traditional Catholic, like Cardinal Ratzinger, came as a bit of a blow. But the key thing was that we had the debate ahead of the white smoke at the Vatican, and our coverage on air was, I hope, fair.

This was a typical pattern: identifying editorial problems and doing something about them. We did it, with a reasonable amount of success, during the Iraq War. There was a disdainful attitude towards George W. Bush from many in the media, including some parts of the BBC. I wasn't alone on news board in being concerned about the incomprehension among some of our staff about why Bush had been elected and how he retained significant support in the US, and, as a public corrective, I gave a newspaper interview about the need for impartiality, which was headlined 'President Bush isn't automatically wrong'. More generally in cov-ering a war, as during a general election campaign, there is such a strong awareness that the spotlight is on the BBC that there is a reduced risk of careless bias. I have never accepted the argument that the BBC was unduly pro- or anti-war. Iraq was possibly easier for achieving balance than some conflicts, notably the Falklands, because the divisions in the United Kingdom were so apparent – including the millions who took to the streets as well as those in Parliament – and they almost broke the Blair government before the bombing started. We didn't lack voices opposing the war.

We made a riveting programme with the Prime Minister in the run-up to the conflict, as part of his so-called masochism strat-egy, in which we brought him together with an audience made up entirely of opponents of conflict. *Newsnight* went to Newcas-tle for what turned out to be a compellingly watchable encounter between Tony Blair at his most persuasive and a group of voters determined to resist him, but it cast light as well as creating heat. During a short break after the programme, Jeremy Paxman and I had a few minutes with Blair and Alastair Campbell – and the talk was about the quest for a second UN resolution and the need for international agreement. Blair had recently persuaded a reluc-tant United States to go back to the UN, which was seen as a win for a renewed diplomatic approach.

I have always been wary about people who use the virtue of hindsight to claim that Blair always knew he was going to war on a false prospectus, because at the time the belief that there were weapons of mass destruction in Iraq was shared by many opponents of the war. The argument of France and Germany was not that they did not exist but that more time should be allowed to find them. I was personally against the Iraq War. However, naïvely or not, I found myself being convinced on that night in the north-east, as we talked overlooking the Tyne, that the Prime Minister was sincere about the need for consensual international action and about the existence of the weapons. That view was, of course, tested during the later Hutton Inquiry. However, I had already experienced Tony Blair's certainty about foreign policy. As the war in Afghanistan started, we did an edition of *Breakfast with Frost* live with the PM from near Chequers, and as we drank coffee afterwards, Blair mused on the difference between domestic and foreign policy. Foreign policy, he said, was much more about 'right' and 'wrong' – pointing then to the Taliban and the links with Al-Qaeda that had brought about the catastrophic loss of life on 9/11. Domestic policy, by contrast, was hugely more complex; it was much harder to work out what the best course was for health or education or crime. There was complete openness on his part about the moral dimension to foreign policy, however unconvincing his critics might find it.

Back in the newsroom, it was the domestic issues of immigration and asylum that were proving tougher to sort out. One night on the *Ten O'Clock News* we broadcast a package from a racially diverse part of Britain, where ethnic minorities had become a majority of the local population. People there were interviewed – vox pops, as they are known in journalism – about how they felt about the immigration that had led to the current ethnic mix. Only one white man was featured, and he said everything

was grand and he was perfectly happy with the way his neigh-
bourhood had developed. Concerned about how representative
he was, I emailed the reporter the next morning: 'Just wondered:
did all the people you spoke to think the majority/minority racial
position was good? I'm just curious. What I wonder is whether
we represent diversity well (which we should) but also whether
we represent diversity of opinion well (which we also should!).'

The reporter, a very good chap generally, replied that the vox
pops had been fraught with difficulty because of the 'problem'
of the white population, many of whom were, in his view, 'fairly
rabidly racist'. It was a nightmare in terms of what could be used
in the piece, he said: if they had used the 'hard' white voices, it
might have been illegal in that it could have been construed as
inflammatory. Hence the decision to use the one man who had
expressed a positive view.

I shared this with colleagues on news board, who were as
appalled as I was. It started, of course, from good intentions: not
to stir up community tension and to think about what is put on
air. But it ended with an unacceptably sanitised piece of reporting, and this was a textbook example of how not to put together
a report with vox pops.

It was around this time, too, that BBC local radio identified
for its staff its typical target listeners, imagined as a middle-aged
couple called Dave and Sue. A leaflet for all local radio stations
included a section on their hypothetical attitudes. 'Now it's an
established everyday reality that Dave and Sue live and work alongside and socialise with people from different ethnic backgrounds,'
producers were told. 'They are interested in and open-minded
about adapting aspects of other cultures into their own lives – in

entertainment, medicine, belief, food, clothes and language. Their community-minded attitudes mean they are interested both in projects which advance social cohesion in this country and in international development issues.' It must have been something of a shock to the writers of this leaflet when many real-life Daves and Sues went off and joined UKIP.

I went into battle in the summer of 2003 with the BBC's Editorial Policy team, who circulated minutes from an advisory meeting about coverage of asylum seekers. This was playing strongly, ahead of the much bigger debate about immigration. The meeting criticised television news for 'muddling up' asylum with war and terrorism, and said that people were 'already making a link' – which was not unexpected given that a story of the time was about some asylum-seekers trying to poison people with Ricin. The Editorial Policy people disliked our use of 'iconic' pictures of the Sangatte refugee camp, whatever that meant, and it concluded that we should take care to use reliable information and not stoke up prejudice – which is correct – but asserted that this area was 'being led by an angry tabloid agenda and extreme right-wing groups'.

I sent a truculent email back.

> I should make it clear that I abhor racism, and I accept 1,000 per cent the need to reflect all debates with balance. But the asylum debate is one where we've done rather badly in reflecting the concerns of our audiences or the genuine crisis faced by the government in dealing with the issue; and these minutes read like a pure liberal-defensive response rather than a quest for range and diversity in our journalism.

I shared the correspondence with one or two like-minded souls, including Jeff Randall, who had been brought in by Greg as business editor to ensure a broader range of real-world views made it on air. Jeff certainly managed that. He wrote to me: 'Does anyone in the BBC's Policy Unit/Thought Police read Richard Littlejohn? They should. He reflects popular opinion far more accurately than the views of those whose idea of a good night out is reading the Indy over a vegetarian meal in a Somali restaurant.'

We had already shown our commitment to broadening the debate on air. A *Newsnight* special with Tony Blair and an audience of voters devoted the first twelve minutes to questions about asylum. Current Affairs did a film for BBC One about our porous borders. I also went further than normal in putting the debate about coverage into the public arena. In the autumn of 2003, I was interviewed by Tim Luckhurst in *The Independent* and I had an uncoded bash at Editorial Policy, arguing that we had been very slow on the asylum issue. 'Two years ago, when it started being raised, we did not realise the level of popular unease about the issue,' I said. 'There was a sort of easy knee-jerk tendency, a kind of metropolitan ease, of saying "Oh, it's all got up by the *Daily Mail* or got up by the BNP or whatever." I don't think that is true.'

This did not make me popular – sainthood was ever more elusive in the hurly-burly of news – and over the years I have lost plenty of battles, some deservedly. But I did feel some vindication when, a few years later, the fact that the BBC had been slow on asylum-seeking and then immigration became the official line of the Trust and the management, with Helen Boaden telling a Trust review that the BBC in general had a 'deep liberal bias' on immigration when she became director of news.

As my boss, after Richard Sambrook had moved to BBC World News, Helen was an ally on another awful policy dilemma, where what seemed at the time to be a lonely position has become, thankfully, orthodox. It was in 2004 that hostage videos started to be part of the weaponry of terror groups, with videos of Kenneth Bigley and Margaret Hassan being distributed to the international media showing them in captivity and begging for their lives. It seemed obvious to me that showing these videos was playing into the terrorists' hands, and I felt viscerally that it was an abuse of human beings to show them on television in a state of great distress. I therefore restricted use to just a still, at a time when other news outlets such as ITN and Sky were showing extensive clips. Many of my editorial colleagues were, according to a subsequent front-page story in *Press Gazette*, 'outraged'. One editor said, anonymously, 'There was a feeling of great despair in the newsroom; everybody else was using it and we were going out on a limb without understanding why.' Looking back at one of my memos to editors at the time, I am not sure what this anonymous individual misunderstood:

> In television news, we will stick with a still, and no audio, from the Margaret Hassan video. This is because she is clearly enormously distressed and under extreme duress. However, we should report in indirect speech some of what she says: in particular, we should include the line that she is asking troops to be withdrawn from Iraq.

The last line was to make sure that we could not be accused of censoring a political message, while being under no illusions about the circumstances in which it was uttered.

With the backing of Helen Boaden and Mark Byford, I was blunt externally too, telling one newspaper: 'The distress is so obvious, it's awful to watch and we didn't think there was any merit in showing it.' I debated the BBC's policy that year on radio and television programmes, in newspapers and on public platforms. I was pleased that other broadcasters gradually came over to the BBC's position – and indeed by 2015 the UK industry standard had become more conservative, often not even showing stills from terrorist videos. The feeblest argument ever is that other people, whether it is rival broadcasters or social media, are doing something so we should too. When I left the BBC, Helen's farewell note to me referred to that episode: 'I was thinking last night of that time when I first arrived in news when you faced down the TV newsroom over showing videos of Al-Qaeda kidnap victims. There was a lot of pompous posturing, but you were utterly resolute and clear.' So, thankfully, was the rest of news management, even when I was being roasted by the *Press Gazette*.

Terrorism was the dominant theme of my last few months in television news, as it had been through 9/11, the subsequent wars, the bombings in Madrid and the murders of the British hostages. July had started brightly with the build-up to an event whose significance for me I could not yet imagine: the awarding of the 2012 Olympic Games to London. In our editorial meetings I had long teased the editors not to bother about London because Paris was going to win the bid, but as we got nearer to the vote in Singapore it was manifest that our capital was more in contention than we had imagined. I gently changed my position on the likely outcome, and promised everyone there would be cakes at the afternoon editorial meeting if the IOC chose London.

We watched the voting process in the TV news office, courtesy of a BBC News and Sport co-production: Dermot Murnaghan in Singapore for news, Sue Barker for sport and Barry Davies doing the commentary. When Jacques Rogge said the word 'London', I think for the only time in my life I jumped into the air with excitement, doubtless to the embarrassment of those nearby. Cakes were ordered immediately, and we put on special programmes on BBC One through the afternoon to celebrate what had initially looked like a most unlikely victory.

The next day we had more news specials that could not have been more different in their content and tone. Bombs had exploded on three London Tube trains and on a bus, and from the initial reports it was apparent that casualties were on a devastating scale. In times like these, journalists can only operate by separating the job in hand from the human reaction to what is unfolding before them. The day was a blur of activity in the newsroom with rolling news on all channels, and a mass of logistical problems for reporters and crews as transport came to a halt and the communications networks collapsed under the pressure of events.

If the public are frightened, journalists and their families are not exempt – and we had our own moment when the threat of terror was literally on our doorstep. Just as we were about to start broadcasting the *Six O'Clock News* from Television Centre, we were told there was a suspicious vehicle right outside. In a building that had been blown up only four years before, we were not inclined to put our staff at risk, but we also knew that, in the aftermath of the IRA bomb, the structure had been made tougher and safety had been increased. More to the point, on the night that more than fifty of our fellow citizens had been killed in a terror attack, we could not conceive of failing to broadcast the main network news. Our staff and presenters wanted to carry on, so we did.

For me, it was only when I got home that night, close to midnight, and watched our output retelling the story that the devastation of the day hit home: the lives lost, the families bereft, the injured whose future had been transformed by fanaticism. I therefore make no apology for my anger when I saw some of the reporting of the aftermath of the London bombings by Fox News. A contributor claimed that 'the BBC almost operates as a foreign registered agent of Hezbollah and some of the other jihadist groups' and Bill O'Reilly wrote a commentary titled 'How Jane Fonda and the BBC put you in danger'.

With the support of the BBC press office, I went much further than BBC management normally does, with this short statement in reply: 'I am writing this in a building which was bombed by Irish terrorists. My colleagues and I are living in a city recovering from the wounds inflicted last week. If I may leave our customary impartiality aside for a moment, the comments made on Fox News are beneath contempt.'

Fox News did not like this. They asked me to appear on a number of their programmes. The O'Reilly show request came on a night when I was with BBC colleagues at a concert in Kew Gardens, and it was an easy choice between expressing solidarity with London by showing the city's life was continuing or sitting in a studio being harangued – and doubtless edited – for the greater glory of Bill O'Reilly. O'Reilly attacked me and the BBC again anyway, and one of his contributors exemplified why 'beneath contempt' was about right for Fox: 'The BBC has a long history of having soft-peddled terrorism in the Middle East. And the

London attacks have exposed them as an unfair, unbalanced, and unreliable journalistic enterprise.' Sitting under a summer night sky in Kew listening to Bjorn Again was definitely a better option than feeding the Fox propaganda machine. I was subsequently put on O'Reilly's 'cowards' list of people who were too afraid to appear on his show – alongside Bill Clinton, Jeb Bush and, even more unexpectedly, Barbra Streisand, and there, in cyberspace, I proudly remain to this day. The episode was a useful reminder that, despite the BBC's inclination to feel more comfortable with a liberal agenda, applying a Fox-style conservative agenda would be a grievous error too. The ideal remains an independent and intellectually rigorous journalism that challenges all shades of opinion.

By the summer of 2005, my energy was flagging after five years of being on the hamster-wheel of news. I had applied for the controllership of Radio 4 in the autumn of 2004 and had rightly been beaten by one of my bosses, Mark Damazer, since he loved the station as a whole while I, as in my *PM* days, only truly loved its news programmes. I have still never made it more than ten minutes into a radio drama, which would have been a poor qualification for the job. But it made me realise how keen I was to move on and how there was a world beyond the News Centre, with all our channels chattering away incessantly. I had therefore watched with interest the departure of Peter Salmon as director of sport, and had idly wondered whether I might be in the running, when two things happened. Peter sent me an email saying I should think about applying for the job, and I bumped into Mark Thompson in the coffee queue at Mangiare in the White City Media Centre. Mark did one of his slightly stuttery bits of musing as we waited to pay for our cappuccinos: had I maybe thought about being director of sport? I still have no idea whether he would have contrived this conversation with me somewhere else or whether he just found it convenient to offer the role to the next person he met in a fast-food shop, but it sent me walking back to Television Centre with a spring in my step. More wars, terrorism and political crises – or on to running a whole division with *Match of the Day*, the Six Nations and the Olympics? I had no doubt which path was the more appealing.

CHAPTER 9

SPORT

I KNEW SOMETHING ABOUT the culture of BBC Sport from my time on 5 Live. It was an impressive outfit: tremendous at covering the set-piece events like World Cups and Olympics, and confident about its importance to the BBC. It had lost some major sports rights, with Formula 1 and cricket creating the most damaging gaps. But the blow of football highlights disappearing to ITV, in the ill-fated form of *The Premiership*, had recently been reversed – and *Match of the Day* was back on BBC screens each week. It seemed a more cheerful place than television news:

it had customised its floor in Television Centre with a running track painted on the lino in the corridor, and a garish rendering of a golf course and assorted-sized balls. But I spotted early on that the devotion to sport of the division's senior producers was absolute. They could never understand why an over-running snooker match was not kept on BBC One, even if it meant vanquishing the news or *Strictly Come Dancing* or whatever else lay in its path, and it was taken for granted that the only sensible course for BBC management was to pump squillions more money into sport and give it as much airtime as it wanted.

At the time of my move to sport, I was busy with another extra-curricular project. Greg's 'Making It Happen' had been replaced by Mark Thompson's 'Creative Future' initiative, which was designed to work out the shape of our programming in what he called 'an entirely new chapter in broadcasting'. I had originally been asked to lead the work on knowledge-building, which was a slightly hazy concept around specialist factual content, documentaries and websites, but, to my relief, Mark suggested that I move over to sport's Creative Future team instead. It would give me a ready-made vehicle for reviewing the strategy of the sport division. However, it meant we had to tackle what people talked of as 'the *Grandstand* problem' right from the start.

I had grown up with *Grandstand*. In the black and white era it had brought sport into the living rooms of Britain, and all the best action was there. ITV's *World of Sport* was never serious competition, since it seemed to be made up of horseracing from minor courses and large men in leotards taking part in professional wrestling. The *Grandstand* brand took in the Olympics and, initially, the World Cup too – though that later moved under the *Match of the Day* banner. But *Grandstand* had been all-conquering and confident, and for decades it was the flagship of BBC Sport. By 2005, though, you could choose your cliché: it was either a sinking flagship or a limping warhorse, but either way round it was in trouble. *Football Focus* had been floated off from the start of the programme, and *Final Score* had become a programme in its own right at the end. In between there were some days with strong live events, but others when there was a menu of highlights from disparate sports: rugby union, basketball, golf and horseracing were on the agenda in one hour of a single programme in the summer of 2005. This might have retained an audience in the analogue days of restricted choice. But in a digital world, where Sky had introduced dedicated sports channels with live action from the start to the finish of each event, the *Grandstand* mix no longer captivated. Nor did it reflect the more enterprising scheduling of events: Six Nations rugby was moving to 5.30 p.m. or even 8 p.m. kick-offs, way outside the *Grandstand* zone. The programme's critics carped that its fading rights portfolio meant it was no longer what it was, but they would have been furious if it had emulated its heyday, when live Test cricket was interrupted for a visit to Royal Ascot. The last redoubt of believers in the programme was in the fifth floor BBC Sport offices of Television Centre.

Fortunately, the sport Creative Future team battered down *Grandstand*'s remaining defences. The group's members included Dave Gordon, as one of the most respected former editors of *Grandstand*, and Clare Balding as a current presenter. They were supplemented by emerging stars in the division such as Jonathan Wall, who went on to become controller of 5 Live. The evidence we looked at was overwhelming: what we needed to do was invest in the digital future, principally our website and streaming services, and to phase out the formats that had dwindling audiences – and were, at worst, a drag on the image of BBC Sport. If we could let our major events stand in their own right, as the BBC's Olympics or the BBC's Wimbledon coverage, then they would achieve greater impact. We also spotted that the BBC could create 'surround-sound' programming that made sport even more appealing to audiences and, importantly, wooed rights holders too. Top of our recommendations was 'harness the whole BBC – local and national – to make the most of events like the World Cup and Olympics', and we showed what we meant with a *Top Gear* special from the Winter Olympics in which the lads drove a Mini off a ski-jump. Impact, indeed.

There was no secret about the way our discussions were going, and that *Grandstand* was destined for the knacker's yard with the unanimous backing of the Creative Future team and even the approval of the executive responsible for the show, Philip Bernie. Its demise also had the enthusiastic support of the BBC One channel team. Here, there is another of the glorious paradoxes of the BBC. At times, even the most secret discussions can leak out into the outside world, whereas some stories remain within the corporation even though almost everyone knows about them. The latter was the case with *Grandstand*.

In early 2006 I took part in a seminar pulling together all the Creative Future conclusions, and we told a couple of hundred of the BBC's senior leaders that we were going to phase out *Grandstand*. The Sport leadership group knew too, as did significant numbers of the programme staff. But not a peep appeared anywhere until the night before Mark Thompson's announcement of the corporation-wide plans for news, sport, drama, entertainment and the rest. It did, however, play big: 'Grandstand Axed' was the front-page splash in the Daily Mirror, and it was in all the other papers too. As usual, it was the BBC who managed to report most negatively on their own story by implying that it was all over for sport at the corporation, and contriving to miss out our reassurance that sports coverage would continue on most Saturday afternoons and we would be expanding our output elsewhere. We were grateful to people like Des Lynam, who got it spot on: 'I'm sad about it in many ways because the programme stood the test of time for so long,' he said, when the announcement was made. 'But with multi-channel television, people will only really watch live events when they are big-time. The days of viewers sticking with the programme for five hours just because it was on are gone.'

After the years of fretting about Grandstand, it felt good for the BBC to have made the decision. The only problem was that sport is a division where producers regard 'decisions' as being the opening of a debate rather than its conclusion, and where there is a profound scepticism about management. One of my moles reported a road trip in which a senior editor spent most of a dinner with junior producers attacking the management as people who simply did not support sport. This was a serious obstacle to productive staff relations. 'Just wait for this lot to move on, and we'll be fine' was the gist of the Grandstand supporters' argument, and there was an immediate drive to make our 'phasing out' of the programme one of the longest transitions in broadcasting history. For some weeks, the discussion meandered around final shows being in 2008, to enable it to reach its 50th anniversary, or even later. One of the team suggested that, given we had London 2012 only six years away, it would be mad to lose the brand before then, given the alleged resonance of *Olympic Grandstand*. It became a hallmark of meetings about the theme music for any event, big or small, that someone would suggest using the *Grandstand* music 'because it's so popular' – which was true about the music, but the motive seemed to be more about keeping the programme on life support.

I did, however, relish a little spat with Steve Rider, a former BBC presenter who had moved over to ITV, from which vantage point he called on us to save *Grandstand*. I wrote to *Broadcast* magazine:

> If ITV's Steve Rider is so worried about the future of *Grandstand* then the solution is in his hands. ITV should bring back *World of Sport*. I gather that Big Daddy and Giant Haystacks are sadly no longer with us, but Steve is just the man to link smoothly between a revived ITV Seven and wrestling from Derby.

One night late in 2006, after a particularly exasperating day with some of the producers, I was sitting on the platform at Turnham Green station, waiting for a delayed Tube train home, when the idea seized me that we should go for a quick 'kill'. The Six Nations would start in February 2007, and just before then was, surely, the right time to take *Grandstand* off the air. We were guaranteed weeks of top action on a Saturday, which would benefit from having a focus on a single sport, and the branding could be the BBC's Six Nations rather than a mishmash involving *Grandstand*. I put the thought to my management team the next day, and they went for it. Again, a decision was better than letting things fester.

We told the team immediately, and I mused publicly in an interview with *The Guardian* in December that the programme would be phased out 'early next year', but we did not make a public announcement about the date of its final edition. This was a mistake. The reason was simply that we wanted to avoid yet another bunch of newspaper articles about 'the end of BBC Sport as we know it', but we got some of that anyway. The *Daily Mail* were tipped off about the last-ever show and weighed in with a piece headlined 'The shamefaced BBC don't want you to notice this, but after forty-eight years they are pulling the plug on a national institution'. Determinedly unshamefaced, I whacked them back with a blog calling their piece 'endearingly bizarre', since we had announced the closure the previous spring with a great fanfare. But they were right that we did not give it the send-off it deserved. The final Sunday afternoon programme centred dispiritingly on indoor bowls, and we laid on some wine and snacks for the team. On that gloomy January day, I felt like a murderer appearing before a panel of victims' relatives, but I have never regretted the decision. It was right, and BBC Sport has been stronger without *Grandstand*. The investment in digital services paid off, and the coverage of the 2012 Olympics was inspired by the belief that there was a world beyond the linear programmes of the analogue era.

The sleepless nights in BBC Sport were, instead, caused by rights issues. From the start, I knew that my key ally would be Dominic Coles, the director of sports rights and my financial right-hand man. It was to Dominic that we owed the deals for the Olympics, including 2012, and the World Cups up to 2014 – which were a reassuring anchor for a new director. He is a formidable rights negotiator and a clever strategist, and we developed a friendship reminiscent of my relationship with Jim Naughtie. We were both in always-on mode, usually about work but also sharing the ups and downs of our respective football teams. He supports Liverpool and I was at that stage on the waiting list for my Arsenal season ticket. Our contact became even more intense when we were in the middle of a negotiation, and we had the heart-pounding combination of excitement imbued by fear that a deal would go the wrong way. Life in BBC Sport was made more perilous by the newspapers' fixations. Even when Peter Salmon had success-fully started to rebuild the portfolio, the single loss of the Boat Race to ITV had provoked newspaper correspondents to further fits of gloom on our behalf. An article at the time noted that the loss of such a symbolic event 'prompted a flood of unfavourable headlines, accompanied by predictable hand-wringing over the BBC's commitment to sport and at least one call for [Salmon's] resignation'.

I, of course, had had some experience of this on 5 Live – when Dominic had been one of the corporate minders ensuring that our bidding was within appropriate financial guidelines. But radio was easy compared with television, and in my first couple of years leading the whole of BBC Sport we knew we faced battles for the renewal of *Match of the Day*, our FA Cup and England deal, the Six Nations, Wimbledon and a range of other events. This was against a background of a vigorous and massively funded Sky Television, competition in the pay market from Setanta, and an ITV hungry for sport. We had even more of a problem when Michael Grade, who loved sport, defected as BBC chairman to become ITV's chief executive. But our first scare came from an unexpected source. In the early summer of 2006 we were bidding for the terrestrial television package of Premier League highlights – the content of the weekly *Match of the Day* and *MOTD2* – in what had initially seemed like an easy process for us. ITV had been so bruised by the experience of *The Premiership* when they had taken the rights from us in 2000 that we were sure they would not be in the market again. We doubted Channel 4 had the money or ambition to come in for the Premier League, and Channel 5's interest had been rumoured in the past but had never come to anything. We were wrong.

The Premier League process was being handled by its chief executive, Richard Scudamore, and by my colleague from *Today* in the 1980s David Kogan, though it is a given in this kind of situation that friendships do not count. David and I understand where friendship ends and business begins. There is, in any case, a rigorous process involving lawyers and scrutineers, which means that the call about whether your bid has won or lost is made from a Premier League control room with the maximum amount of formality. Even so, we expected that after our opening bid the phone would ring with good news: it would be Richard, with David alongside, confirming that *Match of the Day* would be back with us for another three years. Instead, it was a setback. The Premier League was going to take the bidding process to a second round, which meant there must be another serious contender.

Dominic would sometimes give me a lift home, since we lived in the same part of south-west London. That evening we debated all the way through the traffic of Hammersmith and Chiswick, and had to stop for more conversation over a beer in Kew. Who could the other bidder be? And, crucially, how much would we need to bid to make sure that we won the second round? *Match of the Day* was not just a powerful way of attracting football fans who might otherwise not come to the BBC; it was also the core of the BBC One weekend schedule, underpinning *Football Focus* and *Final Score* as well as having a repeat broadcast of the main show on a Sunday morning. The period without it had revealed how big a hole it could leave. We had gone to the BBC finance committee and to the director-general, Mark Thompson, to get approval for a properly costed bid, but we would need to go back again and run through the numbers about how much the high-lights were worth to us – and how highly a competitor might value them. To this day, we have never known officially who our rival was, but we are pretty sure it was Channel 5, for whom this would have been, in every sense, a game changer. They would have had a lot of brilliant content that would be guaranteed to attract an audience. Whoever it was, they must have run us very close in the first round – and the rocketing of the price paid in the second round tells its own story. The published figures show that the BBC had paid £105 million for a three-year deal in 2003; and in 2006 we paid £171.6 million for a similar package. Good news for the Premier League coffers, but bad news for our war chest given the other fights that were looming.

The roughest ride we had was about our support, or not, for cricket. After our loss of the rights in the 1990s, Channel 4 had done a sterling job of showcasing cricket on terrestrial televi-sion. The Ashes series of 2005 was one of the most glorious and highest-rating ever. But the most recent rights deal had whisked away the whole of the sport to pay television, after a knockout bid from Sky. There were four strong reasons for us to be pessimistic about a return of cricket to the BBC's screens. The first was that once a sport has gone to pay television, it seldom comes back to free to air. It was way beyond our resources to imagine that we could recapture the biggest cricket events. The second, related, was that nothing in cricket was a category A-listed event – one that was guaranteed to be available live and free to air. The argument immediately started that it should become so again, but the economics were against this. If the England and Wales Cricket Board got their lucrative deal with Sky because of the inclusion of the Ashes in the overall package, the value would collapse if the Ashes were then removed and handed over to the terrestrial broadcasters. Sky needed the premium Test matches to guarantee their investment and to balance the duty commitment to a dull day of Glamorgan *v.* Essex. Third, the BBC had filled its sporting diary with other events after the removal of cricket from its portfolio. It needed agreement with the ECB about how the year was planned to avoid clashes with Wimbledon, Ascot, athletics and the rest. In Peter Salmon's time, the BBC had had a dozen or more meetings on this theme but had got nowhere, and terrestrial television airtime was still limited if we wanted to do justice to a major match. Fourth, and less important, was that BBC television schedulers were never overenthusiastic about the return of cricket. For them, it went on too long with generally low ratings, and it was subject to rain interruptions or extended sessions of play that made scheduling even more of a headache.

We did, thankfully, have the wondrous *Test Match Special* on radio, and we made an early gesture of our commitment to the sport on television by acquiring the highlights packages for the Cricket World Cup and for the Ashes series in Australia. There are few things I personally enjoy more than a day at Lord's with agreeable refreshments, so there was no animosity in the management team towards cricket. But we had an awkward public position in that, under the previous director, we had not bid even for the highlights package of the most recent domestic contract, and, under new management, we didn't believe there was a real chance of the sport coming back live onto our airwaves. The 'Keep Cricket Free' campaign wanted us to agree a deal with BSkyB that would essentially hand over their best bits to us at a commercial price, which we always thought was an improbable outcome and likely to be way too expensive. However, the battle to maintain listed events is one that is in the public interest – and we didn't want to seem indifferent to the many people in our audience who were now shut out from watching any cricket unless they had a Sky subscription.

All the heads of sport for the main broadcasters were summoned by the Commons Culture, Media and Sport Committee in the November of 2005 to be grilled about why cricket had migrated to pay television, and how it was that the ECB appeared to have broken an agreement with the government that this would not happen. The BBC was in the firing line for not having shown enough enthusiasm for the sport. I found this an unappealing episode, especially with the parliamentary sketch-writers perched on the press benches and hoping for blood. John Whittingdale, the committee chairman, promptly bowled me a yorker by asking me why we had not bid for highlights, and I gave the honest answer that it was because we thought Channel 4 would retain them. Whittingdale replied, to laughter: 'So you did not bid because you thought somebody, who also was not bidding, was actually going to win?' Well, yes, kind of. It is particularly difficult doing

one of these committees when you were not in post when the decisions were made, because you have a choice of sounding weaselly
('I wasn't there at the time') or defending in a corporate way but
being at risk on the detail of something you were not involved
in. But the committee came to the accurate conclusion that the
primary responsibility for the live sport going behind a pay barrier was that the government and ECB had let it be so. We were
criticised for not having offered an attractive enough alternative
option, but in response to the Commons report we said that we
hoped to bid for cricket again in future, subject to two things:
one, that the scheduling around other events was resolved; and
two, that it offered value for money. Those qualifications were
crucial, as we saw later in my tenure at BBC Sport.

Horseracing was a similarly awkward sport for us. We had a
simple view. We really liked the Grand National and Royal Ascot
and the Derby, and all the landmark events of the racing year. We
would have wanted to win back the Cheltenham Festival, which
had transferred to Channel 4, and where I had enjoyed days of
racing and people-watching as controller of 5 Live. It was a compellingly successful mix of the Queen Mother with thousands of
Irish visitors and lakes of Guinness. However, we weren't bothered about the lesser days – what I would sometimes call 'the 2.50
at Wincanton' – because our audiences weren't either. This made
relations with the racing authorities somewhat tricky. They, quite
reasonably, wanted more coverage that they believed would bolster
the sport and encourage higher attendances and more sponsorship.
We thought that the best advertisement for horseracing was coverage of its biggest events in the heart of the BBC One schedule,
with the rest of the sport on Channel 4 or the dedicated racing

channels. We managed a renewal on that basis while I was director of sport, but it was no surprise when, a few years later, this dissolved and BBC television was left without any racing at all. We were proved right, though, that audiences for many of the landmarks would fall if they moved away from us. I read a piece by Greg Wood in *The Guardian* in 2014 reporting the fall in racing's viewers post-BBC in which he spoke of the 'fantastic exposure' the BBC used to give: 'The BBC was often criticised in the past for showing no interest in racing beyond the "crown jewels": the Derby, Grand National and Royal Ascot. What is now starting to become apparent is the sport's extraordinary arrogance ... in the long term, the benefit to racing was immense.' Quite.

We ploughed on, successfully, through the Six Nations and Wimbledon renewals. The latter is the one that is so indelibly associated with the BBC summer that it was unthinkable in those days that we should lose it, and the people who ran Wimbledon maintained a careful balance between implying they thought that too and still striking a tough financial deal. They were, however, a pleasure to work with, and that was not always the case with governing bodies. I never warmed to the Royal & Ancient Golf Club, and it came as no surprise in 2015 when the news broke that they were abandoning their long relationship with the BBC and going off to Sky. One benefit of their new deal, they said, would be 'to plough significantly more money back into participation initiatives up and down the country and worldwide'. It seemed curious to talk about the importance of participation when for so many years golf had not admitted women to the membership at St Andrews and had excluded them from other well-known clubs. My colleague Barbara Slater, then head of golf, would tell the story about planning an Open championship on site. When she and the rest of the logistics team got back to the clubhouse, there was the realisation that she, as a woman, would not be permitted to go through the main entrance. Her approved access that day was through the kitchen. In solidarity, the men in her team walked in through the kitchen with her. The R&A didn't seem to like footballers much either, and were resistant to the idea of Gary Lineker, a golf fanatic, being our main presenter for the sport. A dinner with the R&A never passed without sniping at Gary. But I kept smiling in my dealings with them, and I was amused to be voted the 51st most powerful person in golf – just ahead of Seve Ballesteros in 52nd – in a sport magazine's Top 100 list. This, not for the first time, was an unexpected development in my career, since my golfing ability never got past pitch and putt. The R&A were right that I was not their type of clubbable person.

Next on the horizon was the FA, and the rights package we had for the FA Cup and England home internationals. Presiding over the process was the relatively new chief executive of the FA, Brian Barwick – a former head of BBC Sport and more recently head of sport at ITV. In many ways it is hard to dislike Brian, though his reputation with us hit rock bottom when we emerged bloodied from his rights tender. There were indications in advance that all was not well between us. After a particularly dull draw for the fifth round of the FA Cup, I had posted a blog inviting readers to say which match they would cover and why. This provoked a spirited debate, including comments across a range of BBC outlets – and it went down badly at the FA. Barwick sent me an email saying they would need some convincing that this was the right approach. Even if BBC Sport thought it was a good idea, he argued, we could not manage the coverage elsewhere in the BBC, and we were often let down by another part of the organisation and its negativity. I fired back, unrepentant:

> The latest blog simply invites people to give us their view about the fifth-round picks. Clearly, we make our choices with you in the normal way; but I believe our interactivity strengthens involvement and promotes accountability. That, in our view, is a good thing. On the question of BBC Sport managing its output and the rest of the BBC: I don't think it's remotely fair to talk about negativity ... The BBC as a whole massively supports and promotes the FA properties – but this can't extend to managing every comment ever made about them.

There was a constant muttering from the FA about our star presenters and pundits, too, if they made any overtly critical comment about England or the Cup.

For all that, we went into the rights negotiations in decent spirits. Ours was a joint bid with Sky, and it was hard to see how anyone would gratuitously ditch the BBC – who had revived the FA Cup, as they are doing again today – and the UK's premier pay TV broadcaster. At the time of our putting our bid together, we had no sense of an alliance building up against us, and we were prepared to pay a proper price for what was an extremely attractive contract. But, once again, danger came from an unexpected source. Just before the bid went in, we heard a whisper that ITV might be trying to partner with the insurgent challenger to Sky, Setanta. It was not well enough sourced to dramatically increase our bid, nor did we believe the initial stages were going to be decisive. The usual pattern is for a rights holder to encourage a protracted competition to drive up the price, and it will not normally allow an existing partner to be knocked out in Round One. But the FA chose to play by different, unexpected rules. It soon became clear that they had a very big opening bid on the table from ITV–Setanta, and they no longer wanted to deal with the BBC and Sky. A meeting with the FA intended to set out our case in detail, and fronted by Gary Lineker, convinced us the game was up. The FA team showed little interest in the BBC–Sky proposals, and once again they criticised Lineker and Alan Hansen for the comments they had made about their properties. They seemed to want unremitting promotion of the FA, and none of the journalism we saw as essential.

Michael Grade at ITV was characteristically canny. Having made his eye-catching opening bid, he then asked to go into a period of exclusive negotiation, in which the FA would agree to talk only to ITV and Setanta. This was the right tactic for him, but a peculiar move by the FA, since they could have kept everyone in the frame and tried to push up the price by tens of millions of pounds. And we, with Sky, would have been willing to do that. We were unsure at the time whether an exclusive negotiation was going on, so we rounded up James Murdoch as part of the Sky team and Mark Thompson with the team from the BBC for a conference call. We upped our bid by a large amount, and sent off a fax confirming that to the FA – to get no reply whatsoever. We might well have gone up further still if the auction had continued, but the FA had broken the mould: they had agreed a deal with ITV and Setanta, with none of the bidders tested to the limits of their spending. A senior figure at the Premier League later expressed incredulity at what had happened – both in the FA opting for what he considered to be the lesser broadcasters, and in not squeezing the last drop from the bidders, which is something of a Premier League speciality.

Dominic and I had to make another couple of visits to the pub in Kew to anaesthetise the pain. This was a bad moment for us. Although we had hung on to the rest of our portfolio of crown jewel events, the loss of regular live football was a terrible disappointment. The FA, I am sure, felt they were doing a smart business deal, but for us it felt like a poor reward for the way we had supported their competitions. We also knew that we would have the task of facing the BBC football production team, who would suffer the blow of losing the output they most enjoyed and which delivered their biggest audiences. In the event, it helped that our producers thought we had been treated unfairly by the FA, and our star team of Lineker and Hansen were similarly mature in the way they responded. But they did want us to be aggressive in striking back, with a bid for the Champions League – then held by ITV and Sky – at the top of their list.

We had at this stage of 2007/08 both an opportunity and a problem. The one consolation from losing the FA deal was that the money we had earmarked was still there in our sport budget, as allocated by the BBC's corporate centre, and we therefore had a chequebook ready for use. But the difficulty with the Champions League is that it is heavily sponsored, and we knew that we would have serious branding and commercial policy issues if we were ever to broadcast it on the BBC. In that period, UEFA also had a loyalty to ITV and Sky as their partners, so it added up to a calculation that we would need to pay a whopping premium on top of the going rate if the UK rights were to be transferred to the non-commercial BBC. It was hard to argue why the licence fee should pay for that given that the main matches were already free to air on ITV, and we therefore knew from the start that the Champions League would be the longest of long shots. When we met UEFA to talk about their rights process, they invited us to pose with the Champions League trophy. I did so, sheepishly, hoping that the photos would never see the light of day given the near certainty that this would be a failed rights bid.

The papers knew none of this, though, and their hype for a BBC Champions League bid was enormous. Throughout the process, article after article detailed our 'bid', based on our need for more football, and the lorry-loads of cash we were prepared to pay. On the morning of the bid deadline, the *Daily Telegraph* reported with confidence, and 100 per cent inaccuracy:

> The BBC will today use up to £400 million of licence fee pay-ers' money to bid for the rights to screen Champions League football games. Senior sports executives are said to be prepared to bid 'whatever it takes' to win the rights from ITV and Sky, prompting claims that the corporation is misusing money that could be better spent on high-quality programming.

In reality, we had decided months previously that we would not bid for live matches, but we could not say so. It is a risk under competition legislation if a key party announces it is not taking part, because the market might then collapse – and, in any case, the game of sports rights involves everyone having to guess who is in and at what level. I am a profound believer in the public service case for sport, but the rights cannot be delivered other than by competing in a commercial environment.

What we won instead of the Champions League was something decent that we had worked for, and something else that was marvellous and came out of the blue yonder. The planned-for gain was in football with the Football League contract in partnership with Sky, which gave us a nice set of rights at a modest price: the League Cup semi-finals and final, ten live first-pick Championship matches and all the highlights in what became *The Football League Show*. I always liked this deal, because supporting lower-league football was something the BBC was well-equipped to do across regional television and local radio as well as on its networks. I was disappointed in 2015 when Channel 5 took the highlights rights away from the BBC.

But the big one landed unexpectedly. Dominic hurtled into my office one day with the news that he had had an approach from Bernie Ecclestone's people about the possibility that Formula 1 might be on the market. There was a five-year deal in place with ITV, but – and the initial indications were muddy – either Bernie was able to invoke a break clause, putting the rights back on the market, or ITV had decided that it had too much on its plate and wanted to hand back the final years of their deal. That mattered little. 'This is proper sport,' was the verdict of Niall Sloane, our head of football, when I whispered to him the idea of F1 returning back to the BBC, and it did, indeed, tick all the boxes. It was a sport long thought to be lost to the BBC after its move to ITV in the 1990s. It was a succession of compelling events, including practice and qualifying and the races themselves, lending themselves to the BBC's multi-platform approach. It achieved high audiences, but also what we called 'hard to reach' viewers: people, especially younger men, who might have previously come in only for live football, but would be lured back by the roar of the F1 engines. I bit Dominic's hand off when he first said that the deal could be on offer, and there was a similar reaction from BBC television and from Mark Thompson. This was too good to miss.

As usual, the rights team did the hard work. I was wheeled in to meet Bernie when the agreement was close to being finalised, on a night when I had a severe ear infection, which meant that I could only hear about one word in three spoken by our new partner. Bernie, always softly spoken, faded in and out, but I could hear enough to tell that he has a tendency to make a joke that initially leaves you wondering whether it is a joke or not. We discussed who might present the BBC's F1 coverage. 'Tamara Ecclestone is good,' he said. It was a few seconds before a smile flickered across his face, and we realised that his daughter was not a serious counterproposal to our intended choice of Jake Humphrey. On the way home, Dominic bellowed into my ears the points I had missed through my temporary deafness – and within a couple of days we were ready to go public with the news that F1 would return to the BBC the following year. This had been nowhere on the sporting industry's radar, and not a word had leaked that negotiations were underway.

This turned out to be the same day that UEFA announced the outcome of the Champions League tender. We had a 7 a.m. release time for the F1 news, which was totally unexpected to our staff as well as to the wider public, and I went into Television Centre to do a raft of morning interviews. I was greeted on *Today* by Jim Naughtie with the on-air comment: 'It's very nice to have our old editor back with us', which prompted a grumpy MP to complain about soft interviewing, but there was a heartening deluge of excitement from inside and outside the BBC. I loved the comment from Murray Walker: 'I'm absolutely flabbergasted – I was lying in bed listening to the news this morning and I almost fell out of bed when I heard it.'

When the more predictable Champions League news broke later, it was portrayed as a day of 'won 1, lost 1' for the BBC, since almost everyone was convinced we had staked the farm on the UEFA contract. Indeed, the *Daily Mail*'s sports diarist Charlie Sale refused to believe our press officer when she assured him that we had never bid for the live Champions League. I was at home cooking dinner when Charlie rang me to say that he would accept it only from me and on my honour if I told him there had been no BBC participation in the auction. I was happy to give him that assurance. And we immediately began the exhilarating work of setting up an F1 production team, under Niall Sloane and Ben Gallop, ready to deliver the sport to our audiences. It exceeded our highest expectations, winning plaudits for its digital ambition and awards for the television coverage – and more than filling the hole left by the FA contract. Motor sports are not at the top of my personal preferences, but F1 was, by some miles, the best buy of my time in Sport. It fitted into the story we were trying to tell: that sport would always be important for the BBC and we were emphatically still in the business. As a small supplement to that, the Boat Race – source of the division's alleged misery some years previously when it had been lost – came gliding back onto our screens too.

However, the success with Formula 1 reignited the row over

cricket. We had thought about spending some of the FA money on the sport, but we still came up against the two obstacles. It was going to be difficult to schedule cricket to its best advantage on the BBC given our other events, and it needed to be on BBC One or BBC Two to make the right impact and garner the large free-to-air audiences. BBC Three and BBC Four were not on air during the daytime hours when cricket is played. Then there was the question of how much we were going to have to pay, with the rights inflated by their years at BSkyB. Our calculations suggested this would not pass the value-for-money test that we had set ourselves, and F1 was going to be more appealing to more people. We therefore decided not to bid for Test cricket. The England and Wales Cricket Board seemed to accept this with equanimity: they renewed their contract with Sky. But mid-way through 2008, they belaboured us with their bats. Giles Clarke, the ECB chairman, led the attack:

> I do think it's time for a debate on public sector sports broadcasting. Cricket fans – and there are 19 million who are interested – should have a right to expect the public sector broadcasters to mount bids for the nation's summer sport. After all, how many people play Formula 1? If the BBC is to remain a part of this they must answer to the millions of cricket fans in England and Wales as to how it prioritises its investment in sports rights.

The curiosity about this attack was that it came only after the ECB had signed its new deal with Sky. On their own admission, we had told them that we would not bid for live cricket packages in

March, but they only made a fuss about it in August. We therefore hit back hard through our official statement: 'The BBC is astonished by the comments by the ECB. We've always said any bid for live Test cricket was subject to value for money and fitting into scheduling and in our view neither of these criteria was met.' I followed up by going on the record myself a couple of days later:

> What seems distinctly odd is that the ECB claim we told them we weren't bidding for live TV cricket at the end of March. They then kept silent all through April, May and June. They didn't call the director-general or me or go to MPs or the papers or try to raise the issue in any way. Only after they'd done a reported £300 million exclusive deal with Sky did they attack us and call for a debate about the BBC's sports rights strategy.

Quite reasonably, the newspapers reported that relations between cricket and the BBC were at an all-time low, but we renewed the radio deal shortly afterwards, and despite the vehemence of the debate there was never any personal bad blood between Giles Clarke and me. I may possibly have told colleagues that I was off to sup with the devil, but we had a an enjoyable lunch together in the spring of 2009 to mark my transition to London 2012 and the end of my professional involvement with cricket.

Elsewhere in our programming, we wanted to show we remained ambitious. We introduced a sports news show for television called, unimaginatively, *Inside Sport*. It had its moments, but never achieved what *Sportsweek* had done for radio. It showed, though, that Gabby Logan – whom we had lured across from ITV – was a smart presenter, able to do penetrating interviews as well as anchor live events. More successful was the transformation of Sports Personality of the Year – known internally as 'SPOTY'. For some years, the programme had been broadcast from a studio in Television Centre, and it was an extraordinary event for the relatively few who were present. In my first year I stood at the door of the director of sport's pre-show reception and greeted Virginia Wade followed by Jackie Stewart followed by Bobby Charlton and other greats of the past, and then the current pick of the crop – people like Amir Khan and José Mourinho. I later spoke to a polite youngster who had missed out on the Young Sports Personality award. He was Theo Walcott. SPOTY was eye-popping in its ability to attract celebrities. And yet that was part of the problem of a studio show with a limited capacity: because everyone there was either a high-achiever or a sports administrator, they were more blasé than the public would have been. This hit home when Pelé received a Lifetime Achievement award to applause but no standing ovation, which underlined a sense of flatness in the programme as a whole. It wasn't helped that year by the awards won by the England cricket team, who were in Pakistan, where it was the early hours of the morning. The video link conveyed accurately their feelings of 'we're in Pakistan and it's 2 a.m.' When we saw the ratings, we knew the audience shared some of their joylessness: the figures were the lowest ever, and the critical response was no better. It was time for the redesign of another of our warhorses.

This took the form of taking the show on the road, and letting in the fans who would thrill to the sporting gods and goddesses around them. Under the guidance of Philip Bernie, Carl Doran and director Paul Davies, we made a leap of faith and booked the

NEC in Birmingham for SPOTY in 2006. Instead of the neat rows of blazers in Studio 1 of Television Centre, we were going for a vast arena with a crowd into the thousands. A live orchestra would play the theme tune, and stunts would be attempted live and on a scale greater than had been possible before. There would be no margin for error: every moment would be live on BBC One. It was therefore with a queasy feeling in my stomach that I stood on a Sunday afternoon in December in an NEC hanger, empty of people except for the technical staff, looking at the seats awaiting Midlanders' bottoms. As with the move of the news to 10 p.m., I had an insistent voice in my head: 'If this goes wrong, it will be very, very bad.' It needn't even be our fault. All it would take was a rogue fire alarm and we would have had BBC One showing an apology caption and playing seasonal music.

In fact, the programme was spectacularly better than the previous one – and it came with a talking point that guaranteed newspaper headlines. In what was a relatively thin year for the main award's shortlist, the public chose as its winner the Queen's granddaughter Zara Phillips. She contrived to make one of the more inarticulate acceptance speeches, telling the crowd: 'People have said to me, "Have you prepared a speech?", and I was like, "No," I wasn't expecting it all.' This appeared to be true. She then used the word 'amazing' a lot: 'It's amazing, thanks to all the voters, it's just amazing to be here with all these amazing sports people.' But this was wonderful publicity for us and for the new format, and SPOTY never looked back. By 2008, we had taken over the Echo Arena in Liverpool with an attendance of more than 10,000, and in the years since I left BBC Sport it has grown still further.

That Liverpool event was special because it was the celebration of Team GB's stunning performance at the Beijing Olympics. The Games in China – and then the Games coming to this country – became the ever more insistent theme of my time in BBC Sport. In 2006, I went to China with Mark Thompson for a DG visit with an Olympic dimension, and we got a tantalising flavour of what to expect. Mark had been pondering on the plane on the way over about what he would say if he was asked whether he had been to China before. He had – but it was for coverage of the student protests and the Tiananmen Square massacre in 1989. This didn't seem like the best introductory chat with our Communist hosts, so we allowed a little fog to descend over when precisely he had visited the country in the past.

We found our welcome differed from ministry to ministry. At the foreign affairs ministry, there were sympathetic-seeming and relatively liberal officials explaining the complexity of running a country of China's scale. At the propaganda ministry we were told in no uncertain terms that the Chinese government did not welcome the BBC's broadcasting services and our distorted sense of news values. Perched on huge chairs in ceremonial meeting rooms, I sat alongside Mark as he patiently explained to the Chinese officials via an interpreter the difference in our approach to news. 'If you build a hundred houses', he said, 'and one collapses – in Britain we would focus on the one that collapsed, while in China you might want to report on the ninety-nine that have been successfully completed. But that is how we see news.' They didn't look convinced.

For all that, we had a rattlingly enjoyable trip. We made our first visit to the Bird's Nest Stadium, and we met BOCOG – the Beijing version of LOCOG. There was an insight into the mood of a host city when there's less than two years to go: excited but apprehensive, at risk of drowning in the detail. My caveat about the visit, as someone who is notoriously picky about food, was Chinese cuisine – and in particular an Imperial-style banquet given to welcome their guests of honour. Every course produced a new horror for me to endure, and the only salvation was that everything was placed on a lazy Susan. This allowed me to spin the offending foodstuff – why sinew of deer, for heaven's sake? – round to a neighbour. But the alleged pièce de résistance was a turtle. It arrived in a large dish shaped like a turtle, and the lid was whisked away to reveal a real, cooked turtle underneath, still in its shell. The shell was dexterously removed, and the poor little naked turtle was chopped up in front of us. Mark prides himself on being able to eat anything, and found my squeamishness amusing. 'Try a bit, Roger,' he chirped. 'It's a bit gamey, it's a bit stringy, but it's fine, really.' My mind was set. It was gamey, it was stringy, it was a turtle: I was not going to eat so much as a sliver.

What became cemented in our minds during that trip was the extent to which Beijing would be a news story as well as a sport story. It was impossible to divorce modern China from its Olympic Games, and we would be missing the long-term significance of the event if we concentrated on personal bests and plucky winners to the exclusion of the Chinese Communist backdrop. On the plane home, Mark and I made a decision. We would ask Huw Edwards to commentate on the opening ceremony, the place where China would tell us about its history and its present, and make this a news assignment as well as a sport one. He would also be the commentator for London 2012's ceremonies, because they too would be a news story: the moment when Britain showed whether it could deliver the Olympics. Using Huw on both events would have a pleasing sense of strategy, and it would also show we wanted to bind together the BBC News and Sport operations, which in the past had tended to regard each other as the enemy. They would unite under Welsh leadership.

Beijing 2008 was the most comprehensive foreign BBC outside broadcast. There was the usual brouhaha about the number of staff we were sending: a publicly announced 437. This always generates the most illogical headline: that the BBC is sending more people than there are British competitors. Nobody has ever explained the correlation between the size of a broadcasting team – supplying output twenty-four hours a day from a difficult time zone and with multiple sports – and the number of competitors that have qualified from an individual country. As usual, then, the BBC team set off amid much carping from critics – and, as usually happens too, they came back with praise ringing in their ears.

The coverage was brilliantly marshalled by Dave Gordon, whose experience of Olympics goes back to Montreal in 1976 and who was the guiding force behind the sport broadcasting in London in 2012. It started with the quirky 'Monkey's Journey to the East' promotional campaign, which moved out of the comfort zone of traditional BBC Sport titles and into a world of cartoons, with music by Damon Albarn. The Games themselves had wonderful coverage by the host broadcaster, elevated further by the excitement, emotion and wit from our on-air team. We realised what a fine athletics commentator Steve Cram was becoming, and how miraculous it is that a swimming commentary team makes it onto BBC One only once in a blue moon but they manage to be such fabulous broadcasters when they do.

Mark Thompson and I went out for the beginning of the

Games. The night before the opening ceremony we were at a British embassy reception, and the talk was about the jitteriness of the organisers. There had been terrorist incidents before the Games, albeit hundreds of miles from Beijing, and they had prompted an increase in security. The rumour was that every single bus in the Chinese capital had an armed soldier aboard. I could not help thinking that this was foreshadowing London, where tension would be stoked by the wider range of risks in a free country and by the news-hungry western media. We were struck in Beijing by the sterility of the Games in the interests of security and order: an Olympic Park kept free of ordinary Chinese, and a city where you would never know the Olympics were in town except for the groups of people gathered around television sets. This was not the way anyone wanted London to be – and yet you could see that one tiny incident was all it would take to derail the event. The margin for error was vanishingly small.

Mark was treated as a VIP at the opening ceremony, being entertained for lunch by the Chinese President and travelling to the stadium in a minibus with Rupert Murdoch. I was Cinderella, left in the kitchen – or, more accurately, the BBC offices in the broadcast centre, where I jammed on my headphones and watched the output alongside Dave. On the following day, Mark and I joined together again for a mission around Chinese government departments, where we endured the ritual spanking for BBC executives who displayed journalistic tendencies, and we defended the independence of our output. Then it was time for a visit to the sporting events, with Mark's interest rising more because of our fellow guests than in response to the action on the pitch. We saw George W. Bush and an assortment of Silicon Valley moguls at the swimming and Prince Albert of Monaco at the archery, and bumped into Seb Coe in a hospitality lounge. It was networking heaven. It was also another reminder of what the modern Olympic circus is about, especially in cities with even better power hubs and shopping facilities and hotels than Beijing. The world really would come to London in 2012.

Mark flew home musing, he told me later, about how the BBC would do justice to the London Games. I was thinking the same. I had been in BBC Sport for three years, and I had no idea whether the BBC would want me to do four more years and lead the London coverage. There was the complication of the move of BBC Sport to Salford, which was due in 2011. As a northerner, I believed in the devolution of broadcasting to the regions, but as someone who had been rooted in London for twenty years, I was unsure whether I wanted to move myself. Almost all my friends and my extended family were within easy reach of my London base, and they told me volubly that they couldn't imagine me being transported to Salford Quays. I therefore had a mix in my head of thinking I might need to leave sport and being mulishly resistant to the idea of not being involved in the London Games.

Providence helpfully arranged that Mark Thompson's musing, along with that of Mark Byford, came to the conclusion that I should be offered the job of BBC director, London 2012. It was the perfect outcome for me. They conceived the job as being in charge of everything the BBC was planning: not just the sport and news but digital innovation, the Cultural Olympiad and the London content in every single genre. It was going to be based in the capital, while BBC Sport moved north on schedule. I would report to Mark Byford, with the DG taking a close interest, and I

could build and run a support team as I saw fit. It was an opportunity I simply couldn't resist. I had the chance to lead the BBC
through the biggest event in the UK in our lifetimes, and, although
anything labelled by the BBC as a 'project' was automatically
to be regarded with suspicion, this surely would transcend that.
Even if it did not, I reasoned that this would almost certainly be
the last big job I did at the BBC – so it didn't matter whether it
pushed me up the greasy pole of career advancement or not. For
once, this was simply about getting something right – and something that was of huge significance to the organisation and to the
country. I accepted the two Marks' offer in about five seconds flat.

The BBC's coverage of Beijing ended on 17 September 2008,
with the closing ceremony of the Paralympic Games. Around
42 million people had watched the Olympics and 13.5 million had
tuned in to the Paralympics. The BBC's approval ratings were close
to record highs, driven in part by the sporting summer.

It was a month later, on 18 October, that Radio 2 broadcast
a recorded segment of *The Russell Brand Show* in which the presenter, aided by Jonathan Ross, left a series of lewd messages on
the answerphone of the actor Andrew Sachs. They were about the
relationship Brand had had with Sachs's granddaughter, and they
should never have been broadcast. The resultant furore – named
'Sachsgate' – sent the corporation's reputation plummeting, and
the handling of the crisis was dismayingly shaky until Mark
Thompson flew back from holiday and took control. We felt the
pain of the Ross–Brand affair even more keenly in BBC Sport
because we had worked so hard through the summer to show the
corporation at its best – and now here were out-of-control presenters, and woeful editorial grip, undermining those efforts. A

reputation in broadcasting can be lost as quickly as it is gained. But we did, at least, have London 2012 to look forward to and the chance of a much greater legacy for the corporation.

CHAPTER 10

OLYMPICS

I N THE SPRING of 2009, I moved from BBC Sport, where I had been leading a division of 500 people and a budget that ran into hundreds of millions of pounds, into an office newly created for the BBC London 2012 team. There was me; my PA, Elaine Gold; a terrific project executive, Amanda Farnsworth; and a few empty seats. We had no budget, not even one for ourselves at that stage. We had an uncertain place within the BBC structures, because we did not sit with any of the major power blocs. I had a strong relationship with my successor in Sport, Barbara

Slater, but there was no template for the ultimate authority on an Olympic Games sitting outside the sport division. And we had no output planned for more than three years. My young cousin Damien put it nicely at the time: 'Nobody will have the remotest idea what you're doing now, but there'll be a blinding revelation in the summer of 2012 – for better or for worse.' But I had received a heartening email from Sebastian Coe when my appointment was announced: 'I can't tell you how pleased I am for you and for the project. I've sensed for some time it would need one person to really drive this through to 2012, and by a country mile you are the right person to do this.' Seb alternated this praise with a teasing line on public platforms about my experience of Beijing. I had said, somewhat too simplistically, that my dominant impression from there was just how big the modern Games are. Seb would say, deadpan, 'And this is Roger Mosey, whose revelation from Beijing was that the Olympics are, well, big.' It was fun working with him, and Seb deserves all the plaudits for his leadership of the organising committee, LOCOG.

When I was offered the 2012 job, I consulted colleagues who said that my condition for taking the role should be that I would be given control of the entire BBC Olympics budget. At the time, I said that was not too much of a concern, and I was reluctant to erode the authority of the other divisional directors, notably sport. My main grip on the event was the agreement that I would be the individual managing the BBC's relationship with the International Olympic Committee (IOC) and with LOCOG. This allowed our office to be a 'one-stop shop': any BBC programme wanting do anything about the Olympics needed to make an approach through us, and if the IOC or LOCOG wanted anything from the BBC, they knew who to call. But an intervention from the National Audit Office and the Public Accounts Committee handed the 2012 budget over to us too, because they ruled that the BBC's approach to Beijing – separate budgets for news, sport and other programme departments – was wrong. There should be one individual responsible for the financial control of major events.

The BBC agreed with the recommendations, as it is politically wise to do, and I was handed the spreadsheets. We appointed a head of production for the whole of the BBC's Olympic programming, Jamie Hindhaugh, and Dominic Coles became chief operating officer for the 2012 project alongside his other BBC roles. Dave Gordon, as BBC Sport's head of major events, had a reporting line to Barbara Slater and to me. This was the engine room of the operation, but it fitted within a governance plan that worked extremely effectively. We had representatives from BBC News, Sport and Future Media – the tech guys – at our regular management meeting, and the BBC 2012 steering group was chaired by Mark Thompson or Mark Byford, with all the main directors attending.

This meant that we could operate as 'one BBC', in an echo of what the BBC values had aimed for, and any turf wars were sorted out rapidly. People like Helen Boaden for News, Jana Bennett and later George Entwistle for Television, Erik Huggers and Ralph Rivera from Future Media, Caroline Thomson from Operations, Tim Davie from Radio, Lucy Adams from Human Resources and Zarin Patel as finance director were all involved in the planning; and their enthusiasm played back into their home divisions.

Our team built up steadily in the three years of the project. But the most pressing early need was to define what we were there to do, and what viewers and listeners could expect from the BBC in 2012. Two big ideas were already forming. The first was a commitment we had made that we wanted to cover every event from every venue – which sounds obvious, but had only recently become possible thanks to the spread of digital technology. In the Olympics of the 1990s, the BBC had been confined to its two terrestrial channels. By Sydney in 2000, there was a very basic website, and for Athens in 2004, the red button was becoming part of our Olympic repertoire along with video streaming on the web. But even by 2008, with six red-button channels on offer, we were still only able to offer people in Britain about half the content available from the host broadcasting operation.

In our office in Beijing, I showed Dave Gordon an email we had received from a fencing fan, protesting that we were offering no live coverage of his sport. 'That surely can't be true,' I asked, 'with all the red-button services and online streaming?' But it was correct because 5,000 hours of sport were being squeezed into 2,500 hours of airtime, meaning that half the Games were simply not seen by our audiences. Dave was in the vanguard of wanting to change that, and we made the pledge without being completely sure how we were going to deliver it. It was an example of an editorial ambition being handed to the technology teams for them to solve – and, gratifyingly, they did.

Allied with this was a feeling that 2012 could be the breakthrough year for digital Britain. We presented this as an ambition originating in broadcasting history, though quite who crystallised it for 2012 is lost in the mists of the Olympic project. It had been in 1936 that the abdication crisis had seen the nation brought together by radio, as people gathered around their wireless sets to listen to King Edward VIII renounce the throne. Seventeen years later, television came of age for the Queen's coronation. There was a massive surge in the number of television sets sold to households across Britain; and, for the first time, more people watched an event on TV than listened to it on radio. For London 2012, we could see that we would have more online and mobile services than ever before. Social media would be at its most widespread, allowing people to share the moment. If Dave's plans came to fruition, at peak times we would need a total of twenty-four channels to cover all the Olympic action. Our aim was that whenever you wanted it, and wherever you were, you would be able to enjoy London 2012 from the BBC; it would be the time when digital services came of age. At this stage we did not know that the royal boost to this would come not from a coronation or an abdication, but by the Queen appearing to jump out of a helicopter.

Perhaps as a subconscious tribute to Gordon Brown, we drew up a five-point plan for what we hoped to achieve – and we published it. Number 1 was to offer brilliant coverage of the sport. Number 2, we wanted to bring the nation together round a whole series of events in 2012, including the Diamond Jubilee, the torch relay and the Cultural Olympiad, in addition to the Games themselves. Number 3 was to have wide-ranging and expert news reporting of the events: independent and impartial, but also proportionate to the scale of the year when our capital would be the centre of world attention. Number 4 was to drive digital: to encourage its use, and offer unprecedented choice and personalisation. We wanted to reinforce this commitment to the future by capturing some of the Games for the first time in Super Hi-Vision, a technology developed by Japan's NHK and the BBC; and we would offer some live coverage in 3D. Number 5, we wanted to secure a legacy for the BBC and for the country, by engaging the widest range of audiences and delivering projects with long-term benefits.

The torch relay is one of the examples of the benefit of taking decisions early, with some plans signed off as early as 2009. In LOCOG's research, conducted by their marketing head Greg Nugent, the torch relay was a hazy concept for many in Britain: they knew little about what it entailed. But when it was explained to them that it might mean the torch coming to their town or city, possibly even right along their street, they really liked the idea, and LOCOG saw this as the means by which enthusiasm for the Games would spread across Britain in the weeks before the opening ceremony. This tied in with the BBC's strengths in the nations and regions. It was a gift to local radio stations and regional television, who could have 'the Olympics' on their patch when the torch came to town.

We therefore built into our budget the funding for every region to have a special TV programme for the relay, and for every local radio station to have money for an enhanced breakfast show and extra reporting. Colleagues from the BBC's nations and regions met with LOCOG many times to work on the torch's route, how its journey would be announced and then the detail of the daily schedule. As often as we could manage it, the torch's biggest moments would be 'live' into the BBC 6.30 p.m. regional news programmes. We invested, too, in 3G technology that would allow the relay to be covered live on our website throughout its journey: 'Torchcam' was to be one of the hits of 2012.

But one of the biggest moments was planned to be in a place that didn't exist. We thought it would be an amusing idea to take the torch to Walford, in London E20 – better known as the home of the soap *EastEnders*. I was uncertain whether the people running *EastEnders* would take to the idea, because there is a tricky balance to be struck between real events and continuing dramas. However, the argument was that it was surely impossible for an East End borough not to have any reflection of the Olympics happening in the East End of London in 2012, and we had a gratifyingly warm welcome from the *EastEnders* production team when we put the proposal to them that they could have the actual torch being carried through their fictitious borough. It was they who added the idea that this could be 'live' – adding a live segment to an episode partly on tape. Hence from some considerable time out, the characters of Walford were seized by the prospect of the torch visiting them.

The announcement was made in the Queen Vic on the same day that the route was announced to the real places hosting the relay in the rest of the country, with a long-term plot developing about who would carry the Olympic flame. We had held meetings in which LOCOG had set out their high aspirations for torch-bearers: that they would be an inspiration to others and pillars of their communities. The *EastEnders* producers had explained that most of the inhabitants of Albert Square had lived rather more vivid lives, given the local reputation for crime and lurid personal relationships. In the end, the character chosen was Billy Mitchell, who might have struggled with the real-life vetting process. On the night, LOCOG arranged for a special mini-convoy to break away from the main relay party to go to the *EastEnders* set in Elstree, where the live outside broadcast captured Billy's run on BBC One. For students of the media, there was the additional pleasure of watching the BBC News channel simultaneously broadcasting a scene from a soap opera with the caption 'Live from Walford'.

This customising of the relay reflects the close relationship we had with LOCOG. I had a formal opposite number in Jackie Brock-Doyle, their director of communications and public affairs, and we would meet or speak every week, or, in 2012 itself, almost every day. We didn't always agree about everything, but when action was needed the system worked. Dave Gordon phoned me in considerable alarm one day when he saw that a crowd direction pylon was being erected in a place that would be right in the middle of the shot from our Olympic studio window. It meant that instead of viewers seeing the Aquatic Centre behind Sue Barker's head, they might witness a revolving electronic message about delays on the District Line.

Within an hour or two, Jackie had sorted it out – at some cost to LOCOG, since it involved digging up concrete foundations – and the nation was spared unwanted travel news on our flagship broadcasts. Jackie's deputy, Joanna Manning-Cooper, was similarly adept at reconciling the needs of the organising committee and broadcasters, and was a neighbour of mine in Richmond and a drinking companion on tough days. All of this was outside the International Olympic Committee's playbook: in their theology, the IOC dealt with the organising committee, and their partner was the official host broadcaster, Olympic Broadcasting Services, who provided core coverage of the Games for the whole world. There was no formal role for the rights-holding broadcaster of the host nation, but LOCOG and ourselves ignored that protocol. We saw our partnership as essential to making the Games a success within the UK.

It meant that we had privileged access to London's Olympic story. Five years before the opening ceremony, we walked around the site where the main stadium was going to be built, and we were there after the first concrete had been poured, when you could start imagining where the track and the stands would be. I recall a visit to the Olympic Park on a bitingly cold but sunny morning in January 2008, with Beijing still to come, in which the team and I felt for the first time that this was truly going to happen: the athletes of the world would be running and swimming and cycling here, in what had previously been a wasteland in an unfashionable part of east London. Later we worked with LOCOG on a series of countdown events, with 'three years to go' somewhat predictably being followed by 'two years to go'. There were attention-grabbing moments such as the first run along the Olympic track, and sporting heroes marched live on network television across one of the bridges newly installed to convey the crowds from transport hubs to sporting venues.

However, the public relations impact of these events could often be hijacked, in an apparently amiable way, by the Mayor of London. The idea of a media visit to the velodrome when it was partially completed was to showcase cycling stars spinning round the track, but Boris Johnson spotted an opportunity. He climbed aboard an unused bike and set off himself, a little uncertainly, round the velodrome – pursued, of course, by a phalanx of photographers and video crews. Those pictures made the news bulletins and the following day's papers, and it was characteristic of the mayor's ability to win over some and to leave others grinding their teeth.

For a couple of compelling meetings, I was co-chair with Johnson of the London telephony working group. It was set up to try to resolve the enormous pressure there would be on the mobile networks, and Amanda Farnsworth's early intelligence had been alarming. She came back from a meeting where the operators had predicted that not even voice and text services would run flawlessly, because of the unprecedented demand. Our aim of offering video services to mobiles was impossible: there was not the digital capacity in the UK to enable that, and nor were there enough phone masts in east London.

Hence a planning group comprising the mobile companies, the mayor, the BBC and LOCOG. Johnson would start by brandishing some huge old mobile phone at the operators. 'What am I going to be able to get on this gizmo?' he would boom, apparently oblivious to the smartphone generation. But you could spot his political savvy too. The mobile companies' standard response was to call for more investment – either from the government or from the city authorities. They wanted someone else to put in the infrastructure, if needs be from the public purse. The mayor would have none of it: he was not going to spend his budget on something that would benefit the phone operators or the video suppliers. After the clowning around at the start of a meeting, it would become apparent that he was no soft touch.

There were, unavoidably, some bumps in our relationship with the organisers. LOCOG awarded the rights for the Paralympics to Channel 4, much to our unhappiness at the time. We had seen the possibility of a Channel 4 bid because it looked commercially attractive to them, but they came in at an offer way above what we thought was realistic. It was a blow to Dave Gordon in particular, because he had championed disability sport for many years and had pushed BBC Sport to bring it into its mainstream coverage, so it was galling that the International Paralympic Committee did not support that long-term commitment when the Games came to London. But it was, possibly, the right decision. Channel 4 covered the Paralympics well, and, as I watched our television team drive themselves to exhaustion during the Olympics, it would have been tough to ask them to do it all over again two weeks later. A fresh perspective was of benefit. For ourselves, we were proud that Radio 5 Live managed to do justice to both the Olympics and Paralympics.

More of a conundrum throughout the Olympic project was what to do about the Cultural Olympiad. This is intended to be a feast of the host country's arts, running from the handing over of the Olympic flag – so in our case from 2008 – to the Games themselves. The words 'Cultural Olympiad' were, and remain, a mystery to most people, and I always had a suspicion that LOCOG's high command regarded this as a distraction from the main business of getting the Games right. But they dutifully set up a Cultural Olympiad team, and it churned out a number of forgettable small-scale events from some years out. These events ate up Cultural Olympiad funding, and by 2009 there was an unhappy conjunction of no compelling story about Britain's Olympic arts, with much of the money already allocated to dull initiatives.

To the rescue came a figure from my past: Tony Hall, then chief executive of the Royal Opera House, now the new chairman of the Cultural Olympiad board, and Ruth MacKenzie as the director charged with putting together something the public would want to see. Almost every arts panjandrum in London was by now on the board, so it was made up of people like the directors of the Tate and the British Museum and the Royal Shakespeare

Company along with the mayor's cultural adviser – and Mark Thompson from the BBC (when he was not otherwise engaged) or me (when he was, which was often).

I found it partly amusing and often infuriating. The wilful ignorance of sport on the part of some members was a shock, though I know they regarded me as annoyingly resistant to their vision of the arts. More worrying was the attention given to getting public funding for work of questionable value to the taxpayer, of which the Arts Council's 'Artists Taking the Lead' was a prime exhibit. Immediately nicknamed 'Artists Taking the Piss' by wicked folk at LOCOG, it gave six-figure sums to decidedly peculiar initiatives. A column of steam was promised for Merseyside: 'a slender, sinuous spinning column of cloud rising into the sky from the surface of the water on East Float in the Wirral'. It never happened. The London project was Bus Tops: 'a public art installation on the roofs of bus shelters. LED panels became canvases, showcasing digital commissions by a range of established artists, as well as allowing Londoners to display their creativity, play games and express what is special about their city.' I never met anyone who had seen one, let alone played games with it. 'Nowhereisland' was a travelling island, which even *The Guardian* said 'deserves to sink'. The East Midlands got some crocheted lions in glass cages. 'Godiva Awakes' was a giant Lady Godiva, only slightly compromised by being clothed and propelled by bicycles. All of them were routinely described by the arts types as 'spectacular' and 'extraordinary', of which only the latter was true for me – and not as a positive. The total cost was £5.4 million. Jackie Brock-Doyle and I would sit within each other's sight and roll our eyes in bafflement or outrage at the latest idea, and

I could have sworn that there were points when even Tony's eyebrows were raised a little too.

We had hoped for some of the artistic projects to be good enough for broadcast on BBC One. When I observed that it all seemed a bit BBC Four, if that, I was reprimanded by a panjandrum. 'In that case it's simply a matter of putting that BBC Four material onto BBC One,' he said, primly. One of the icons of the arts world also sighed about the relationship between the Olympics and sport. 'Wouldn't it be nice', he mused, 'if we had some sport supporting a major arts festival, rather than the other way round?' Sadly, the world still waits for a West Ham *v.* Stoke match to build up excitement for the Turner Prize.

I came to like and respect Ruth MacKenzie a great deal, and she and Tony grabbed the Cultural Olympiad agenda as best they could and reshaped it into the London 2012 Festival, which was more comprehensible to the public. But at the BBC we mainly did our own thing and simply commissioned some decent programmes that would fit under the Festival banner – hence the Shakespeare season, with the memorable *Hollow Crown* series; the Radio 1 Big Weekend in Hackney; and the 2012 Proms, which had already been promised as having an Olympic tie-in. I enjoyed escorting the BBC Trust chairman, Lord Patten, through the muddy fields of Hackney Marshes for what was possibly his first live experience with Dizzee Rascal and Plan B.

Throughout the long planning period, we found dealing with the BBC Trust to be a dispiriting part of the job. Chris Patten, who arrived only just over a year before the Games, was the exception to the rule: he understood sport and was enthusiastic about the Olympics. Many of the rest were the spiritual siblings of the folk on the Cultural Olympiad board. In our update sessions that started after Beijing, trustees would always have questions about the arts or education initiatives around the Olympics. But I cannot recall any significant issues being raised about covering the sport of the Games: nothing about building a profile for minority sports or ensuring excellence around the athletics, swimming or ceremonies. When we set out the audience figures for Beijing and made our predictions for London, one senior trustee asked dismissively, 'Are you really sure people are going to want to watch this in those numbers?' – to which our answer, even in 2009, was an unequivocal 'yes'.

As we got closer to the Games, the seeming misery of some trustees increased. In a textbook example of looking through the wrong end of telescope, one Trust committee obsessed about our need to provide alternative coverage to the Games. They extracted guarantees from the management that none of the beastly Olympics would encroach into peak time on BBC Two or BBC Four, without considering the storm there would be among viewers if a gold medal cycle race was chopped off in its prime, or factoring in that there were hundreds of alternative channels available. Almost never did we get a spark of enthusiasm from them that this was a once-in-a-lifetime festival of sport and the BBC should do it justice on those terms.

There was further frustration in dealing with the Trust bureaucracy. It is right, of course, that new services should be subject to scrutiny, and regulation is essential for broadcasting. But when we started to imagine, prompted by an enquiry from Sky, that our twenty-four online channels of sporting action might become twenty-four Games-time television channels, we realised how much more complex our regulatory framework had become. In

2011, one of the BBC management team who dealt with the Trust gave us the timeline for approval of what was being construed as a suite of new services – even though they were only going to be there for seventeen days. He noted the likely need for a public value test, the required consultation periods and the rest – and concluded that everything might not be fully approved until September 2012. Amanda Farnsworth and I tried to discern whether he was joking or not, but there was no flicker of a smile on his face. The Trust did, fortunately, recognise that approval for Olympic services after the Games themselves might not have been the smartest move. Indeed, having the twenty-four channels available, not just on Sky but on Freesat and Virgin cable, became a great success, thanks to the ease of finding sports live and uninterrupted via the programming guide on a digital box.

The contrast between the Trust and the staff of the BBC was striking. Even three years out, I had been surprised by the large turnout and the warmth of the reception at the headquarters of BBC Scotland at Pacific Quay for our presentation on what the 2012 project was doing. That is always a tough venue for a London-based manager, especially when he is talking about an event that is unavoidably centred on the capital; but in Glasgow, and in Belfast and in Cardiff and right across England, there was a faith in what the BBC could do. This was never uncritical, and I emphasised at every stop that the journalism must be independent. If things went wrong, as they did with the G4S security fiasco, then the BBC must be leading the coverage, and I was pleased in Games-time that BBC London managed to irritate LOCOG considerably with their reporting on empty VIP seats. But colleagues from many different departments wanted to be involved in the Olympic story too: some, like BBC Drama, in a way that we had never expected.

On a sticky afternoon in the summer of 2011, I took the Tube over to LOCOG's ceremonies team at their home in Three Mills: an unexpected oasis of the creative arts near Bromley-by-Bow station, chosen as an antidote to the tower blocks of Canary Wharf, where most of the Olympics organising team was based. We were going to be shown the plans for the opening ceremony of the Games; an event that had the lowest of expectations in a British gloom-fest about how London 2012 would most likely be truly terrible. Our host was Martin Green, the head of ceremonies, who had chosen Danny Boyle as their creative director. Martin was an example of the strength of the LOCOG team, combining imagination with a shrewd business head.

The first glimpse of what they were planning at Three Mills was not reassuring. There was a scale model of the stadium with a green mound at one end, and the field of play was dotted with plastic models of sheep and cows. A cotton-wool cloud dangled overhead, held in place by a piece of string. But what emerged after that prompted a dramatic swing in my mind from 'they've gone crackers' to 'this is creative genius'. The ceremony on that summer's day a year out was represented by models like the one of the stadium, sketched drawings, pieces of archive film and snatches of music. There were the 'mood boards' beloved of advertising agencies: a visual attempt to show what it would be like – the feel, the colour, the atmosphere. The whole thing was stitched together in a presentation that lasted roughly an hour, but what drove through those sixty minutes like an express train was Danny Boyle's vision. I had argued in a blog in 2009 that the worst outcome for the opening ceremony would be to have it designed by a committee – and this certainly was not. It was one man's view and what is remarkable is just how much of those 2011 plans were seen by the world twelve months later.

It was an achievement because the ceremony was the most scrutinised aspect of the Olympics, and it was overseen by a whole range of bodies: from the British Cabinet to the IOC, and from the Mayor of London to LOCOG's panoply of boards. Danny and Martin had to get all of them to agree to it, and there were many times the omens were far from propitious. There were government statements about the need to show just how great a triumph Britain had had in the Second World War. Jeremy Hunt told Andrew Marr a few months ahead of the ceremony that it was vital to show how we had stood alone against fascism, and the people of Lincolnshire lobbied to get a Vulcan bomber flying over the world leaders assembled in peace in Stratford. Much of Britain's history was strewn with metaphorical landmines, whether it was the risk of offending the nations we had beaten in wars or the countries we had ruled during the age of empire, or even in the relationships within the UK between the English and the Scots, Irish and Welsh.

But Danny sailed through all this. His idea of basing the first part of the ceremony around the Industrial Revolution was inspired: a non-contentious piece of our past, and a beacon for the world. For the second section, honouring the National Health Service, a Conservative-led government – especially a Conservative-led government – could never have vetoed a tribute to the NHS, however bemusing it turned out to be to the rest of the planet. And Danny's other touches – the suffragettes, the Windrush generation,

Liberty's Shami Chakrabarti carrying the Olympic flag – were all defensible in their own right, while making it abundantly clear where his heart lay.

There were some changes, of course, from the 2011 template. One of the most celebrated moments on the night was when the Queen appeared to jump out of a helicopter. When this idea was revealed to Huw Edwards in a planning meeting, before the royal approval had been given, he was certain: 'She'll *never* do it.' In the storyboard of the film, an additional gag was that the helicopter pilot would be revealed to be Prince William – but that fell foul of the Palace's aversion to 'double-teaming': for special events like these, the Queen's role is solo.

At that stage, too, Danny simply had 'a comedy moment' in his demonstration video, illustrated by old Monty Python clips – and it was this gap that was filled by the Rowan Atkinson Mr Bean sketch. But otherwise the biggest elements were there: from smoke-stacks crashing out of England's green and pleasant land and J. K. Rowling reading a bedtime story through to Paul McCartney singing a concluding 'Hey Jude'. In the recording, it was even in tune.

It would be wrong, though, to imagine this process was easy, and there were indications in the year running up to the ceremony that crockery was sometimes being thrown in the LOCOG kitchen. Danny was never one to dance to the tune of the Olympic sponsors, for instance, and after the Games he described the behaviour of one of them as 'disgusting'. In an interview with the *Mail on Sunday*, he said:

> The battles were exhausting. My lowest point was the Rapier missiles, which were positioned on buildings near where I live.

The Olympics is a festival of peace, for God's sake. I was very close to walking away. I thought it was morally wrong. I wanted to go out and say, 'I would prefer to risk being blown up and all 80,000 of us die than have Rapier missiles on top of buildings.'

This sometimes felt like one of a number of plots foreshadowed by the funny and prescient *Twenty Twelve* comedy on the BBC, though the tension within LOCOG was real and it would have been a disaster if Danny had walked out. But in the BBC Olympic planning team we were most aware of budget problems. Danny had a Hollywood film director's urge to make it big and bold even if it cost a shedload of money, while LOCOG had an understandable wish to stay within their (still pretty big and bold) budget. In true creative fashion, if he was challenged on budgets Danny would use the 'shoot and the baby gets it' technique – which meant it was the things he believed the bosses most wanted that he would threaten to drop if he was at risk of overspending.

That was how BBC Drama ended up making the Queen/James Bond film. It was going to be a startlingly expensive five minutes of television: edging into seven figures. In one of the behind-the-scenes crockery-throwing moments, LOCOG and Danny disagreed on the funding from within the LOCOG budget. It was at risk of being dropped from the running order, and we therefore had a plaintive request put to us: either we made it – and paid for it – or an astonishing moment might be lost to the globe and posterity. As it happened, the BBC Olympic budget was slightly underspent and we could afford it. But a decision to make the film was one that I felt needed to be shared with Mark Thompson. Happily, he took the view that any television producer would take. If you have the chance to make a film featuring the Queen and James Bond, and it will be seen by a few billion people, then it would be mad to turn it down.

We therefore commissioned our Drama colleagues to do the filming to the directions of Danny Boyle, and miraculously – especially for the BBC – almost none of this leaked. At the Buckingham Palace shoot there were 135 crew involved, given the complexity of the operation and the limited availability of the star performers, but only one relatively small and inaccurate story emerged from it. Even when we had a pair of helicopters flying through Tower Bridge, and the Port of London authority unhelpfully told the papers, 'That's the BBC filming the Olympic opening ceremony,' nobody put two and two together. The film on the night was an electrifying surprise. And in the days ahead of the ceremony I came across Nick Brown from BBC Drama in the cutting room as the final edit was underway, and he said that each time the editing machine disgorged the clip of the actual Queen performing with Daniel Craig he had to pinch himself and ask, 'Is this real?'

As the Games drew nearer, we spent ever more of our time in Stratford in the International Broadcast Centre. IBCs for sporting events are the same each time: vast aircraft hangars with space carved out for the broadcasters of the world, and a depressing catering operation with queues for bad coffee. The spaces were massive and luxurious for the Americans of NBC, and relatively cramped and functional for the BBC. An inflatable kangaroo showed where the Australians were, and then the smaller nations hung their flags and emblems outside tiny offices shared with others. The miracle of these operations is that the thousands of miles of wiring does what it is supposed to, and the build by the broadcast engineers was flawless.

Our operation spread outside the Olympic Park, too. In a deliberate attempt to separate the up-close BBC Sport operation within each venue from the more objective news coverage, the news presentation location was on the highest floors of a block of council flats overlooking the park. It had a wonderful shot of the Olympic activity in one direction and the London skyline in another, though it was a rough and ready location for the star presenters. There was inadequate air conditioning on baking hot days, fuelled further by studio lighting, and a preparation area that had the ambience of a shower block at a budget camp site. But everybody was thrilled to be there; it was a great assignment, even though for most there were no tickets available for the sport events. Dave Gordon and I moved into a flat in Hackney Wick ready for our 24/7 Games-time roles, prompting jokes from our colleagues about us living together like Morecambe and Wise, only less funny.

In the days immediately before the Games, I felt satisfied that everything was coming together: the robustness of the planning meant the BBC machine was swinging smoothly into action. In the Broadcast Centre, Dave and I had wandered into one of the technical areas and had seen the test cards lined up for our twenty-four feeds of live action: we really were going to launch twenty-four television channels in a few days' time. Our trails and the splendid title music, commissioned from Elbow, were unmissable across BBC television and radio. There was also the backdrop of the torch relay doing exactly what we had hoped. Massive crowds lined the route all across the United Kingdom, and there were knockout moments: the aerial shots of the relay reaching the summit of Snowdon on a sparkling summer day, the zip wire ride for the torch in Newcastle, the disabled war hero Ben Parkinson being cheered through Doncaster. The mood in the country seemed to have become exuberant. People wanted a party, and they wanted the Olympics to work. But I never lost the feeling of just how easy it would be for that to change and for disaster to strike.

The experience in Beijing of the oppressive atmosphere generated by terrorism hundreds of miles away had stayed with me, and we used to talk within our team about the catastrophic effect of even a minor bomb incident anywhere in the UK but especially in London. The Olympic Park was as secure as humanly possible, but what if there had been an explosion in a supermarket in Newham or in Kensington or beyond? The effect on foreign competitors and visitors, and on the spirit of the Games, would have been terrible. We felt some reassurance after visiting the secret command centre for London 2012, where all the key agencies were working together: transport, the police, the armed forces and, I assume, the intelligence services. Everything that could be done was being done, though the fear of a 'lone wolf' attack never went away.

The other worry remained the opening ceremony, because it would so much define London's Games. Even knowing that its concept was brilliant and so were many of the elements, I was beset by doubt in the run-up to 27 July. Our team knew there were so many things that could go wrong. Early rehearsals had revealed that a downpour significantly affected the timings: the green and pleasant land became much heavier, composed as it was of proper turf, and was therefore much slower to rip up and carry away. But it was wind rather than rain that was thought to be the bigger enemy. If the wind was too strong, the parachute jump at the end of the Queen/Bond film would be ruled out on the grounds of safety. The weather forecast became a subject of obsessive study.

There were public dress rehearsals for the ceremony in the final week of preparations, but before those we had a private run-through in the stadium on a warm and lovely Saturday evening. We made our way to our seats as some of the cast were arriving, with sheep being guided across the concourse and a flock of geese being released into the bucolic setting. The audience comprised LOCOG officials, a BBC team and the folk from NBC. NBC had a barbecue to mark the occasion, while we shared LOCOG's curled-up sandwiches. It was that night that we knew what an incredible moment the Industrial Revolution sequence would be: the visceral thrill of the shout of the workers as they flooded onto the field of play, and the brilliance of the creation of the Olympic rings out of molten steel. But we saw how easy it was for things to go awry. A chimney stack stuttered rather than soared skywards, and the inflatable house for the big dance number didn't inflate properly. The giant baby at the end of the NHS sequence wasn't ready – a blessing, thought some – and came close to being axed from the show. If you watched from the stadium, some of the dancing by NHS staff was, understandably, a bit of a shambles because they were not dance professionals; and in none of the rehearsals did the Queen and Bond film appear. Some secrets were too good to share, even given the impressive discipline of the cast and preview audiences.

We never saw the lighting of the cauldron being rehearsed, either. This was also intended to be a moment of wonder, though

– like many things – it had come close to being revealed ahead of the Games. One night in the spring I had been called by Jackie Brock-Doyle about some aerial footage being shown on BBC News of the preparations being made for the ceremonies. 'Get it taken off,' she said, with the hard edge in her voice that I had come to recognise and fear. 'You can see the outline of the cauldron, and it blows the entire secret!' And it was true that, if you knew what you were looking for, the design of the cauldron was exposed on some of Britain's top news programmes. Fortunately, nobody did work out what it was, and my iron rule – never to interfere with news programmes – held.

That said, there were some oddities about sponsoring both news and sport coverage. Some of the people working for me in the online news area of the 2012 team were trying to find out about Games secrets that were known fully by other people in my team sitting just a few desks from them. This respect for 'Chinese Walls' reached its height in an interview with Danny Boyle, done ahead of the event by Huw Edwards, who also knew everything that was in the ceremony. Huw tried to tempt Danny on air to reveal a secret or two. Unsurprisingly, he didn't. Again, this represents the balance we had to strike between journalism – which should be sacrosanct – and not spoiling the surprises of the most spectacular show in Britain for generations. We treated it like a story where there is an embargo and details cannot be released ahead of a specific time. The other part of the balancing act was to make a successful television programme out of the sometimes frenetic goings-on in the stadium. But that had been sorted for us and the rest of the world's broadcasters by the Boyle vision: his ceremony was always conceived as a television show, or indeed a live film. Hence his prolonged battle with the host broadcaster OBS to ensure that it was his own cameras and directors who captured the ceremony, and that they had been involved from the start, rather than entrust it to people flown in a fortnight before the event. He had also thought carefully about the role of TV commentary. There was one of those 180-degree inaccurate stories in the papers that had said Danny was bothered by the idea of Huw Edwards and our commentators talking all over his beloved ceremony, when in fact Danny had told us from the start that he had imagined the points where Huw would need to speak. There were points of transition where an explanation was necessary, and he had always heard them in his head being spoken in Huw's voice.

The morning of the day of the opening ceremony was enlivened by one of the more amusing manifestations of the Cultural Olympiad. At twelve minutes past eight, we broadcast Martin Creed's 'Work No. 1197'. This had the rubric 'all the bells in a country rung as quickly and as loudly as possible for three minutes', which prompted the excitable arts community to proclaim that 'everyone will ring a bell!', while our communications chief Louisa Fyans asked plaintively how this could be construed as an art work. But it felt appropriately celebratory. It raised interest from Chris Evans on Radio 2 and from breakfast television – and then from all news outlets when the Culture Secretary, Jeremy Hunt, managed to propel part of his bell towards a bystander thanks to his enthusiastic ringing. There were jokes about dropped clangers, and worse, but it added to the gaiety of the nation.

Back in the office, I watched the final versions of the films made by BBC Sport for the two hours of live coverage before the ceremony began, and they lived up to my hopes. There was the wonderful 'opener' featuring Benedict Cumberbatch, adding poetry to the excitement of the day, and in the immediate run-up to the ceremony we played a beautifully crafted history of London by Andrew Marr. It included the way London had come through the Blitz and more recent challenges like 7/7, and it was high-end, ambitious television. This was not a night for easy populism: it deserved the care and professionalism that it got.

The success of the 2012 opening ceremony, and of the BBC's coverage of it, are now accepted facts. I watched it on the night amid a group of BBC Sport colleagues with my heart in my mouth – knowing how fine the line is between triumph and tragedy. But walking home afterwards in the early hours of the morning to our flat in Hackney, I passed groups of people still out on the canal towpaths who had been watching the ceremony on their mobiles and, across the water, in real life as the fireworks had illuminated east London. Judging by the number of empty bottles on the grass, they had been having quite a party. If ever you could say there was a 'buzz' it was that night: there was an unmistakable sense that it had been not just all right but breathtakingly brilliant. It only remained to see what the television audience numbers had been like, and here we had had relatively conservative predictions. Given that a home nation's World Cup match gets around 20 million viewers, we would have been pleased if we had matched that. Very few programmes these days break the 10 million barrier. But when the ratings popped up on our computer screens at 9.30 the next morning, we found we had exceeded our expectations by a mile. The average audience throughout the period of 9 p.m. to 1 a.m. was 23.4 million, with a market share of 84 per cent. The peak was 27.3 million, and more than 20 million were still watching at half past midnight. These were the best figures since the current television ratings systems began, and the largest audience on any channel in the twenty-first century. We press-released and tweeted and Facebooked the glad tidings: we wanted to reinforce the story that this was already a success, and there were sixteen glorious days yet to come.

I would never have imagined that those sixteen days could run as smoothly for the BBC as they did. After the Diamond Jubilee pageant disaster, which involved muddy lines of communication and confusion about who was in charge, Mark Thompson had designated me to be the single point of referral below him. If anything cropped up – from national emergencies and editorial crises through to scheduling clashes – I would be on call to deal with them at any hour. There was a fantastic team around me, of course, but I expected to have interrupted nights and early morning conference calls and executive meetings to deal with whatever the Games threw at us. I thought it would be like being back in news at the time of war: unrelenting and difficult. Instead, it was unrelenting but surprisingly easy. Dave and I were in the office from before eight in the morning and left usually after ten in the evening, and there were television schedules to debate and plans to be tweaked and feedback to be given. But I have never been so impressed by the enthusiasm and dedication of the BBC's staff, exemplified by the lads (they were almost all lads) in the video editing area. They put in long shifts in an oppressive room buried in the middle of the IBC, crafting the montages of the day's action, which never failed to capture the emotion of each event as well as its thrills.

What became clear early on was that alongside the raw material delivered to us by LOCOG and the IOC, it was the broadcasting that was winning the nation's admiration. We had not put a lot of money into our studios, which, to ensure that we had a backdrop of the main venues, were in the park about ten minutes' walk away from the IBC. They were made up of the World Cup studio from 2010, recycled and plonked on top of giant containers, along with a roof terrace where BBC Three plied its trade. To comply with IOC rules, they were not branded, and we were unable to advertise where the BBC was in the park. But the public immediately worked it out, and the studios were routinely besieged by large crowds – especially in the late evening when Gabby Logan's highlights show was on air. That was when the day's medallists would arrive to be interviewed, and we sometimes took them into the mêlée accompanied by a roving camera so that we could capture the triumphant athletes meeting their fans. Viewers at home seemed to be enraptured too. The ratings remained at stratospheric levels, and our stars' popularity shot up.

The most notable phenomenon was the nation finally recognising what a great broadcaster Clare Balding is. In our discussions with the BBC television channels a couple of years out, the one thing that tended to make the schedulers' lips curl was the idea that the early days of the Games would be dominated in the peak schedule by swimming. For them, swimming was something for BBC Two on a Sunday afternoon, if they really had nothing else to show, and less of a crowd-puller than athletics or the major cycling events. But we were sure that swimming presented in the right way would be a winner for BBC One, and Clare was central to that. We always wanted her to be 'on location': in the heart of an event rather than spending too much time in the studio. She is at her best prowling round the winning post of the Grand National or on the towpath for the Boat Race. And, as we watched her in the opening nights of the Olympic swimming, bantering with Ian Thorpe and interviewing Bert le Clos, awash with pride after his son Chad's gold medal, we knew that was the right call. 'Why can't everyone be like Clare?' asked Jan Moir in the *Daily Mail*. *The Guardian* agreed: 'The biggest national treasure to emerge from the 2012 Olympics may be the BBC's Clare Balding.'

This is the kind of thing that tends to curdle the milk in other presenters' morning coffee. They all want to be a national treasure because it is in the bloodstream of anyone who ventures in front of a camera. But the team stayed remarkably harmonious because, in my view, they were all at the top of their form. I think Gary Lineker is consistently underestimated: it is a miracle that a great footballer can also turn into one of the best television presenters of his generation. He and Sue Barker and the rest of the studio anchors created the relaxed, informed atmosphere we wanted on air – from opening to closing, and at all points in between.

It was unashamedly patriotic coverage, too. Everyone remembers the behind-the-scenes footage of the BBC athletics team going crazy as Mo Farah won his gold medal, and it was, of course, our doing that those pictures made it into our main broadcasts and onto social media. We were rooting for Team GB, and we wanted everyone to know. Critics sometimes misunderstand this as compromising our journalistic integrity, but to me it has always been simple: sport coverage can be partisan when a national team is involved, while the news output retains an obligation to be measured. Audiences can perfectly well understand Gary Lineker willing on England in a World Cup, but would be less understanding if Fiona Bruce read the news wearing a Three Lions shirt. And there was a marvellous alchemy in the summer of 2012: Team GB were putting in the performances of a lifetime; LOCOG had created a Games that fired up British pride; and the BBC was the means by which this reached the public. One night I stood on the BBC roof terrace with Mark Bright, who was working as one of our football pundits, and, as he surveyed the crowd below and then looked over to the Olympic Stadium, he said simply: 'I have never been so proud to be British.' Millions of people would have joined him in that.

There was, though, a small media flurry about whether we were being over-patriotic. This arose from our regular conference calls between the Olympic Park and BBC headquarters, in which Mark Thompson took part, along with the major divisional directors. It had been a theme for a day or two in the middle of the Games that we were bothered about the news programmes over-focusing on Team GB, and we had discussed the fact that a British bronze was often getting a higher place in the bulletin running orders than even the most stellar gold-winning performance by a foreigner. There was no concern at all about the sports programming, but the message had been passed on to the news division – with, seemingly, little effect. We therefore decided to make the case a little more strongly, and Helen Boaden sent some of her editors an email marked 'An order from the DG'. She wrote: 'Mark Thompson is increasingly unhappy that we are focusing far too much on Team GB's performance to the exclusion of all else … As editor-in-chief, he has issued a directive that this needs to change from today. So you need to get cracking on making that shift.'

In the finest traditions of BBC News, it took mere minutes

for the memo to leak to the press. They ignored any distinction between news and sport, and went for the predictable headlines: 'BBC ordered to stop being "too patriotic" over Olympics coverage', with stories saying that 'channel controllers' had been told to switch their focus away from Team GB. Initially, we thought this had the potential to be detrimental because we believed we had overwhelmingly got the content and tone right, and the idea that the director-general was unhappy with it, or disliked patriotism, was damaging to us and to him. The moment the leak received publicity, there was a rumbling about 'bloody management' within the IBC. The press office therefore took the relatively unusual step of issuing a statement in Mark's name, with a careful delineation between the different areas of output:

> I am as delighted as our audience and the whole BBC team about the brilliant performance of Team GB – and it is quite wrong to suggest otherwise. The BBC has been right to focus on sporting achievements which the whole country has been celebrating and we will continue to do so with pride. We can do that while at the same time making sure that our news programmes fully reflect some of the other great sporting achievements and human stories of the London Games.

With this, and some robust briefing, the story rapidly deflated.

And those were our tactics throughout. We knew we had a lot at stake in the Olympics and the scrutiny of our output would never be more intense, so we had a team trying to squash erroneous stories before they became damaging. When there was a Twitter campaign against Trevor Nelson's commentary on the opening ceremony, we answered the complaints as soon as they arose, and later tweeted the audience survey results showing that he was liked by the majority of viewers. It was via Twitter that we were first aware that there were problems with the on-screen data from the road cycling. Again, we were able to explain what was happening – that it was a problem outside our control and originating from the organisers and the host broadcasting operation – and Gary Lineker was tweeting an apology within a few minutes of the issue arising. This may sound an obvious thing to do for anyone familiar with the modern practice of PR, but it was less than automatic for the BBC. Indeed, much of the crisis around the Jubilee Pageant had been caused by the failure to explain what was going on and the absence of suitable BBC representatives for interview. Instead, we had locked ourselves in the bunker and received a more prolonged kicking. This was a lesson learned, though arguably forgotten again after the Games.

All of us in the leadership of the BBC Olympics spent long days in the Broadcast Centre obsessively monitoring the output and the reaction to it. The peaks of each day were when the production staff would stand around the monitors, yelling for Team GB competitors as they went for a medal – and a gold always generated a cheer to lift the roof. By the time of the start of the athletics, just over a week into the Games, I was feeling sufficiently confident about the operation to give myself a break from the IBC and go to hear the cheers of thousands more people at an actual event. The irony of having a pass that would get me in to any venue was that I saw almost nothing live. But its virtue was that when I did, it was in the VIP area: the seats designated for 'the Olympic Family'. I therefore got myself into the main stadium with Dominic

Coles watching Mo Farah strike gold, with the Duke and Duchess of Cambridge just ahead of me, Ed Miliband appropriately to the left, and the Prime Minister, David Cameron, with Boris Johnson just behind. This led to a moment of misfortune. We were naturally proud of our twenty-four online streams and our mobile services, and the opportunity occurred to show them off to the Prime Minister. The amazing night of athletics was drawing to a close in London, but Team GB's men footballers were locked in a battle with South Korea in Cardiff. It had been 1–1 at full time; extra time had failed to break the deadlock and it was going to have to be resolved by penalties. David Cameron asked us what the score was, so Dominic brandished his smartphone. There, courtesy of the BBC's innovation, was the penalty shoot-out being streamed live. Cameron, Johnson and ourselves huddled over the screen – only for it to freeze just before the crucial moment when Sturridge missed his penalty. Cameron took it with the good spirits of a man who knew he had no need of football to make London's Games a success, while Dominic tried to grab what advantage he could from the disappointment. 'That shows why we need more money for the licence fee,' he said. The Prime Minister laughed.

This struck me later as being the opposite of what normally happens. An innovation can be demonstrated successfully to the top brass, only to fail when it reaches millions of regular viewers. Thankfully, we had almost no glitches at all in the streaming and the catch-up services or in the delivery of the twenty-four channels. To our pleasure, they ended up being among the most popular of all digital services, taking around 5 per cent of total television viewing, despite the dominance of the flagship coverage on BBC

One and BBC Three. One day I went into the newspaper shop in the Olympic Park and heard from the assistant, who had no idea I worked for the BBC, the perfect self-portrait of the digital generation. 'I was watching BBC One on the TV last night', he said, 'and I had another event streaming on my iPad. And then I was tweeting to my mates about the British golds. Fantastic!' He was not alone. Our slogan – 'Never miss a moment' – was coming true, and you could take delight in sharing the moment with family and friends and the whole nation.

They, and I, wanted it never to end. But on Saturday 11 August, I sat with Mark Thompson in the video editing area of the IBC, watching the montage to end all montages: an item for our programme on the next day, the final night. It played images from the Games accompanied by the words of Seb Coe from the opening ceremony: 'There is a truth to sport, a purity, a drama, an intensity, a spirit that makes it irresistible to take part in and irresistible to watch.' The pictures were of Ennis and Hoy and Bolt and Phelps and Wiggins. 'For us too, for every Briton, just as the competitors, this is our time. And one day we will tell our children and our grandchildren that when our time came we did it right.' The tape ended with pictures of the cauldron that was still flickering a few hundred metres away from us, but would soon be extinguished.

Tears were flooding down my face. 'Oh look, Roger's crying,' said Mark, loudly, but not, I hope, too unsympathetically. And they were not the only tears of those closing hours of the Games. I have never known such shared emotion as in the production gallery when the final show came to an end, and among the presenters and commentators. We made our way home through the crowds of people who had been there for the dying moments of the 2012 Olympic Games, savouring the memories they would never forget. Britain had done it, London had done it and we had done it too: we were elated and knackered, and proud and bereft. Now that golden time was over, never to return.

CHAPTER 11

DIRECTORS-GENERAL

W
HEN I BECAME director of sport, and again in my last year as director of London 2012, I joined what was claimed to be one of the BBC's top decision-making bodies: BDG, which stood for BBC Direction Group. Those executives outside it wanted to be on it, while those on it never quite figured out what it was there for. Actual decisions seemed to be made somewhere else in the organisation, but the greatest benefit was hearing direct from the boss about what was on his mind – and Mark Thompson's mind was always a subject of fascination.

One evening our meeting stretched into a dinner and we started talking about Lord Reith: how he had been the founding father of the BBC but had ended up estranged from it, consuming little or no television and radio. This set Mark and the rest of the table ruminating about how few directors-general ended their time at the BBC happily. We went backwards: Greg, who had come a cropper over Hutton; John Birt, who had seen his inheritance handed to Greg, the candidate he didn't want; Michael Checkland, who had lost out to Birt in seeking to continue as DG; Alasdair Milne, who had been unceremoniously sacked by the chairman. Indeed, said Mark, it seemed that the last DG to leave cheerfully and on his own terms was Ian Trethowan in the 1980s. 'It makes you wonder why anyone wants to do it,' he mused – a man who had been appointed only the previous year to the job he had always seemed destined to do.

I never imagined at any point in my career that I would be DG. It had never been on the radar when I was in radio, and if I had wanted to build a Thompson-like career I would have moved earlier to television. But watching DGs close up, I lacked what made each of them distinctive: the precision and long-term strategic vision of John Birt, the ebullience and showmanship of Greg Dyke, the tactical brilliance and the rhinoceros hide of Mark Thompson. Thankfully, I always knew that was the case for me: it is a terribly difficult job, with the bodies of the defenestrated as its proof.

John Birt was the first DG I witnessed at the top level. He was not popular with the staff, and that included senior staff: the most common occurrence was to come across someone leading a division or a project who was fuming about the DG's apparatchiks sending back the latest version of a paper because it didn't fit the approved corporate approach. 'Iteration' became word of the day, meaning endless rewriting of papers for a sclerotic bureaucracy. I saw the worst of this in the high temple of Birtism: the annual performance review. I was part of this for BBC News in 1999, and the best part of two days was set aside for it. Enormous amounts of work from our strategists went into capturing every factoid and number that might be required by the corporate centre, and as news board, led by Tony Hall, we had rehearsed our lines and were ready for scrutiny.

It turned out to be one of the most peculiar experiences of my working life. I had imagined we would talk about the content and strategy of news programming; instead we devoted hours to baroque performance indicators which were grouped graphically into something called 'the BBC cathedral'. Birt was worried that we hadn't captured the most meaningful data properly and we fretted collectively not about the main TV news bulletins or the *Today* programme but about whether the colour-coded scorecard had properly changed from amber to green. My colleague and friend Linda Anderson gave the south-west London contingent of news board a lift home in her car, and colleagues who had worked on the review uttered a cry of anguish: 'It's mad, completely mad.' A few years later, performance review under Mark Thompson was done in ninety minutes for the whole of the Journalism group, which then included not just news but BBC Sport and the controllers of BBC Scotland, Wales and Northern Ireland.

Some of those close to Birt at the time say that what provoked this behaviour was fear of his own instincts. He had studied engineering, and one of those who observed him at close quarters said he sometimes seemed to yearn to think like a machine: if all the data could be collected, the answer could be definitively nailed down.

He was not a compelling public speaker, and his meetings with staff tended to be stiff and over-formal. A briefing with a group of editors before the start of the Gulf War in 1991 needed an Agincourt-style rallying cry as we began one of the most challenging and intensive periods of broadcasting, but instead he turned in a stumbling performance – which, I wrote later, 'left us thinking it might be better to strap ourselves to an Iraqi power station than cover the war Birt-style'.

Yet his instincts, as I had found when I took over 5 Live, were good. And actually I enjoyed most of my encounters with him, as long as they didn't involve the BBC cathedral. He would send notes about incidents on 5 Live, which proved he was listening. I had a handwritten note from him in April 1997: 'Roger – out of curiosity: why did the line go down so many times during the Liverpool *v.* Man United match? John.' He also did more than any other DG in my time to invite middle-ranking staff to dinners and social events. The dinners in the Broadcasting House executive suite had a Birtian twist: you had to look under your plate at the start of the evening to see if it had a red dot underneath. If it did, it meant you had to move four places to your left after the main course to ensure a circulation of hosts and guests around the table. After he had left the BBC, I sat alongside him at the Germany *v.* Argentina match in the 2006 World Cup, with his passion for football overflowing. But he allowed himself a wry joke about my transfer from news to the former lads' paradise of BBC Sport: it proved the critics wrong, he said, in that the BBC had clearly moved upmarket since his departure.

But Birt's personal style mattered much less than his achievements, and here I am an unalloyed fan. He came to the BBC as Michael Checkland's deputy after one of the routine periods of internal turmoil – in this case the sacking of Alasdair Milne – and he captures the scale of what he faced in his autobiography: 'I battled on many fronts. Against old Lime Grove, against green-eyeshaders in the newsroom, against bone-headed baronialism and obstructionism in the television service, against an illiberal government – all under the eye of a hostile press. I experienced deviousness, lack of steadfastness and dishonourable behaviour.' That could have been written by any number of senior BBC folk over the years, though I used to call the old guard in the newsroom 'the men in cardigans'.

But Birt managed more than anyone else to change the organisation. He rightly invested in news and in journalistic specialism. He was correct, in my view, that BBC News needed to be distinctive and what we reported should pass a test of its significance, and he saw the potential of digital technology way before anyone else. As far back as my *World at One* days we were contemplating a future in which people could opt for the news they wanted to consume in the order they themselves chose – a decade or more before this became mainstream. When I went on a course to the INSEAD management school in 1999, expecting the public service BBC to be way behind the curve in modern business, I was surprised to find that we were talking a language that private industries were still struggling with: I knew a lot more about the potential for e-commerce than they did.

It was smart of Birt to seize on the possibilities of 24-hour news after the experiment with Gulf FM – the Radio 4 rolling news service – during the first Iraq War. That led directly to Radio 5

Live. Then he pushed the BBC into online news and the launch of BBC News 24, all the time taking money out of the conventional services and investing in digital to a background of incessant moaning from the people who were losing out. He was right and they were wrong, and the BBC's benefits from its first-mover advantage in online are visible to this day.

There were also positives from John's emphasis on management. The flipside of the frustration of senior managers as they ground through their iterations was compensated for by the process, at least, being clear. There was a corporate machine that took in the data and eventually churned out a signed-off plan. This was a contrast to the Dyke and Thompson years, when at times it was difficult to work out where decisions were made. There was a helpful image in the offices used by the different DGs. Birt's was oak-panelled, at the front of Broadcasting House and was used by the great figures of the past. Dyke and Thompson moved into modern spaces, even open-plan, and there was something of the spirit of the time in their move towards sofa government.

The immediate thanks that John Birt got when he left was his replacement by Greg Dyke. There was a telling vignette about the way power changes in the BBC at the leadership lunches, which Birt had introduced. They had no seating plan and for years ambitious executives manoeuvred their lunch tray to sit as close as they could to Birt. At the first meeting when Greg was in attendance as DG-designate, the crowd had moved on: John sat at a sparsely attended table while Greg was surrounded by courtiers and job-hunters. The Vicar of Bray came to mind. Later, Greg cheerily described his manifesto for the job as 'anti-Birtist' and, in an entertaining clash of autobiographies, Birt claims he helped Dyke get the job, while Dyke asserts he knows how hard Birt worked to stop him. In this case I think we can safely say that Greg is right, and when he started working at the BBC he found the outgoing DG and his senior team 'were disliked, even loathed' by large numbers of the staff. Within the executive itself, he wrote, 'they had learnt how to operate as competing individuals within a climate of fear'.

Within BBC News, there was trepidation about the new regime. Birt had, rightly in our view, transformed the resourcing of the news division; Dyke was seen as more of a showman, with his LWT background and his fostering of Roland Rat at GMTV. Our boss Tony Hall had been his rival for the director-general job and, in what had been at times an unedifying campaign, there had been leaks and insinuations about all the candidates, leaving an atmosphere of mistrust. Indeed, we were marched off to a news board away-day at which the facilitator said that we should have the same mentality as a company that had just been subjected to a hostile takeover. In the event, Greg left news largely untouched, except for the hugely enjoyable *Ten O'Clock News* campaign, and Tony's departure for the Royal Opera House removed any remaining tensions as the calming figure of Richard Sambrook moved into the top job in news.

I owe my best time in the BBC, outside the Olympics, to Greg. He was determined to change the culture of the place. To do that, he set up what seemed initially like another set of task forces and working groups, so loved by Birt, but Greg's 'Making It Happen' project was different. He wanted to involve all the staff – and he meant all the staff – in debating how the BBC could be better: being more creative, hacking back the bureaucracy and finding

the best leaders. He signalled his intent by theatrically brandishing a yellow card and proclaiming his mission to 'cut the crap'.
Initially, my role seemed unpromising. I was put in charge of the
group called 'We are the BBC', which Greg explained to me as
trying to counter the apparent view that 'the BBC' was something
alien to its own workers: staff would blame 'the BBC' for decisions
they didn't like, and they would regard the corporate centre as 'the
BBC', which was somehow in a different universe to their daily
lives. My job was to identify how we could become 'one BBC',
with everyone feeling they were part of the same enterprise, and
I was charged with defining the values of the organisation to help
that along. Greg emailed a brief after an exploratory visit he made
to US companies:

> In every organisation we visited, the values that organisation
> lived by were clear and were articulated to everyone in a sim-
> ple way. At the BBC we don't do that. We need to be very clear
> about our objectives and the values that support them and then
> we need to tell our staff and the world what they are and make
> sure we all live by them. Simple.

This fuelled what turned out to be the most interesting of the
Making It Happen groups. Despite the predictable sniping from
inside and outside the organisation, most of the staff loved the idea
of being able to nail down what it was that made them proud of
the BBC. Discussions were held from Aberdeen to Truro. Cynics
were gratifyingly outnumbered. The coalition of the willing relished the chance to define how people should behave: respecting
each other as colleagues, and showing the right attitude to the

public who funded us. I would not pretend that the values we came up with are quite the equivalent of the Gettysburg Address, and I still have some friends who ruthlessly mock them, but they felt right to people within the organisation and are still to this day on the back of every BBC identity card:

- Trust is the foundation of the BBC: we are independent, impartial and honest.

- Audiences are at the heart of everything we do.

- We take pride in delivering quality and value for money.

- Creativity is the lifeblood of our organisation.

- We respect each other and celebrate our diversity so that everyone can give their best.

- We are one BBC: great things happen when we work together.

Hearing from the staff, and realising that we wanted to achieve the same thing, was uplifting, and presenting the values back to the BBC was a strangely emotional experience too. We held a management conference in the Custard Factory in Birmingham, as a mark of Greg's funky new BBC – and Peter Salmon, presiding over a session in his customary folksy way, urged everyone to thank me for my work on the values by giving me a hug whenever they next met me. The result was being pursued around Birmingham by tipsy members of the Human Resources department, keen to capture the hugging spirit of the times, while other colleagues moved smartly in the opposite direction to avoid the embarrassment of it all. But I felt Greg gave us permission to be ourselves. It was at that conference that I talked in a plenary session about growing up adopted in our post office in Bradford, to fill in some of the story about me as an individual and to enable others to feel that, whatever their background, the BBC was for them too.

Some of this openness was inspired by a visit to companies in the United States that Greg laid on for the Making It Happen team. It started farcically. We were in the departure lounge at Heathrow when one of our number spotted two men unknown to us who were perusing photographs of the BBC senior management team. This could mean only one thing: the *Daily Mail* were on our case. We could see the headlines about BBC profligacy as we boarded our plane, business class, en route to the agreeable W Hotel in downtown San Francisco. An in-flight emergency conference decided that we would split up when we got to San Francisco to avoid the photo that would make the story complete: a luxury bus-load of BBC executives busy metaphorically shredding dozens of licence fees. It was only some days later that we saw the two men again. They were Europe-based executives of one of the companies we were visiting, who had been innocently doing their homework about the BBC people they were going to meet in America.

But the trip made me and others think radically about the world of work. We criss-crossed the US, visiting a restaurant run by former convicts in California, and a shampoo factory in Chicago. We loved the spirit of Southwest Airlines and their willingness to bust conventional ways of doing things, and we shied away from the over-formality of Ritz-Carlton Hotels. We realised that creativity isn't achieved by waiting and hoping that someone comes up with a good idea, but by working at it and understanding audience needs, before you test ideas and shape them again and again. Most of all, we understood what it means to be a team. One night, weary after an early start on the west coast, we flew into Dallas just as the city was emptying for the night. Most of us wanted to go to the hotel and crash out before another working dinner, but Greg had other ideas. 'We gotta go see the grassy knoll,' he proclaimed, and redirected the bus to take us to the Texas School Book Depository, where he marched us round the JFK museum just before its closing time. He was right, of course, and the week in America was when I felt closest to my senior colleagues in seeing what Greg's BBC might become.

This is not to say that Greg was relentlessly sweet and fluffy. Like anyone who gets to the top of the media industry, there was a core of steel, and you wouldn't choose to get on the wrong side of him. I had a flavour of that when a lecture I gave at St Andrews University displeased him because of my criticism of some aspects of digital television. I had run the speech past an array of senior colleagues, including the press office, before delivery, so the DG's indignation turned on them and I came across Richard Sambrook doing a version of the old sight gag of holding the phone a distance from his ear while Greg berated him for letting me say what I had said.

Which brings us to Hutton. This was the prolonged crisis started by Andrew Gilligan's report on the *Today* programme about the intelligence assessments of Iraqi weapons and whether they had been sexed up by Downing Street. It is, looking back more than a decade, one of the oddest of all the BBC's crises because Gilligan was overwhelmingly right, and Greg's instincts were right in defending the BBC against the bullying of No. 10. It is Lord Hutton's report into the affair that has not stood the test of time, looking more one-sided than ever and uncomprehending about the nature of journalism. And yet it was while events were unfolding, rather than with hindsight, that there was unease about the way Greg handled things: one of his strengths became, in that unremitting spotlight, a vulnerability.

Even as head of television news, I was an observer of this crisis rather than a participant. It was one of the hallmarks of the way it was handled that it was kept to a small core team: Greg and his people in the corporate centre with Richard Sambrook and Mark Damazer from news. I remember anguished conversations with senior colleagues claiming that the Gilligan affair had barely been mentioned at executive board and asking what I had gleaned from news board – to which the answer was the same: very little.

It is, of course, perfectly understandable that the DG would lead on a matter of this gravity, but what he lacked in enough volume were the voices of caution asking what the exit strategy was from his increasingly ferocious war of words with Alastair Campbell. As John Ware said in a *Panorama* report on the crisis, Greg effectively bet the farm on Gilligan's 100 per cent accuracy – and, even allowing for the flawed Hutton process, almost no daily journalism can bear that kind of stake. I was reminded of what I had told Peter Oborne for his study of Alastair Campbell, published in 1999, which described the rapier strikes within the bludgeoning by Campbell and his spin doctors: 'Often Labour complaints had some substance. That was their cleverness. If there was a glimmer of an inaccuracy they were on to you.' Alongside the incoming fire on the corporation from Downing Street, I was receiving emails from Labour MPs who were friends of the BBC, questioning our approach. 'What is going on, Roger?' said one. 'I have the impression the BBC is still in total denial. The very future of an organisation that I love and value is being put at risk.'

In his book, Greg describes it as a mistake that he responded too quickly and too vehemently to one of Alastair's provocations, and it was: the approval from the staff for Greg's 'standing up for the BBC', perhaps fuelled by the spirit of Making It Happen, drowned out the more measured arguments about de-escalating the row. The model of how to handle it was already there: Thames Television's setting up of an independent inquiry into its documentary 'Death on the Rock' showed how a broadcaster could best retain control of a spiralling controversy. Greg could similarly have told Alastair he wasn't going to reply to any more of his letters until an investigation had got the bottom of Gilligan's story. This may sound like the caution of someone wearing the grey suit of the BBC bureaucracy, but it is in the nature of the BBC that its independence has to be defended with care and due process. The point at which your employees are cheering you on and the adrenalin is coursing through your veins is the point at which you need to pause, take a deep breath and call for a few wise old birds from the corporate backroom who will guide you through.

Yet, despite any misgivings about how he had handled it, it felt like a terrible blow to the BBC when Greg was forced to resign immediately after the publication of Hutton. What was unedifying was that this had been a battle that the BBC collectively had waged, and at key moments the governors had backed the position of the DG – which then made it illogical that they demanded his head based on a strikingly unbalanced assessment from a judge. But yet again there was no room for a wider assessment of the DG's worth or any sentiment about an individual who had fought bravely for what he believed to be right. I have never before or since seen the mass emotion from the staff at anyone's departure, let alone a senior manager – and I watched as the normally cynical television newsroom gave Greg a standing ovation as he made his farewell tour of the building. The contrast could not have been greater with the joyless 'clapping-out' of John Birt by a small number of corporate centre apparatchiks when he left Broadcasting House for the last time.

At this point, Mark Byford made a five-month appearance as acting director-general. I had not encountered Mark much before, but what I had seen hadn't created a favourable impression. There was puzzlement about how someone so young and so professionally Yorkshire had got to the top of the BBC, fuelled by a question about who the real Mark Byford was: the populist, bear-hugging enthusiast or the strategic wise-head who had ended up as John Birt's preferred successor. He had then been propelled into the deputy DG role towards the end of the Gilligan crisis, allegedly at the behest of the governors, and people muttered darkly about the nightmare ticket for creative freedom if Gavyn Davies and Greg Dyke were forced out: 'Pauline Neville-Jones or Richard Ryder as chairman, Byford as DG.'

Mark's early moments acting as our leader didn't win hearts and minds. The unreserved apology he and the acting chairman Lord Ryder made about the BBC's errors over Hutton was unavoidable for any corporation after a public inquiry, but the awful staging of it and the repetition in subsequent days of the word 'sorry' meant that morale sank still further – especially in the journalism areas, where people could see the brutal consequences of the slightest mistake. Mark was also unlike any other BBC leader we had come across. He turned up at a news board meeting to try to cheer us up after the traumas, and immediately told us how he planned to do that: 'I will love you.' He repeated the words, more slowly. 'I. Will. Love. You.'

And in the months that followed, Mark Byford did a wonderful job in healing the BBC when its wounds ran deep, and he became one of the people I most liked and respected in my time there. He was always on hand with advice, and it was invariably wise. The more you knew him, the more his personality became endearing rather than irritating – which is the opposite way round to many media folk. The hand he had to play as acting DG was a difficult one: the staff still yearned for Greg, which made new leadership a tougher challenge, but normal business had to resume with the right balance between journalistic enterprise and accuracy. There was also political pressure, most conspicuously from some BBC governors, for an accounting for the errors of the past. If the chairman and the DG had lost their jobs, what about the people on the coalface who had brought about this collapse, in their view, in the reputation of BBC News?

If you know the people involved, that was an absurd position for anyone to take. Richard Sambrook, Mark Damazer, Kevin Marsh and the rest are journalists of the highest integrity. The idea that people like Kevin should be subjected to what he calls 'the process' in his book about Hutton – essentially a disciplinary process without using the 'd' word – was only compounding months of external mauling. Some years later I read Charlotte Higgins's excellent essays about the BBC in *The Guardian*, and Richard Sambrook's quote leapt from the page:

> After Hutton, I'd say it was about two years till I got over it. It was the first thing I thought about when I woke up in the morning and the last thing I thought about when I went to bed at night, every single day. What happened there? What could I have done differently? To what extent was I culpable, or not culpable?

I never experienced horrors on that scale, but I witnessed enough people who did – and I had enough troubled hours of my own caused by lesser stories – to know the emotional truth of what Richard said.

George Entwistle, even more bizarrely, was dragged into the process because of *Newsnight*'s alleged failure to connect a Susan Watts briefing from David Kelly with the Andrew Gilligan story based on the same source – despite the fact that both had generated stories on flagship programmes and nobody else made the immediate link either.

There was a view at the time that the process was Mark Byford's fault, and he should have stopped it. In reality, my sense is that the process was foisted upon him and he did his best to manage it humanely and to keep all the individuals on board. In that, he succeeded. It would have been an unforgivable outcome if more heads had been placed on spikes outside Broadcasting House.

With his reputation for possessing a safe pair of hands, Mark came within a few days of being appointed the BBC's next director-general when the date was set for the job interviews in April 2004. But then Michael Grade was selected as the new chairman of governors, and the DG race was suspended. Things within the BBC are sometimes taken as established facts even if nobody's quite sure of their evidential base, but there was an immediate assumption: Byford wasn't Grade's type of chap, whereas Mark Thompson was. And so it proved.

Mark Thompson was the man everyone always thought would be DG. On the day he was appointed as editor of the *Nine O'Clock News*, the same day I became editor of *PM*, he was tipped as 'the man most likely to rise to the top'. There was a presidential air about him even as a 29-year-old. What was unusual about him when he became DG was that, even as someone who had been at Channel 4 for a couple of years, he was 'one of us'. John Birt, as he once said himself, to much chortling from the staff, came from another world, and the showmanship of Dyke was different galaxies away from BBC traditions. Between them, they had run the BBC for more than a decade, and the previous incumbent had been an accountant. But Mark was a BBC programme maker through and through: graduate trainee, news editor, channel controller, regional director, head of television. It felt like someone like us was back in charge.

I enjoyed working with Mark. Most of the time when he was DG, I was in sport – an area that interested him personally not one jot. But he knew the importance of sport for the BBC, and I learned to admire his ability to improvise on subjects about which he knew little. At an early meeting with BBC Sport producers, he was asked what he thought about our coverage of live golf. I am close to certain that his golf-watching had been confined to ten minutes a few years previously while he'd been waiting for *Newsnight* to come on, but he delivered an articulate and editorially credible analysis of BBC golf from flimsy foundations. When it came to sports rights negotiations, he was tigerish in his competitiveness. There was never any chance we would lose *Match of the Day* under his watch, and he gamely flew out with me to Georgia to profess an enduring love of the Masters to the Augusta Club when we thought the rights were vulnerable to Sky. He was unflinching in his commitment to the 2012 Olympics.

For the BBC, this was the era of Mark T and Mark B. Mark T performed the smart move at the start of his director-generalship of entrusting Mark B with the whole of the journalism portfolio, thus putting distance between the DG and the kind of news issues that had brought down Greg. Watching Mark T announce this at a leadership session, it struck me as both right and tactically brilliant: Mark B was there to catch the crap. What soon became apparent, though, was that the two Marks were complementary. Mark T was at his best in his lightning assessments of changing circumstances and his ability to seize advantage from them, while Mark B was the person at his side saying, 'But if you do that now, Mark, you'll be giving yourself a problem in three years' time.' Michael Grade had described Byford as 'the conscience of the BBC', and Mark T said he 'never had a closer or more supportive relationship with any colleague'.

I can vouch for it being an excellent combination, and its strengths were manifest in two of the bigger crises of the Thompson era: the mess over rigged competitions and the meltdown caused by Jonathan Ross and Russell Brand careering out of control in their programme on Radio 2. After losing a DG over assessments of weapons of mass destruction, to have lost the next one over the naming of the *Blue Peter* cat or rudeness towards an actor from *Fawlty Towers* would have been bathetic; yet there were moments when the edifice felt close to collapse, and it was the Thompson–Byford partnership that shored it up.

But these turned out not to be the real crises burrowing away underneath the corporation. It was only after both Marks had left that we found out about the horrors of Jimmy Savile, which had been unknown to us. But the problem about money was more obvious as something that had been building up for some years: at its baldest, everyone at the top of the BBC – and I include myself in this, with a salary that reached £270,000 a year – was being paid too much. The figures from 2010 are noteworthy for being so much more than the same roles attract now. The DG received a total remuneration package of £838,000, close to double what Tony Hall gets; Jana Bennett as director of television was on £517,000; and Mark Byford was receiving £488,000 per annum. A key figure from the Trust floated the idea that it was possible the next DG would have to be paid £1 million a year if the BBC was to attract the best talent in the world, and internal minds boggled at the people in the HR department earning around £200,000 a year, with their director on £320,000.

In fairness, this madness was apparent across the public sector in the pre-crash years in the pay given to council chief executives and university Vice-Chancellors and NHS administrators. But some things were unfortunate for the BBC. It was a problem that John Birt and Greg Dyke and Mark Thompson could all have earned much more elsewhere. Mark's successor as chief executive

at Channel 4, Andy Duncan, was paid a grand total of £1.48 million in his final year there. This meant that chief executives who
had made a real sacrifice were probably slower to see that the
corporate pay bill was still way too large. It was also unhelpful
that Freedom of Information made all top BBC salaries visible to
everyone in the organisation. What it did was fuel pay requests
from staff who saw what their colleagues were earning, and it
ratcheted up inflation. It would also have been better if a Fran-
ciscan nun had been chairing the BBC's executive remuneration
committee instead of the chairman of Barclays Bank.

Curiously, though, it was in tackling this – arguably somewhat
belatedly – that there was a fateful moment for Mark Thompson
and the BBC. The priority in 2010 became cutting pay and being
seen to be run in as lean a way as possible, and as part of those
discussions Mark Byford did a very decent thing. He offered to
leave the BBC if his presence as deputy and his salary were part of
the problem. Byford would never have made that offer if it hadn't
been a serious one, but it must nevertheless have been a traumatic
moment for him when, after a period of consultation, Thompson
accepted it. I, more than most, knew how little Byford wanted
to go. He was chairman of the London 2012 steering group and
he had set up the structure I was running, and there was no one
more passionate about delivering the Olympics. He also loved his
job chairing journalism board, in charge of news and sport and
the nations. So it was a shock when his senior team was called
into his office one by one in the October of 2010 to be told: 'I'm
going. I'm leaving the BBC.' For once, I wanted to give the famed
bear-hugger a big hug himself – but, fortunately for the dignity
of the occasion, we managed to restrain ourselves. The emotion

was real, though, and Byford's departure turned out not to be just a moment of personal sadness.

For a start, Mark got a pay-off that ultimately made him the poster boy for the deficient executive culture of the BBC. As far as he was concerned, he took what he was offered. As far as the BBC was concerned, it was trying to do the right thing for a long-standing servant of the corporation who had sacrificed his job. As far as the public was concerned, it just didn't wash – and the grisly parliamentary hearings in 2013 were a reminder of the disconnect between the media culture and the real world, even though there was a credible underlying story about the millions of pounds of savings, far exceeding the redundancy costs, that the BBC had made in its executive ranks.

But worse than that, Byford was absent when new crises hit the BBC. I cannot imagine the Savile affair spiralling out of control if Mark had been sitting alongside George Entwistle. Mark would have had a grip on all the Diamond Jubilee coverage in the same way that he did for the royal wedding. Even in the routine day-to-day affairs in the closing months of Mark Thompson's director-generalship, we missed the steadying hand of Byford. The re-created autonomous news division never had the steadiness that it had gained within journalism board, and the nations' directors saw less of their boss when that boss was the DG rather than the DDG. What it had needed, of course, was a piece of classic Byford advice when Thompson came up with the politically smart idea of making him redundant: 'But if you do that now, Mark, you'll be giving yourself a problem further down the line...' Byford was, arguably, the best DG the BBC never had. He was certainly the deputy that every DG needed. It is hard to think of anyone more devoted to the BBC and its ideals, and his energy was formidable, even if it meant for people like me a constant bombardment of ideas throughout the day and into the night.

His reputational reward was much less than he deserved, though that applies too to the people who made it to the very top: Greg having to resign, John Birt being derided as a Dalek, Mark Thompson being assailed after his departure on pay-offs and Savile. Thompson was right to muse about why people wanted to do the job at all.

But, as ever with the BBC, there is a test greater than the corporate reputation, and that is the strength of its programme making and the level of audience trust in its content. When we think back to the political hostility to the BBC at the end of the Thatcher era, and the explosion of competition in the digital age, the fact is that the BBC at the end of the Birt, Dyke and Thompson directorgeneralships was in far better health than anyone would have predicted in 1990. It was still the dominant broadcaster of its age, buoyant because of the robust health of the flagship services such as BBC One and Radio 4 and the innovation of online and iPlayer and the rest. If the buck stops at the top for things that went wrong, it should stop there too for what went right.

CHAPTER 12

TRANSITION

A s I was being ferried back home on the day after the Olympic closing ceremony, Chris Patten phoned me. It was a call of congratulations on a job well done by the BBC team. Curiously, though, that was it from the Trust. Given their inclination to break open the white wine for what some would deem to be lesser events, like the retirement of a trustee from Wales, it is in retrospect perhaps odd that they never gave the Olympics leadership team a drink or sent a thank-you note. We must assume many of them had been watching BBC Two and BBC Four for their alternative content. By contrast, we had a glowing public tribute from Mark Thompson:

> As a once-in-a-lifetime broadcasting moment draws to a close, I want to pay tribute to every single person in the BBC who has helped to bring London 2012 to our audiences ... It's needed total commitment and great stamina through very long hours, but everywhere I've been over the past fortnight I've seen amazing team-work, passion and utter professionalism. The result has been the best coverage of any event by a broadcaster that I have ever had the privilege to witness.

The team and I also had a wonderful email from the former BBC chairman, Michael Grade:

> I am lost in admiration for your virtually flawless coverage. I watched wall to wall, HD, Red Button, Radio 5 Live, Olympic DAB channel, online, you name it. If ever there was a killer argument for the licence fee, this was it. For less than the cost of a day ticket to the hockey, you got the full Olympics, pick and mix, all you could eat! A total triumph, editorially and in every way ... Congratulations, Team GB and Team BBC delivered way beyond expectations. You should be SO proud of what you planned and executed. The Corporation will be calling your achievement in aid for the next 100 years!

The week after the Games I slept more than I was awake. Long nights, supplemented by afternoon naps, got me over what felt like an extreme version of jet lag, and my only disappointment was not having the Olympics to watch when I woke up. But I had an intriguing few weeks ahead of me. Working as director of 'Vision' – as television was then, irritatingly, still called – was a decent prospect while I sorted out what my post-Olympic life was going to be like. I could think of nothing in the BBC that would ever give me the thrill of London 2012, and my inclination was still to leave rather than to stay. I did, however, like the idea of working with George Entwistle as he established himself as director-general, and television was the powerhouse of the whole organisation, with a budget of more than £2 billion. An immersion into that world for six or seven weeks, until a permanent appointment was made, could only be a good thing. In fact, I was there for nine months and served under four DGs: Mark Thompson, George Entwistle, Tim Davie (acting) and Tony Hall. This was a period with diminishing amounts of joy in it, and the source of cheer in the gloomiest hours was plotting how to escape. It was a year without any sense of mission.

I started in television just a week after the Olympic closing ceremony to find that most of the rest of the division had gone on holiday, exhausted by the Games. So I enjoyed myself by going on a day trip to Cardiff to see the Drama Village and walking around the sets of *Doctor Who*, *Casualty* and *Pobol y Cwm*, the Welsh soap. I caught the train to Bristol and met the amazing team behind BBC Natural History, who were attracted by the lessons from the Olympics about creating 'event television' alongside their crafted films. I found most of the people in television to be welcoming, though the BBC edged back to type after the collective effort of the Olympics: there was a sense of some folk playing politics and eyeing the succession, and it is never easy to be in an acting role.

The best you can do is keep the business of a division moving along, which I think we succeeded in doing; though the weeks of the Savile crisis made that extraordinarily difficult.

What you cannot do in those circumstances is duck decisions. The recent history of the BBC shows that a decision not to broadcast can be worse than a decision to transmit, and one of the examples of that involved Donald Trump. In October 2012, as the Savile affair was raging around us, BBC Two had scheduled Anthony Baxter's documentary film *You've Been Trumped*, which was an unflattering but funny account of the tycoon's creation of a golf resort in Scotland. This had gone through our compliance procedures in the usual way, but on the Friday afternoon ahead of a Sunday transmission we received a humdinger of a letter from Trump's lawyers. If we went ahead with the broadcast, they said, they would complain to Ofcom and the BBC Trust and reserved the right to take legal action. A Trump spokesperson described the documentary as 'a piece of propaganda that is wildly inaccurate, defamatory and deliberately misleading'. We went through Friday night in a flurry of legal and editorial policy consultations, and I phoned George to let him know what was going on. My instinct was that this was a classic example of last-minute pressure around an unfriendly programme, but we didn't want to take needless risks. If this went wrong, it would feed powerfully into the 'BBC crisis' story. I certainly got no sense of equivocation from the Trump lawyers. They even called me on my mobile on Saturday when I was pushing a trolley round Waitrose. I was being lectured by New York lawyers alongside the cheese cabinet.

We decided to broadcast the programme as scheduled and without any cuts. A strong defence was that it had been shown as a film in cinemas in North America and in Europe, and it was only when it made the transition to the BBC and a mass television audience that the rhetoric against it built up. The Trump people asked for a right of reply for one of their representatives immediately after the programme, potentially standing alone as a piece to camera, and we denied them that. We said, however, that we would be delighted to welcome Mr Trump as a guest on *Newsnight* the following night if there were points he wanted to make. Paxman *v.* Trump would have been marvellous box office. But our invitation was declined, and instead there was a barrage of condemnation from the Trump organisation. Donald himself tweeted: 'The BBC is widely criticized for a lack of professionalism. We dealt with a Roger Mosey – a total lightweight who doesn't have a clue.' I had never previously been called light. George Sorial, Trump's chief counsel, was quoted in *The Guardian*:

> The BBC is now an active participant in what many … know is a complete false telling of the story behind the construction of Trump Golf Scotland. I would say Roger Mosey should certainly resign or the BBC should consider firing him. We're filing complaints with Ofcom and the BBC Trust and are considering other available legal actions.

To the best of my knowledge, no complaint was received, and in this case it is apparent that the alternative course, of delaying the programme, is what would have added to the momentum of a 'BBC crisis'. It would have been about loss of nerve, and giving in to corporate interests. But these decisions are never so clear-cut at the time that you have to take them.

The other challenge was maintaining quality on air amid the management meltdown. The Saturday evening on which George Entwistle resigned was part of Remembrance Weekend, with the commemoration at the Royal Albert Hall next in the BBC One schedule after the newsflash that he was stepping down. The following day we were live at the Cenotaph for one of the nation's most solemn moments, the two-minute silence. On Friday it was Children In Need. All of these needed to be as flawless as possible to avoid another wave of controversy washing over us, and Children In Need was a particular test. We were concerned that trust in the BBC had slumped to such an extent that people might not donate to the charity, especially given the stories emerging each day about Savile and children he had met on BBC premises. To address this, Terry Wogan delivered a script about the effects of child abuse, which began simply and unequivocally: 'Children should be able to trust adults. That should be a given. Our role is to protect them.' There was relief when the money raised beat the totals of previous years, and Children In Need avoided any damage through its association with a tarnished BBC.

We needed to make sure, too, that the appalling acts of previous decades were not made worse by bringing them into the present. That is why a commemorative plate painted by Rolf Harris did not make it onto Children In Need. We knew by then that the police were taking an interest in Harris's crimes, though at that point there were only allegations and he had not been arrested. I later saw a website which, not knowing the true reason, apologised to customers:

Earlier this year, there was talk of manufacturing a Diamond

Jubilee plate designed by Rolf Harris to raise funds for Children in Need. Despite having received numerous enquiries from customers, we are sad to report that this project will not be going ahead. No doubt the BBC has other things on its mind.

Few people had spotted the omission, but it was impossible to explain why it had happened when investigations were continuing. That was a problem that came up time and again through that autumn. We could remove the known guilty from the air, as in the case of Savile: we dropped all editions of *Top of the Pops* that featured him. We could not edit out of archive programmes, or withdraw from advertised live appearances, those about whom there were suspicions but not yet charges, and all the time we bore the risk that a wrong call would result in another reputational blow. 'They knew he had been accused of something serious, but the programme still went ahead.'

In television, the fact that benign Savile obituary programmes had been broadcast the previous Christmas increased the nervousness. Every time someone died, or a tribute season was planned, I would receive a call from a scheduler in my role as divisional director and gold commander: 'Is there any reason you know why we shouldn't broadcast a programme about X?' We never lost sight of the fact that it was the victims of sexual abuse, and our audience's understandable anger about the past, that necessitated this caution. But it was a jittery few weeks, working with Tim Davie as acting DG, as we tried to balance maintaining normal business with minimising the risks of further damage to the corporation.

If there was any light relief, it came from the impending move of BBC television from its home of more than fifty years, Television

Centre, to New Broadcasting House (NBH) in London. As divisional director, I oversaw the transporting of many of our staff and their belongings along the Westway to what was, in all sorts of ways, a wonderful new space. However, I had experienced some of its pitfalls already. NBH was predominantly open plan: it was designed to increase interaction between different teams and to break down barriers – or, as we called them in the BBC, 'silos'. The intention was that I would have no individual office myself, and I would be perched on a chair at one end of an area shared with television HQ staff and some programme makers. I worked from there during some of the Savile crisis, and discovered immediately that conversations from the far end of the office were transmitted perfectly to my ears by the excellent acoustics. This made me sure that any of my confidential chats or phone calls would go back the same way. I asked to move into one of the small conference rooms to ensure privacy, and was granted my request – only to find that, even with the door shut, I could hear every word spoken by a woman ordering coffee outside. It turned out that some of the walls deliberately did not reach the ceiling, for reasons of air conditioning, and there were ducts in the floor that relayed sound along them to the outside offices. I learned to speak much more softly than I had been used to.

Many television colleagues were also less than keen initially on their new home. The channel controllers had chosen a space on the sixth floor of the building which, at first sight, had looked as though it gave them a quieter area than most. When they got there, they discovered that they fronted onto what had become a busy walkway. They sat neatly in a row, accessible to all, and at one point were 'door-stepped' by a visiting journalist. Someone described them as sitting there like disconsolate check-in staff for a budget airline, and they soon demanded new desks and – where possible – partitions and defensible space.

Humour was to be found, though, in the meeting rooms. The excellent sitcom *W1A*, whose commissioning I approved while I was in television, must have found it hard to satirise their names, because we really did have finance meetings in 'The Del Boy Room'. My windowless meeting room for guests was called 'Nice to See You', and it must have been a narrow squeak that its companion space was not called ''Allo, 'Allo'. Up on the seventh floor, the break-out area used for conferences and seminars was splendid – except for its literal openness, which allowed guests for Radio 1 on the eighth floor to march along a corridor directly above, either chattering to each other or ear-wigging on the discussions below.

This is not to detract from the success of the building overall, because most of the time it worked: you bumped into people much more often than in Television Centre, and it broke down the hierarchies in a refreshing way. It was just not the ideal place for the most sensitive of conversations, as the controllers pointed out to me every time they had to have 'secret' talent negotiations in glass-walled rooms with a hundred pairs of eyes looking in. It was not all done without cheerfulness, though, and I became fond of Janice Hadlow on BBC Two and Richard Klein on BBC Four, both of whom did a tremendous job in commissioning shows that were a pleasure to watch.

As if my life was not complete with being responsible for the whole of BBC television, I was given the additional role of chairing the BBC's Editorial Standards Board. As its title suggests, this looked at standards and policy across the organisation, and it was paralleled by the Trust's Editorial Standards Committee, which would receive reports from the management as well as running its own complaints process. I went into this with reasonably good spirits, but it soon became the most tiresome of chores. I had, up until this point, got on fine with most trustees, despite my differences with some of them about sport. But after George's departure, and with the cathartic thought that 'I really don't have to work here any more', I didn't hide my feelings when I found Trust processes baffling or irritating. This included having to deal with their impartiality reviews, which took an enormous amount of Trust and management time to little apparent result.

With the one exception of Anthony King's work on devolution, which changed the BBC's journalistic output for the better, I am not sure any of them made us much wiser. On rural affairs, for instance, which was underway during my time there, it was predictable that the report would conclude that there should be more about rural affairs, or, as the Trust put it, the BBC 'must tackle the deficit in its network coverage of rural England'. It was also inevitable that the review would call for the reintroduction of a rural affairs correspondent. Most reviews demanded new on-air or off-air editors to pursue their subjects. I had once, in television news, drawn up a list of all the things that well-intentioned regulators wanted us to do more of: arts, business, sciences, religion, European affairs, the developing world – the list went on and on. But there was almost nothing anyone wanted us to do less of, and the network bulletins remained stubbornly just twenty-five minutes in length. I am not aware of any BBC Trust report into a specialist area that called for less of it.

Rural affairs was actually one of the more sensible reports, but others contradicted each other. The science review by Steve Jones concluded that climate change was settled science and that we should reflect that – only for the impartiality review by Stuart Prebble to criticise a piece on the College of Journalism website because it was 'entirely devoted to sustaining the case that climate change is effectively "settled science" and that those who argue otherwise are simply wrong'.

For the most part, journalists simply shrugged their shoulders and got on with the job. In so far as the reports had an effect, though, they were about greater co-ordination and centralisation of policy. This is a good thing on issues of fact or legal matters. It is more of a problem if it seeks to shape opinion across an organisation with as many outlets or as much market share as BBC News. I have always believed in editors editing their individual programmes and fostering as much diversity as possible. It is better if they choose different stories and fresh treatments, rather than offer a table d'hôte menu cooked up by the centre. My worry was that the Trust's wish for 'compliance' across the BBC, with their view of a desired agenda, would erode programmes' autonomy – the right, sometimes, to be contrary.

The one thing that kept me sanguine throughout this was the knowledge that I didn't have to stay: I could retire from the BBC when I turned fifty-five in January 2013. I could do what I thought was right in television without bothering about the politics, or the obsession in some quarters about ratings, and I could say what I believed to be true to the Trust. This made my relationship with them even chillier. But there was the backdrop of the appointment of Tony Hall as director-general, and the dilemma that caused for me. I liked and rated Tony, and we had kept in touch throughout his Opera House years. I had phoned him after George left and told him he was the person the BBC needed as DG. We therefore had a number of meetings about the organisation and its challenges after his appointment had been announced, and while he was still at Covent Garden, all of which were warm if slightly fuzzy. At one meeting, in a supposedly out-of-the-way coffee shop, the Arts Council chairman Peter Bazalgette was on a nearby table and waved cheerily at the BBC conspirators. In truth, we were skating around the question of what I might do – with Tony saying appropriately kind things, and me wishing there would at least be a concrete proposal. I hoped to conclude my unexpectedly long role in television and to get some certainty back into my life. I had not been offered a permanent job after the Olympics and nor had the BBC served me notice of redundancy. The previous autumn's jitteriness was still hobbling the organisation, and that was worse for those without a guaranteed role. I was in limbo, with a not altogether helpful thought in my mind: I wanted to be allocated a new post, but I was also pretty sure I would turn it down. The best thing for me to do was to leave, and yet I would have preferred to have an external job to go to, and the autumn of 2012 had offered no time to look for one. We meandered through the early weeks of 2013, with some of Tony's pieces slotting into place but warm fuzziness still the order of the day for me.

It was in the middle of February that I got an email from one of my colleagues, Barnie Choudhury. He attached an advertisement from an academic website for the Mastership of Selwyn College, Cambridge, with a note: 'Just in case you need a new challenge… I think you'd be great.' I later saw the ad in the *Sunday Times*. Being head of a college was something I had considered before: I had enjoyed the many visits I had made to universities and colleges in the build-up to the Olympics, and my Wadham heritage still meant a lot to me. I decided to apply, though with the belief that it was the longest of long shots. This was Cambridge, which I had visited only half a dozen times in my life, and I was a broadcasting executive seeking a role at a college where all the previous Masters had been academics or ordained priests or both. I sent off my CV and a covering letter, and thought little more about it.

The BBC wheels continued to grind slowly. Eventually they disgorged advertisements for two roles: director of television and director of news. Both were jobs that I might have been qualified for, though neither excited me, and in any case I was clear with Tony that I was not going to start putting myself through an application process. He had agreed that I would be offered something at an appropriate level, and I received an email from the HR department accepting that I would not run for television or news and saying, 'The key thing, Roger, is that we want you to stay and we need you. We're doing everything we can to resolve this quickly.' It was therefore useful to bump into a Media Guardian journalist at an awards ceremony and to give an honest answer to the inevitable question about my intentions. Ben Dowell asked me, 'So are you going to apply for both jobs, then?' and I said, 'No, neither' – which took him aback because there is normally hedging, or straightforward lying, when personal prospects are discussed. He wrote a piece, which got the story out ahead of any interviews. I had previously experienced *The Guardian* being convinced that I was a candidate for director of radio in 2008, when I had never applied, and it was not unknown for colleagues to express sympathy on losing out even when you had no interest in a role. Ben's report said:

> Roger Mosey, the BBC's acting head of Vision, has not applied for the senior posts of director of television or director of news and is thought to be ready to take on a new role at the corporation. Mosey, who was regarded as a potentially strong candidate for either role after overseeing the BBC's successful coverage of the 2012 Olympics, is understood to have spoken to incoming director-general Lord Hall over continuing his 33-year career at the BBC with a new post. He declined to comment.

That last bit was odd, really, because I had not only given *The Guardian* their story but I had said I was happy to have it on the record.

Tony finally arrived at the BBC at the start of April. I tweeted supportively after his first executive meeting on 2 April: 'Tony Hall's first management board has just ended. It felt cheerful and upbeat.' It did. Tony's gift is to make it feel that a grown-up is back in charge, and he has a fundamental optimism that is reassuring while also being a silky political operator. I then showed that I wanted to get away from the BBC and its burdens by flying off to Australia two days later for my first visit there and a first long break since the Olympics. I loved it. Drifting along the Swan River outside Perth on a glorious autumn day, consuming the wines of South Australia in Adelaide, and eating fish and chips in the shadow of the Sydney Harbour Bridge: it was a marvellous antidote to what had felt like a long, grey winter in the BBC. I took the boat out to the Olympic Park from 2000 to check that there is life after the Games, but I spent almost no time at all thinking about work, which was a contrast to my quest for news and BBC gossip when I had been on long-haul holidays in the past. In those days I used to reach for my phone or laptop at every moment. In Australia, I needed them mainly for the football scores from back home. I did, however, get an email from Selwyn College while I was away, in which they invited me for a first interview at the beginning of May.

I arrived back in London in late April in a relaxed frame of mind, though my role in television was ending in about three weeks' time following the appointment of Danny Cohen. That appears finally to have galvanised the BBC into making me a job offer, and when it came it was a decent one. I was walking through East Sheen on the way to meet George Entwistle for a long-arranged supper when HR head Lucy Adams called me to float the idea that I should become editorial director. I would be working direct to Tony on three things: big editorial issues that cut across BBC divisions, longer-term editorial policy, and overseeing major events. It was obvious that there was a flavour of the old Byford role about this, including the bit where you do the things the DG wishes not to do.

A revitalised George, who was generally positive about me taking the job, spotted the downsides as we chatted over dinner: 'It's the Hand of the King from *Game of Thrones*,' he said. I was unfamiliar with the show, but when I checked it out later – he was right. I was used enough to catching the flak, or worse, that this aspect of the role was fine, and being involved with the Commonwealth Games and the First World War commemoration was appealing enough too, though I kept thinking that neither of them was quite London 2012. I edged from 'say no and leave this summer' to 'maybe give it a go'. The next day I went to see Tony to talk about the role, and afterwards I reasoned that I would enjoy working with him again and it was a credible way of spending the next year or two. I was pushing thoughts of retiring from the BBC to 2015, after the general election, rather than straight away. I did tell him that I had a 'live' job application externally. 'I hope you don't get it,' he said. 'Don't worry, I won't,' I replied. I accepted the job of BBC editorial director, not convinced I was doing the right thing, but feeling I would at least give it my best shot.

In the following couple of weeks, my Australia-induced calm was tested. I was winding up my time in television, getting ready for the new job and also dashing round the country – first to Cambridge for the Selwyn interview, and then to Lincoln, where I had put in an application for the unremunerated role of chairman of the council at Bishop Grosseteste University. It is a former teacher training college that became a university in 2012, and it owes its splendid name to the theologian and scientist Robert Grosseteste, who lived in the thirteenth century. My thinking was that the experience would be good for my CV, and it might help win a role in higher education further down the line. Rather like being editorial director at the BBC, I was unsure whether Bishop Grosseteste was right for me, but I knew it to be a decent place, and I had the family loyalty to Lincolnshire that made it more compelling. So I stayed in that process as well as the Cambridge one.

I had never been to Selwyn College before my interview on 2 May. From the website, I had formed the image that this was Cambridge's version of Keble College, Oxford, which I had always found a rather forbidding piece of Victoriana, based on experiencing it on a foggy day in December 1976. In fact, sur-rounded by spring blossoms on a sunny day, Selwyn felt like Keble's much prettier sibling, and I liked it from the start. I also immediately warmed to Michael Tilby, the Vice-Master, who was organising the Mastership election and greeted candidates with sandwiches and coffee in his rooms overlooking the Old Court. The first round's format was simple. The college's Fellows had signed up for one of three sessions with me, and I had to take questions from the different groups over post-lunch coffee, after-noon tea and pre-dinner drinks. I was not short of refreshments. I had no idea beforehand about the culture of the college, which in Oxbridge can range from the pleasantly informal to the frankly stuffy, but Selwyn had an instant appeal. The Fellows seemed to be down-to-earth and practical – not playing politics, and seemingly engaged with what I had to say. I told friends afterwards that I sensed one or two people at this stage saying to themselves, 'Elect the man who brought Formula 1 back to the BBC? I don't think so!' But I felt heartened by the reaction in each of the sessions, and I went to the next part of the ordeal – dinner – in good spirits.

I can now say with certainty that if you are invited to dinner in Cambridge while you are applying for a role, then dinner is emphatically part of the process. The college may smile and say that it is the social finale after the hard work of selection, but can-didates should not believe them: how you handle conversation and the giving or receiving of hospitality is part of the scrutiny. This is not for snobbish reasons. It is important that heads of col-leges can be sociable and make guests feel at ease, because they deal with literally thousands of different individuals each year – academics, students, parents, alumni and distinguished guests

– and being a hermit would be an inappropriate qualification. So your first dinner is monitored closely. I had an enjoyable meal. Possibly humouring the broadcasting executive who had landed among them, some of the High Table conversation was about *Britain's Got Talent* and *Doctor Who*. The Law Fellow was debating whether the victory of a Hungarian dance troupe was quite in the spirit of Britain having talent. There was also a lobby for Joanna Lumley to become the new Doctor Who.

Another kind of doctor, the Vice-Master, walked me to the college gate afterwards. 'Thank you so much for coming, Mr Mosey,' he said. 'You have been most...' (and here he paused, briefly) '... entertaining.' Entertaining? On the train home I had two thoughts in my mind. The first was that Selwyn was a lovely place, and it had been a stimulating way of spending a day. I relished the combination of friendliness with intellectual skirmishing. The second was that 'entertaining' must surely, in a Cambridge context, be a bad word, rather like 'brave' when attached to an editorial decision. It conjured up images of BBC One Saturday night, not the magisterial figure who had typically led a college. I concluded that it had been a worthwhile experience, and I would know in future not to be entertaining, but I should apply myself to the editorial director role at the BBC and put aside thoughts of the outside world.

Five days later I was in Lincoln for my interview at Bishop Grosseteste University. It went smoothly: so well, in fact, that they called me back in immediately afterwards to offer me the post. By coincidence, this was also the day that the BBC decided to announce publicly my new role, and I was therefore pacing the corridors of the university talking to the BBC press office about their media release as well as thanking the Vice-Chancellor for inviting me to be his chairman.

Afterwards, I met Les Sheehan on Lincoln's Steep Hill for some pasta and beer. 'Congratulations,' he said, cheerily. 'Today is the day you got two jobs you didn't want!' That was, of course, overstating it, and I have enjoyed my role at Bishop Grosseteste. But I felt mildly depressed that night about the BBC job, seeing the risk of a grey, corporate and uncreative future for me, even though the media comment was positive. *The Guardian* said I would be the 'go-to man' for handling major editorial issues, and *The Times*'s headline was 'Roger Mosey to make the BBC's big calls'. In *The Observer*, Peter Preston wrote: 'Applaud gently as Roger Mosey, all-purpose BBC troubleshooter, becomes Tony Hall's Mark Byford (without the deputy title, or the salary). That makes perfect sense: a seasoned broadcaster able to watch the boss's back.'

Home again in London, I set to work back-watching. I was stationed outside Tony's office in an open-plan area with the rest of the HQ team, and, since access is essential to making this kind of role work, I could grab hold of Tony any time I wanted to. I had teams to oversee, too. There was an area working to me that was led by David Jordan, who was director of editorial policy – which sounds satirically similar to being editorial director, and indeed our titles were often muddled up. The difference was that David and his colleagues would offer advice based on their expertise in guidelines and broadcasting regulation, while I was there to help editors by making decisions and taking responsibility for them. I also started getting stuck into the major events, and especially the Commonwealth Games. I realised that part of what had made London 2012 work was the knowledge I had of how to get the best out of the BBC machine, having run sport and television news and being able to drop a word in the ear of the people leading television or radio. It was tougher for the BBC Scotland people trying to build up the Commonwealth Games, most of whom were unaware of some of the foibles of channel controllers and knew less about which corporate button to press to get something to work.

The atmosphere in the BBC in the spring of 2013 had been lifted by Tony's arrival. It is hard to imagine anyone doing a better interim job than Tim Davie had done, but it was Tony who had to move the BBC forward. Watching from close quarters, I was unconvinced that the structures around him were a help in doing that. The DG is chairman of the executive board and, as part of the reforms of the mid-2000s, the board has non-executive directors too: outsiders to the BBC. They were good people to have around, but they not unreasonably took the view that one of the lessons of the catastrophe of the previous autumn was that the NEDs should be more knowledgeable about what was going on in the BBC, and sometimes more assertive in making their presence felt.

The problem was that was also the lesson that had been taken away by the Trust. They wanted to scrutinise what the BBC executive was up to, and they too had some wise trustees. One issue apparent to the management was that some of the cast lists could have been interchangeable: the former news executive Samir Shah had been an NED, while the former news executive Richard Ayre had become a trustee. What this structure had done at its worst was to make the DG and his colleagues have to jump through two hoops not one to get something done: they had to get NED approval and Trust approval for some courses of action. But even on routine business, many items went through both the executive board and the Trust – and if you factored in the management's own routes for approval, through the various lesser boards, it too often felt like *Groundhog Day*. Greg Dyke's mantra of 'Just do it' was some miles away from reality, and Mark Thompson's hope of creating a simpler organisation had similarly not been realised. Tony was right to promise 'a bonfire of the boards', though the unwieldy structure at the top remains.

This headache might not have mattered if doing all this committee work had ensured watertight compliance and excellent decisions. We were about to be shown that this was far from the case. Tony had brought his optimism, but the sky was still full of black clouds. The first one to dump its rain upon us was the Digital Media Initiative, or DMI. Technology projects are often complex and have a high failure rate, but this was a shocker. It had started as the idea of bringing almost all the BBC's content together digitally, allowing sharing and archiving and editing across divisions. I had encountered it during Mark Thompson's time, when it was a brilliant concept but not actually functioning. There was one management awayday in the mid-2000s when we discussed DMI as potentially being the BBC's gift to the media industry; something that could be shared with independent companies and partner broadcasters. But at that point it could not even connect two rooms within Television Centre, and it got little better. By early 2013 it was apparent that it just did not work, despite expenditure of around £100 million. As a management board we took the decision that it was better to kill it than try to cure it, and we went public with the admission that £98.4 million of licence fee money had been written off.

We knew another storm was imminent. In the aftermath of

George Entwistle's departure, the National Audit Office had asked if it could examine George's pay-off and report on it to MPs. The BBC Trust refused to allow that, but instead, in December 2012, it asked for the NAO to take a broader look at severance packages for BBC executives. It was already known that Mark Byford had received a settlement of £949,000 and Caroline Thomson, more recently, £670,000 – with George's pay-off put at £450,000. The Trust commented in a press statement: 'We have received [the NAO's] schedule of work for 2013, and we are pleased to see that they will take this approach in a planned review for next year.' When the report reached them in late June, they were markedly less pleased. The NAO revealed that the BBC had breached its own policies on severance

> too often and without good reason … This has resulted in payments that have not served the best interests of licence fee-payers. Weak governance arrangements have led to payments that exceeded contractual entitlements and put public trust at risk. The severance payments for senior BBC managers have, therefore, provided poor value for money for licence fee-payers.

In the weeks ahead of the NAO report, our management board had taken the best pre-emptive action we could by radically changing the pay-off structure. Tony was able to declare that in future it would be no more than £150,000, which was a potential cut of hundreds of thousands of pounds for people like me who had previously been entitled to two years' salary if they were made redundant. There was a raft of other measures to tighten up procedures. The management response included the context that the £25 million spent on pay-offs would deliver savings of more than £90 million, but that was lost in the understandable public outrage at what had been going on. What then happened in the response to the NAO was that the Trust, in the view of many of us on the management board, overplayed its hand. It went into battle with the previous management. When we saw their statement in response to the NAO, we were dismayed by its vehemence – and partly because we could see that the Trust was not going to escape the criticism raining in on the BBC. The Trust talked of a 'fundamental failure of central oversight and control', and then noted – correctly – that they are 'not empowered under the Royal Charter to intervene directly in decisions around individual employment arrangements'. But they encapsulated the confusion in this area by adding that 'although the BBC Trust cannot play a part in approving … individual remuneration or severance packages, we do, as the BBC's governing body, have an overall responsibility for value for money'.

It was correct that the Trust constitutionally could not and did not approve the severance packages, but it was also manifest that they knew they existed and the level of them, if only by reading about them in the papers. Mark Byford's had been in the BBC Annual Report. Mark Thompson said they had been fully briefed, though the Trust denied it. In fact, my experience is that the Trust often asked the management for more information about issues like this, even if it was only by informal routes. Therefore, cried the outside world, if the Trust knew this has been going on for some years, and they are responsible for value for money, why did they do nothing about it? The 'fundamental failure of central oversight and control' was a criticism hit straight back at them.

In fairness to the Trust, they had been facing an existential crisis for some years. They were not loved by the management and the staff; they were still a shadowy force to the public; and they increasingly failed to convince politicians that they were the answer to regulating the BBC. It was understandable for them to seek to whack the management over pay-offs, but the result was that the BBC was once again at war with itself: Chris Patten's Trust at odds with Mark Thompson's management, and some terrible scenes were enacted in public before parliamentary committees. It might, with hindsight, have been better if there had been a collective statement by Trust and management: 'Sorry. We all got this wrong. We'll put it right.'

While this was starting to play out, I was called for a second interview at Selwyn College. I was surprised, but excited. I still thought I had very little chance of being elected, but I reasoned that the odds must be moving slightly in my favour. However, I almost pulled out of the contest. As editorial director I was responsible for major obituaries and a couple of days before I was due to go to Cambridge we had the breaking news of two significant admissions to hospital: Nelson Mandela in South Africa and Prince Philip in London. I was sure that being interviewed for an external job would not be a convincing reason for being absent from New Broadcasting House if the worst happened in either case, so for some hours I wavered about whether to pull out and avoid a crisis of conscience. I then decided to let fate take its course. If one of the two aged gentlemen died, I would not set off or I would hurry back to London. If they lived, I would stick with Selwyn. I have never been so grateful for medical science's work as in that June.

The Selwyn interview started in Cambridge at 10.15 a.m. and I caught the 9.15 p.m. train back to London. It was exhaustive and exhausting. I was interviewed by, seemingly, everybody – including student representatives, heads of department and finally all fifty-seven Fellows. The biggest challenge was to chair a mock governing body, again with every Fellow present, at which I had to referee a concocted dispute between the bursar and the senior tutor. There was also a ten-minute presentation at which I was invited to set out my vision for the college. I emphasised the obvious point: I was not an academic, and I was new to Cambridge – so I would have a vast amount to learn. But I believed in what they were doing, in academic excellence and creating a strong community, and I felt my own life, and the benefits I had received from education, would help in making that case. I did something that I would have found difficult in my early life. I talked about my adoptive family and my natural mother, and what linked them. They wanted, in their different ways, to do what was best for a child: a strong family is an ideal, but it is education that can be transformative. I argued that Cambridge must be open to all. There should be no selection by wealth or postcode, but a true meritocracy in which every child who is bright enough, and works hard enough, can aspire to become a member of the college and the university. I was reassured by seeing nods of agreement around the Senior Combination Room – and I tried not to cloud the serious message with too much entertainment.

Another dinner followed. During it, I spoke to the director of music, Sarah MacDonald, who was preparing for that night's choral compline. She suggested I should drop in to the rehearsal on my way out of the college, so I did. As dusk fell on a perfect

English summer's day, I walked with Michael Tilby across Old Court to the soaring Victorian chapel. Inside, softly lit, the Selwyn choir were singing the plainsong of compline. It was an utterly beautiful sight and sound, which moved me close to tears: talented young people, in a wonderful environment, combining tradition with their limitless potential for the future. I caught the train from Cambridge station feeling, quite simply, happy. I had had a marvellous day at Selwyn, even though – or perhaps because – it had been tough and challenging. The next stage of the Mastership process, they had told me, was the vote, in which each Fellow would plump for whom he or she wanted from the final shortlist, and I would most likely be informed of the outcome in a fortnight. But I thought I might never see the college again: it was surely impossible that something I realised I wanted to do so much would become a reality.

The following evening, Michael Tilby phoned me. I had been nominated by the Fellows of Selwyn to be the college's next Master. In a long and overwhelmingly joyous conversation, there was a flicker at one stage as if Michael was concerned that I might say 'no'. The chance of that was zero. It is extremely rare in life that a decision is 100 per cent clear in your mind, but this was one of those cases: when it came to the moment to choose between the BBC and the outside world, it was the world that won by a landslide. I was sworn to public secrecy for an agonising two weeks before the formal election took place, and I was only allowed to tell my family and the most senior members of my kitchen cabinet. But I never hesitated for a moment. When I was finally able to talk to Tony Hall, he was gracious and encouraging: 'I'm delighted for you,' he said. 'Cheesed off for me, but delighted for you. It's like when I took the Royal Opera House. I knew it was something I really wanted to do, and I can tell you're like that with Selwyn.' We told the BBC management board, which was meeting on the morning of the election, about my new destination, and it must have come as the greatest surprise to Tim Davie, a Selwyn alumnus. One of the student papers took a suitably satirical line. 'New Master to make Selwyn "more like London 2012"' was the headline, claiming that 'the current Dean of Degrees, due to retire imminently, is set to be replaced with Clare Balding' and 'the Selwyn Ball has been cancelled in favour of artistic opening and closing ceremonies at the beginning and end of every year'. The reminder of other events of the past year was in the final line: '"It sounds really awesome, but I'm not sure that the proposed inquiry into the culture and practices of Selwyn Fellows in the 1970s is really necessary," said Lisa Stone-Jones, second-year Selwynite.'

I negotiated a relatively speedy exit from the BBC – without, of course, a pay-off, because I was leaving of my own volition. I would go at the end of August, and for much of the time I would be acting director-general because of Tony's holidays and a business trip he was planning. This had been the case a couple of times before, but never for such a long spell: a month in total. It was a month that confirmed that being DG was not for me, and that it is an extraordinarily tough role. The crisis still running through that summer was about pay-offs. We knew that there were bruising parliamentary battles ahead in which the Trust *v.* management war would continue, and we needed to be sure that all the skeletons were out of the cupboard. The initial NAO report had sampled a few prominent cases, but we had to get a picture of everything that had gone on. It was around this time that a senior colleague said to me, 'I can never answer the phone without a sense of dread,' and as acting DG I knew that feeling: someone inside the organisation had found a new problem, or the papers were in pursuit of a previously unknown transgression, or we had been freshly lambasted by a politician. There was one day when the press office phoned me with updates on four damaging stories, on a range of issues, that might appear in the next edition of the papers – only to discover in the first editions that we were back with pay-offs and the claim splashed across page one of the *Daily Telegraph* was that the BBC might be investigated by the Fraud Squad over the alleged misuse of public funds.

There turned out to be nothing new in the story, not least because the NAO had found no evidence of criminal wrongdoing, and the police ruled out an investigation a few days later. But we had already decided to invite the auditors, KPMG, to review any cases where guidelines might have been breached, and the NAO was back at the BBC looking at outstanding severance payments made in the three years up to 2012. Many an executive's summer holiday was interrupted by conference calls with the office in which we tried to make sure that every angle had been covered and that we had credible replies to the questions that were being asked. This was a depressing way of spending July and August for those of us manning the bridge.

To our relief, there was a lull in the 'BBC crisis' story in the second half of August. I looked forward keenly to Tony's return from holiday, and to the start of my new life. Meanwhile, I was able to invite some of my future Selwyn colleagues to lunch or dinner in London, with a short tour inside Broadcasting House to show them what I had been used to for so many years. Watching the

Six O'Clock News with them from the gallery, I remembered why my pulse had raced whenever a story broke and what had been so magical about working in broadcasting. I was sure, though, that I didn't want to go back to it: the journalism was now safely in the hands of the next generation. It served to remind me, too, that dealing with the shenanigans between the Trust and the executive had not been the life I expected when I joined the BBC; for multiple reasons the year from the end of the Olympics to my departure from the BBC had been the toughest of times for my colleagues and for me.

I didn't, however, want to leave downcast. I wanted my memories of my last working day in New Broadcasting House to be good ones, and, with a little re-arrangement of the diary, they were. On Friday 23 August, ahead of a bank holiday weekend, I managed to make all my calls ones that I could do from home, with laptop and mobile ready for any crisis on what was also my last day as acting DG. I didn't go into the BBC buildings. This allowed me to have tea and cakes to celebrate my departure with friends in the DG's office on the afternoon of Thursday 22nd, and then go that night to a Radio 2 concert with the Stereophonics in the BBC Radio Theatre. I took along my godson Jules, a music-lover who is always the most pleasant of companions, and we watched and adored the show – before repairing to the top of the nearby St George's Hotel for a couple of beers. We looked out across the night-time London skyline, and down onto a floodlit Broadcasting House below, and I thought then that I would never regret working for the BBC. But every instinct had been right: it was time to go. Bowing out on a day of cakes and Stereophonics, and as acting DG, was a decent result.

CHAPTER 13

CAMBRIDGE

SEPTEMBER 2013 WAS my first ever month off: free from the
BBC after thirty-three years, guaranteed to be unbothered
by breaking news and not yet in my new role at Cambridge. In fact, I was already spending quite a lot of time around
Selwyn, watching the finishing touches being put to the repaint-
ing of the Master's Lodge and attending my first college events
as Master-elect. But there came a day when I was in my kitchen
in Richmond, surrounded by newly packed boxes, and I had
the most powerful memories of a similar moment in Bradford

thirty-seven years previously. I was once more getting ready to go to university. I had gathered together books and duvet covers, and I had bought a new kettle. A couple of London houseplants were also ready to make the journey to the east. I remembered the pride of my parents as they drove me to Oxford in the autumn of 1976, and I wished they could have been there to see me arrive in Cambridge. But my spirits were lifted by the good wishes of my extended family and friends as I made the move, and by the warmth of the welcome at my new home.

The Master's Lodge is rather more spacious than my undergraduate rooms at Wadham. It was built in 1883 for the Master and thirteen servants, though the servants' quarters have subsequently been hived off from the rest of the building. The ground floor is largely 'public' space, where we have receptions and dinners. It can accommodate up to 100 guests at a time. The first floor is my flat, and the second floor has the guest rooms. It isn't particularly private because it sits in the heart of the college, and people are coming and going all the time – including my terrific assistant, Sheila Scarlett, whose office is in the Lodge. I like having the activity going on around me, and it is a glorious place to live, though it can sometimes be disconcerting to arrive home and find the maintenance team in a bedroom or the catering team clattering round and preparing for an event in the dining room. It took me some time to get used to my title, too. On my first day in the Lodge, when I was upstairs unpacking, I heard a voice from below trying to find out where I was and shouting, 'Master! Master!' I realised after a few seconds of bafflement that they meant me. This was not the way I tended to be addressed at the BBC. However, there is plenty of space to get lost, and the most terrifying thing is when my youngest relatives come to visit and they announce they are going to play hide and seek. It could take weeks to find them.

There is an installation ceremony for a new Master, and mine was conducted by Rowan Williams, the former Archbishop of Canterbury, who is now also a Cambridge head of house. I was allowed to have fifteen guests, so I mixed family with the friends who had meant so much to me over the years, and they watched in the packed college chapel as I was led to the Master's stall by Rowan, reflecting the literal meaning of 'installation'. I felt for a moment that I was being made a bishop rather than becoming an academic. There was music from the college choir on that dark autumn night, reminding me of when I had first heard them, and been so moved, on a summer's evening. Around us were Fellows in the scarlet gowns reserved for special occasions, and representatives of the students and the college staff. I was particularly touched that Owen Chadwick, the longest-serving and most distinguished of Selwyn's Masters, now in his ninety-eighth year, was among the congregation. This exemplified how much community and Fellowship matter in a college, and how change must be accompanied by a respect for traditions.

I then did what I had promised, and set about learning about the college and the university. I went to see students and academics in their lecture theatres, labs and seminar rooms. I visited the Cavendish Laboratory to see a new generation of solar panels being developed; I had a look at the wind tunnels and robot test-tracks of the engineering building; and I watched the dissection of a dog's leg conducted by first-year students in the veterinary laboratory. Everywhere I went, I found incredibly bright, committed people – and some of them had amazing stories to tell. If I had still been on the *Today* programme, I would have had a dozen cracking items about research being done in Cambridge. I redis-covered my roots as a historian, too. Within a few days of each other, I visited the library at Corpus Christi College and gazed at a letter handwritten by Anne Boleyn, and I was taken round the archive at Churchill College, where the original text of Winston Churchill's 'Blood, toil, tears and sweat' speech is kept in a plain box folder. It was extraordinary to see the yellowing, typewritten manuscript, with the sentences set out like poetry, that Churchill had held in his hands in the House of Commons.

Within the college, I relished the discussions with Fellows about their work and I rapidly discovered that chatting with the students is one of the greatest pleasures of all. They are almost all hard-working, super-intelligent and much more socially poised than my generation. Our suppers in the Lodge for the first-years, where we shipped industrial quantities of chilli con carne and curry to the new students, were hugely entertaining, and the conversations often ran an hour or more past their scheduled finish.

Being head of a college entails operating much more as a chair-man than as a chief executive. The idea that you could sit in your study and issue orders to the academics is ludicrous. Despite the grand surroundings, it is still a job: there are the scrapes students get into, the personnel issues, the tasks of refurbishing historic buildings and the ever-present need to keep our finances on track. Selwyn is one of the poorer colleges, with an endowment of around £40 million compared with the hundreds of millions that the richer colleges receive. But I am well supported by an excellent bursar in Nick Downer, who belies his Twitter handle

@grumpybursar, and by a constructive and non-factional governing body. Selwyn, like the other Cambridge colleges, is an
independent entity operating under statutes approved by the Privy
Council – so we hold our destiny largely in our own hands, and
day-to-day college life is a model of simplicity. We have a college
council, including student representatives, which meets every
three weeks or so, and the governing body, with all the Fellows
present, meets once a term and is where sovereignty rests. Where
the complication comes into Cambridge life is in the cherished
independence of all thirty-one colleges, which means agreement
on a common line can take a while to achieve. Then there is the
relationship with the university. For a newcomer, the university's structure of Regent House and Senate and Council and the
General Board of Faculties and more is complex, and it is sometimes hard to know where decisions are made. Some of those
involved aren't too sure either. A senior figure in the university
headquarters at the Old Schools on Trinity Lane advised me that
the process is actually that you put policy documents in front of
every committee you can think of, and when everyone has lost
the will to object it is deemed finally to be agreed. This may be
unfair: there is leadership from our Vice-Chancellor, Professor
Sir Leszek Borysiewicz, who is known to all as 'Borys' and has
the added distinction of being an Arsenal fan. And most of all:
Cambridge works. It is Britain's leading university, and in every
survey one of the best in the world, and it has deftly combined
the needs of the modern world with its 800 years of tradition.
Cambridge is able to boast that it has backed more than 300
high-tech companies and 200 computer-based companies to the
tune of £1 billion, and its links beyond the city and the region

meant that in 2014 *The Independent* could write the headline 'Why Cambridge is at the heart of Britain's economic recovery'.

We sometimes discuss whether the rituals and dressing-up of academic life hinder the image we want to project of a world-class university helping to drive the UK's economy. When I am wearing my cap and gown and processing with colleagues, I am always amused when we are spotted by tourists and there is a shout of 'There they are!' followed by a rush of cameras to capture the lesser-speckled academics in their natural habitat. For a new head of house, some of the rules of academic dress are puzzling. We wear caps and gowns and hoods for some occasions, and doff the cap on entering the Senate House, but no hoods on days of mourning like Remembrance Sunday. Scarlet days mean full finery. Caps are not worn when walking through a college that is not one's own.

Then there is the language of degree ceremonies: Latin. I never thought I would be so grateful for my O-level Latin from Bradford Grammar School. Sitting in the Vice-Chancellor's seat wearing the robes of office with a packed congregation around you is nerve-racking enough, but having to greet the graduands in Latin is an extra trial. We begin '*Auctoritate mihi commissa admitto te ad gradum...*' ('By the authority committed to me, I admit you to the degree of...') and I have come to fear vets and engineers for the '*veterinaria*' and '*ingeniaria*' – each made up of six syllables – that loom in their section. There is room for some playfulness. When I received my own Cambridge MA, a conversion of my Oxford degree, the Vice-Chancellor's role was performed by Stuart Laing, Master of Corpus Christi College. As I went forward to kneel before him, and for him to clasp my hands and confer the degree, he greeted me with a cheerful '*Salve Magister!*' ('Hello, Master!') I doubt that it would have had them rocking with laughter at the Bradford Alhambra, and the truth is that all of this is endlessly parodiable. The people who do not like it will never like it. But I have seen that it matters to the students and academics here, and it respects the traditions of a university that goes back over so many centuries. The important thing is to remember that it is both 'traditions' and 'the future', inseparably linked, and not one or the other.

I am impressed by how hard academics work. There is the cliché about them having long holidays, but almost all of them have a towering pile of commitments. Teaching and looking after students during term-time; preparing series of lectures; helping to run their colleges and their faculties; and, most acute of all, the need to show that they are active in their research – making an impact in their specialist field and regularly publishing their findings. Many are practitioners too, most conspicuously our medics, who are also consultants at Addenbrooke's Hospital. The pay of most academics is low compared with what people receive at the top of the creative industries. A junior research fellow with a doctorate might expect to get around £20,000 a year and a relatively experienced college teaching officer might be on £45,000. Rewards for professors are, naturally, higher, but attracting academics on this kind of pay scale will be an increasing challenge in a city where the property market is almost as crazy as London's.

This was one of the themes we tackled in an informal strategy review during my first year at the college. I was conscious of the need to avoid a media-type consultant-driven exercise, though simply mentioning the word 'strategy' in an email to students prompted a diary item in *The Times* saying that, thanks to me, 'management-speak has invaded Selwyn College, Cambridge'. But the conclusions were resolutely practical: we came up with a set of measures to strengthen our teaching and to reinforce our commitment to academic excellence, and we know we will have to increase our support for less well-off students in the coming years. There are two things which reinforce each other: aspiring to be excellent, and also being a nurturing community. I have been reassured that the people who emerge as Cambridge alumni, like my friends from Oxford, are the very opposite of pompous or self-satisfied, and they are not driven by a sense of entitlement. Most of them have put back into society far more than they have ever taken out, and they are proud of the education and of the values that inspired them.

In a Cambridge autumn, surrounded by novelty, New Broadcasting House seemed a long way away. But I wanted to keep an eye on media issues, and I had always intended to use the freedom I had to comment on current topics. I had made a pledge to the staff newspaper when I left the BBC: 'The most dreary thing in the whole world – and shoot me if I ever do it – is people who write to the newspapers to say things were better in my day.' But I did plan to talk about the future of broadcasting, and ideas had been swirling round in my head during my early weeks in Cambridge. I believe unequivocally in the BBC as a force for good in British life; it would have been odd to stay there for thirty-three years if I did not. But the most dramatic change for me had been leaving an organisation that from the inside often felt beleaguered and battered down, and realising that from the outside it looks surprisingly formidable. When you are a BBC executive, you start the day reading the collated newspaper cuttings about how beastly the press are being to you today, and when you are not a BBC executive, the criticism drifts past you and makes little impact, while the strength of its programmes is manifest. But it seemed to me that the organisation needed to think boldly about its future, and to learn the lessons from what had gone wrong in the recent past. I bounced ideas around with friends and some former colleagues.

The trigger for going into print, which I did in *The Times* in early November, was reading a couple of pieces in other newspapers which seemed to define being a friend of the BBC as supporting a higher licence fee and not requiring much in the way of reform. I felt this was wrong. I therefore argued that more account needed to be paid to the age of austerity in which licence fee-payers were living, and to reassuring them that the BBC was the optimal size for its public service mission. If this was done with skill, and included some measured retrenchment, it might make the corporation simpler to run – which had been the goal of recent directors-general. There was also a balance to be struck between areas where the BBC is under great competitive pressure, such as among young audiences, and those where it can be argued that the BBC is itself too dominant, such as news. It is uncomfortable that the BBC has a market share of at least 70 per cent in both television and radio news, especially when there is an itch for greater central control of the agenda. Plurality and diversity are important in public media, and that is harder if there is one man or woman at the top with the ability to shape so much of it. I noted that the BBC had admitted that it had not, with the virtue of hindsight, given enough coverage in the past to people opposed to immigration or who believed Britain should withdraw from the EU. I went on to make the argument for the BBC to be slightly smaller, and for the BBC not to be the only vehicle for public service media in the UK. There is already some top-slicing, as it is known, in the BBC's support for S4C in Wales, in its subsidy for content from city television stations, and in its levy for the rolling out of rural broadband. I said that 'none of this is an argument for taking a wrecking-ball to the BBC. Its strengths remain manifest', and concluded:

> The BBC should not have to contest its funding year-by-year and should have a guarantee of the dominant slice of the licence-fee pie. But the hard question for the corporation is why in a digital age it should have the whole pie to itself for-ever – when doing something different might be better for the public good.

In its reporting of my article, *The Times*, possibly predictably, went further than I had done by claiming that I believed the BBC was biased to the left, and the piece encouraged grumbling about left-wingery in the usual quarters. I should have been even clearer that the real enemy was homogeneity in news output. Other reaction was rich in its variety. 'Mosey unleashed!' said an email from one of my friends. 'More please.' A number of BBC staff texted their support, and one – Mark Urban – went public describing it on Twitter as 'excellent piece in the Times. I share your view BBC no longer dominated by left. But its liberal values can be suffocating.' More compliments came from people at ITV and Channel 4 and from the independent sector, principally around the idea that there might be financial support for high-quality non-BBC news services. A former chief executive of the Royal Television Society described it as 'thoughtful', and the letters I received at Selwyn were all positive. The official BBC response was measured: 'We want every licence fee payer to have a part in the conversation about the future of the BBC. This is one strand of that.'

Soon, however, there were signs that some BBC insiders took a dimmer view. There was the traditional punishment for dissent: a couple of catty pieces in the *Guardian* diary. Friends still in the corporation conveyed the image of dark corners where pins were being stuck in a voodoo doll. At no point, though, did anyone from the BBC engage with the arguments I had made. My views may be right or they may be wrong, and I would never claim a monopoly on wisdom. But seemingly the only on-the-record response came from the director of television, Danny Cohen, in a speech at a Christmas programmes launch. In the previous weeks, I had not been alone in questioning the size of the corporation. David Dimbleby, Jennifer Saunders and Lord Sugar had all made comments about the size or alleged overstaffing of the BBC, and they were to be followed by Jeremy Paxman and John Humphrys. Danny Cohen started sensibly by saying that 'the BBC is an imperfect institution and "critical friends" are an important way for us to keep improving'. However, he then went on to question why 'some of our on-screen talent and some former members of staff choose to attack or undermine the BBC in public rather than express any concerns they have in private conversations within the BBC'. I tried to imagine that conversation. 'Danny, I'm a bit bothered about homogeneity in news.' 'Thanks so much for calling, Roger, we'll attend to it right away.' I failed.

It seemed peculiar to try to shut down a debate and to exclude from it people who know the territory.

What also seemed to be playing out in some quarters was the view that friends should publicly support all BBC policies, while anyone who questions any of them is slotted into the 'hostile' camp. In fairness to the BBC, this is partly because critical comments are seized on by genuine enemies in the press and Parliament, and there is an unforgiving harshness to much of the debate about broadcasting. But this cannot be the reason for not having the discussion about the size and shape of a great national institution. What, for instance, if someone had recommended in early 2010 that the BBC should have a frozen licence fee for five years, incorporate World Service, help fund S4C and buy newsgathering from rival local television services? The less wise within the BBC would promptly have parked any such views into the 'enemy' camp – but that is the deal that emerged in the summer of 2010. It was markedly better than what much of the public sector got, and towards the end of those five years the BBC was trouncing its competitors in the television, radio and news ratings – and still delivering exceptionally good programmes and services.

A debate about what happens next should never be a bad idea. The BBC is not a little pink sugar mouse that will melt away at the first drop of rain. A few months later, when Rona Fairhead was appointed to chair the BBC Trust in succession to Lord Patten, I gave a comment to *The Guardian* recommending that she do three things: 'Act radically about the BBC's governance; fight for its independence; and be free-thinking about the future shape of the organisation.' I'm pleased that she has come round to the view that the days of the Trust in its current form should be severely limited, and I hope the BBC will step away from the position that it alone must do everything from the licence fee.

These brief episodes of putting my head above the parapet were followed by a multitude of requests from BBC programmes to go on the air to be critical of the BBC. I turned them all down. The only interview I did after the *Times* piece was a slot on 5 Live about why listed events should remain to protect free-to-air sport. Subsequent BBC imbroglios got the phones ringing again.

In the spring of 2015 there was a reminder that the director-general is only a steak dinner away from another crisis, when reports emerged of an assault by the *Top Gear* presenter Jeremy Clarkson on one of his production team. The reason was apparently the lack of hot food after a day's filming, and the offer of a cheese platter instead of the star presenter's desired steak and chips. Given the importance of *Top Gear* as BBC2's most watched programme and a major source of commercial revenue for BBC Worldwide, firing Clarkson must have seemed initially like a nuclear option. Friends inside the BBC spoke of it being back in 'full crisis lockdown', and one emailed me to say, 'The BBC is its usual bonkers self with a bit of added bonkersness right now.' I resisted multiple invitations from *Today* and *Newsnight* to comment while the story dominated the headlines, mainly because it is daft to express an opinion on this kind of thing before the facts are established. I sensed that the BBC had made the crisis rather worse for itself by having placed Clarkson on a final warning when it wasn't altogether clear that his past transgressions were serious enough, and its external communications had wobbly moments, as ever, while the controversy raged. But when it was proven that there had been a physical attack, Tony Hall was right to brandish a straight red card. It was a proper corrective to the culture of presenter power that has lurked in too many programme areas.

Otherwise, I continued to be engrossed by life in Cambridge and I realised that one of the most striking things was how self-contained it could be. Everything I wanted was within a few minutes' walk of the college. Some of the first-year students talked to me about feeling they were in 'the bubble': their whole existence was college, work, lectures and university social life, and things happening in the world outside felt distant. I knew what they meant. One fellow head of house asked me: 'Don't you miss the phone constantly ringing?' and I was happy to say that was precisely what I did not miss. It was a joy to live life as a normal human being, away from the maelstrom of broadcasting. Having spent so many years scouring the papers every day and obsessively watching and listening to bulletins, it was a blessed relief to tune in to a music breakfast show and to catch only the occasional *Ten O'Clock News*. This has its risks, of course, in the jibes about ivory-tower detachment, but the global connections of people in the college and university, supplemented by a stream of visitors from London and beyond, has kept things in balance. The former colleagues who jumped on a train to Cambridge ranged from John Humphrys and Jim Naughtie to Bridget Kendall and Jeremy Vine. Jeremy went punting with his family, disdaining the offer of a professional puntsman. To our collective disappointment, and despite some wobbles, he stayed upright and avoided creating a Radio 2 talking point out of a fall into the Cam.

In my first year I also acquired an unusual animal: a basset cat. I had long wanted a dog, but it had never been an idea that was compatible with my BBC commuting lifestyle. Now, with a flat above the shop, it was achievable. Since animals are banned in the college, save for the Master being allowed to keep a cat, I asked the permission of the college council for a dog to move in – and it was readily granted. It was remembered that Owen Chadwick had kept dogs when he was Master half a century ago. The council secretary, Rupert Thompson, wrote a jokey minute: 'College Animal. Noting precedent under the mastership of Professor Chadwick, Council approved the Master's request to adopt a Very Large Cat in the Master's Lodge.' I duly acquired a sweet-natured basset hound named YoYo, who needed to be rehomed from a pack in Hertfordshire. She moved into the Lodge in January 2014, took over the most comfortable sofa for her personal use and immediately became a favourite with students and the wider college community.

Later in the year, I wrote a *New Statesman* diary which included a few lines revealing her feline secret – and we were astonished by the interest this generated. The story was picked up by British newspapers and then by websites and broadcasters around the world. As correspondents to *The Times* noted, there was nothing new in the dog-cat concept. The Dean of Worcester College, Oxford, had been granted this kind of permission in the 1960s, and the memory in Cambridge was that Rab Butler had been given the same privilege at Trinity College even before that. But proving that there is no such thing as an old story, the YoYo publicity machine steamed on. She was featured by the official Chinese news agency, by websites in Brazil, and was named 'Woof of the Week' on Sky News. I was interviewed about her on an American radio station, which did a protracted and deeply unfunny probe about what YoYo herself was thinking

about all this. I played along gamely, and resisted the tempta-
tion to shout, 'She has no idea – she's a sodding dog.'

Aside from canine diversions, the more serious corrective to
being captured within 'the bubble' is the mission we as a college and as a university have set ourselves of breaking down the
myths about Cambridge and doing our best to ensure it is open
to all. One of the most persistent erroneous beliefs is that we are
dominated in our intake by independent schools, and at a recent
Department for Education event I asked teachers from acade-
mies what percentage of state school pupils they believe we take.
The estimates were mainly around the 20 or 25 per cent mark,
and only one teacher guessed it might be 60 per cent. In fact, in
autumn 2014, Selwyn's new intake from the UK was 70 per cent
from state schools. The college has official outreach areas in West
Yorkshire and East Berkshire, and a great deal of work goes on
there and across the country on broadening access: telling every
school student who is bright enough that they can get to Cambridge if they put in the effort. I saw this for myself in a lively
session at Greenhead College in Huddersfield where I talked about
life in the media and in Cambridge to a group from Years 11 and
12. As well as going out to see them, we welcome thousands of
prospective students to Cambridge every year at open days and
in school visits.

It was one of those school trips that brought home the connection between my old world and my new. We hosted a group that
was younger than usual: largely nine- and ten-year-olds from the
London borough of Newham, the site of the Olympic Park. They
were predominantly from ethnic minorities. We gave them drinks
and cakes, and I did my standard short talk about the college. This is

intended to show that we are welcoming and friendly, and that it is a place where they might like to be in a few years' time. But there is a tough message too: they need to work hard and stick with education. For this group, who were still full of the enthusiasm of the Olympics, I was able to underline that almost all the people running the Games and the coverage of it had degrees, and that academic success opens doors that failure does not. They fired more questions at me than many groups, and their interest and engagement were uplifting. I remembered the spirit of the summer of 2012. I fervently hope that they and their teachers will keep at it, because we need more schools that set the standards high and tell their students that this and the other higher education institutions can be for them.

When we get this right, every year we take people at an exciting stage of their development, and we give them the teaching they need and seek to burnish their intellectual ambitions. Just as important, we want them to be suffused with the values of the college and to share those in their future lives with their families, their friends and their communities. As I meet the eighteen-year-olds who come here each year, experiencing their first time away from home and nervous about their new environment, I am full of anticipation about what they can achieve and how they might shape their own future and ours.

Broadcasting at its best is about social good and – at the heart of John Reith's mission – educating as well as informing and entertaining. That was the BBC in which I believed. To be able now to immerse myself in education at one of the world's greatest universities is a privilege for which I give thanks every day. It is not a life I expected to have, but it is one that education has enabled. I am proud to be in that world. I want every child in Britain, born in Warrington or Bradford or anywhere else, to believe they can be part of it, too.

INDEX

313

and directors-general 267, 275–6,
278, 280, 283, 284, 285, 290–91
and Dyke 249
and Labour 122
and news 148
and Radio 5 Live 126, 127, 143
Hanley, Jeremy 113
Hansen, Alan 189, 190
Harrabin, Roger 77–8
Harris, Rolf 270–71
Hassan, Margaret 166
Hayes, Brian 131
Healey, Denis 95, 96
Heath, Edward 95–6
Heggessey, Lorraine 152, 155, 158
Heseltine, Michael 85–6, 87
Hindhaugh, Jamie 209
Hobday, Peter 66–7, 101, 106–7
Holland, Julian 59, 61, 65
horseracing 185–6
hostages footage 166–7
House of Commons 56–7, 100
Howard, Michael 110–11, 113, 124
Howe, Geoffrey 68, 84
Hoy, Chris 240
Huggers, Erik 209
Hume, John 89
Humphrey, Jake 193
Humphrys, John 20, 101–2, 103, 107,
110–11, 305
and Aitken 112–13
and Major 117–18
and Thatcher 67, 68–9
Hunt, Jay 155
Hunt, Jeremy 223, 231

Hurd, Douglas 87
Husain, Mishal 156
Hussey, Marmaduke 90–91
Hutton Inquiry 4, 25, 162, 253–8

immigration 31, 162–4, 165
Inside Edge (radio show) 139
Inside Sport (TV show) 196–7
International Broadcast Centre (IBC)
226–7, 233
International Olympic Committee
(IOC) 2, 167–8, 208–9, 214, 234
Inverdale, John 48–9, 145
Iraq War 160–62
ITN 166
ITV 7, 25, 42, 180, 181, 304
and football 173, 187, 188, 189,
190–91
and Formula 1 192
and news 150, 151, 152

Jenkins, Roy 53, 95
Johnson, Boris 215–16, 239
Jones, Steve 275
Jordon, Darren 156
Jordan, David 13, 19, 283
Joseph, Keith 42

Karadzic, Radovan 83–4
Kelly, Danny 135
Kelly, David 258
Khan, Amir 197
Khomeini, Ayatollah 83
King, Anthony 274
Kingsbury, Jimmy 46

INDEX